So —
You Want
to Be
an Innkeeper

The Complete Guide to Operating
a Successful Bed & Breakfast Inn

So —
You Want
to Be
an Innkeeper

The Complete Guide to Operating
a Successful Bed & Breakfast Inn

MARY E. DAVIES   PAT HARDY   JOANN M. BELL   SUSAN BROWN

Illustrations by
JEN-ANN KIRCHMEIER

Assisted by
SHARYL DUSKIN

Chronicle Books • San Francisco

Printed in the United States of America.

Library of Congress Cataloging in Publication Data

So—you want to be an innkeeper : the complete guide to operating a successful bed & breakfast inn / Mary E. Davies . . . [et al.] ; illustrations by Jen-Ann Kirchmeier, assisted by Sharyl Duskin.
    p. cm.
  Includes bibliographical references (p.   ) and index.
  ISBN 0-87701-721-2
  1. Hotel management. 2. Bed and breakfast accommodations—Management. I. Davies, Mary E.
TX911.3.M27S624   1990   90-1946
647.94 ' 068—dc20   CIP

Book and cover design: Robin Weiss
Cover photo: Michael Long

Distributed in Canada by Raincoast Books, 112 East Third Avenue, Vancouver, B.C., V5T 1C8

10 9 8 7 6 5 4 3

Chronicle Books
275 Fifth Street
San Francisco, CA 94130

CONTENTS

ACKNOWLEDGEMENTS

Mary thanks: The gang at Ten Inverness Way for holding the fort while I wrote; and my husband, Jon Langdon, who never doubted for a minute that it would all come together right and on time.

Pat and JoAnn thank: The Bed and Breakfast Innkeepers Guild of Santa Barbara, including the Old Yacht Club, Bath Street, Parsonage, and Bayberry inns, without whose willingness to collaborate for work and for fun and to indulge "ideas and brainstorms" this project might never have begun; the subscribers to *innkeeping* newsletter and members of the Professional Association of Innkeepers International, who keep us honest by reminding us what it's like to run an inn daily; and the guests and staff of the Glenborough Inn who for eight and a half years taught us lifelong lessons about ourselves.

Susan thanks: The marvelous innkeepers who kept the Bath Street Inn going while I was writing; the workshop participants who kept asking for things I didn't have on paper, forcing me to write it all down; and the guests, who every time I think I have them categorized surprise me and show me a different reason for being an innkeeper.

And we all thank each other for a wonderful collaboration.

THE SPIRIT OF INNKEEPING

We four each had different reasons for becoming innkeepers. What we left, what we found, and what we made of it tell the story of what innkeeping is about. For every innkeeper, the story is different. And that, in a way, is the point.

Susan Brown spent ten years as a personnel-employee relations executive, three of those years with a Fortune 500 company for which she criss-crossed the country almost weekly. Susan snapped on the day she couldn't get the manager of the Skokie Hilton to recognize her as anything other than Room 212.

"I'd been assigned to the room in error," Susan says, "I'd ask for the room change, and he'd say, "You're Room 212,' I'd say, 'No, I'm Susan Brown, and I'd like a different room.' When I started yelling and stamping my foot in the lobby, I realized I'd had it. I took the 'red-eye' home to Los Angeles, sold my house, and quit my job. Hello, Bath Street Inn!

"I didn't even talk to other innkeepers about how to proceed," Susan says. "I knew what I wanted to create, because I was doing it for myself, almost in direct opposition to what I had experienced in the previous several years. For me, creating the inn was stage-managing my own fantasy."

For Pat Hardy too, her inn represented what she wants most when she travels. "I want quiet," she says, "and a chance to choose whether to be alone or with other guests. The Glenborough Inn is equally comfortable if you prefer to curl up in a guest room and read, or come to the parlor and visit."

Pat's parents owned their own business for thirty-five years, and Pat started and operated her own employment business at age seventeen. She has been a full-time mom and wife, a Girl Scout leader, a camp director and counselor trainer, and both development officer and fill-in cook for a private school. During four years as executive director of a nonprofit agency, Pat took it from two and a half employees to twenty-five, from a $25,000 annual budget to $225,000, and from a single-community program to a county-wide one. "I wanted to put the skills honed there to work in a business of my own," Pat says. "I also wanted work that would allow me to be around when my daughter Colleen, now age eighteen, got home from school. The inn met both these needs. It was also great for Colleen. Because of her experience as an assistant innkeeper, handling almost every part of the business, her confidence in the workplace brings her kudos wherever else she works."

Having developed their own inn, Pat and partner JoAnn Bell, along with Susan and other members of the Innkeepers Guild of Santa Barbara, developed workshops to share their knowledge and experience with prospective innkeepers. People of all ages, sizes, incomes, and intelligence levels come to the innkeeping workshops with high hopes.

"It's exciting that this entrepreneurial opportunity exists in the United States," JoAnn says. "You don't need half a million dollars, a franchise, and somebody else's rules and concepts to make your own business.

I didn't like corporate life, to put it mildly. I didn't like wearing dark suits and high heels. Santa Barbara, our home, was wide open with no inns at all. Developing the Glenborough Inn felt like a wonderful option. Which is not to say that I wasn't terrified I'd use all the money I'd ever had on an inn — and nobody would come." The proverbial farmer's daughter from upstate New York, JoAnn might have been worried about the money, but she was fearless when it came to the work. Until the day they sold the Glenborough, whenever a faucet needed repair, JoAnn just gathered up her tools and did the job.

Both JoAnn and Pat are also active directors and fund raisers for non-profit agencies in their community, and feel strongly about the importance of this work for its own sake, as a matter of personal responsibility, and as an opportunity for balance in their lives.

Mary Davies enjoyed some of the most exciting and satisfying work of her life before she decided to move to the California coast. "I was deputy director of the Employment Development Department of the State of California, doing their lobbying in Sacramento and Washington and directing a staff of analysts. Matching that job, for challenge, support, and fun, would be impossible. But it ended, and in Inverness, with one grocery, a service station, a post office, and miles of beaches, the opportunities for corporate success weren't overwhelming in any case.

"In 1979 my friend Stephen Kimball and I were working with our local realtor to find investment property. The realtor told us about a house and suggested we make it an inn. Stephen said he didn't have time to run an inn. Did I? Hey, I was Betty Crocker Homemaker of Tomorrow in high school — no problem! Ten Inverness Way was a dream come true before we had time to dream it!"

Eventually, reality sets in. In mid-1982, Mary was discarding in disgust an unsolicited publication with a name like "Fast-Food News," wishing there was a publication that addressed her needs as an innkeeper, when she decided to write it herself. Her monthly newsletter, *innkeeping*, has since become the basic tool for professional innkeepers across the country. In 1985, Mary had to make a choice between full-time innkeeping and full-time publishing. The inn won out and she bought out her partner. And the newsletter? She sold *innkeeping* to Pat Hardy and JoAnn Bell!

How has innkeeping met our needs and expectations? Susan likes seeing results. "Most of us came from a business world where so much is nonproductive," she says. "As an innkeeper, everything you do counts. For the first year or two, you get direct, immediate feedback on almost everything. What *must* be done somehow *gets* done. You do it." As an executive, Susan unwound by wallpapering, slipcovering, and painting. Today these things are "work." She also puts her background in business administration and psychology to work in conferences and training sessions at the Bath Street Inn, as well as in everyday guest encounters. "I'm immensely curious about people, and whatever else our guests may experience, they definitely get treated as whole individuals," Susan says.

After eight and a half good years of innkeeping, Pat and JoAnn launched the first inclusive association focused on the innkeeper, the Professional Association of Innkeepers International (PAII). Shortly thereafter they sold the Glenborough Inn. Now they have the chance to share their own and others' expertise, and to speak up for inns on an international level.

JoAnn's delight has been the chance to utilize her training as a licensed social worker and her experience with community organizations to help innkeeper associations develop and grow. She also speaks "computer" to anyone who will listen. Pat's phone conversations with PAII members — innkeepers and aspiring innkeepers — are the highlights of her days, as she provides some new idea or resource to callers who can find answers nowhere else.

For Mary, Ten Inverness Way is a chance to share what is important to her. "I'm always saying Ten Inverness Way is an inn for hikers — we're right on the edge of the Point Reyes National Seashore — and for readers, especially those who think inns were invented for curling up in front of a fire with a book after a walk in the rain. I love breakfast, so at our inn, breakfast is serious — Mom's home cooking. To me, the worst thing at an inn is an innkeeper who talks too much. We often fall into wonderful conversations here, but I recognize that my guests haven't trekked out here just to spend their wedding anniversary with me. I love the fact that I can make the inn be just the way I want it."

Naturally, we all make adjustments. As Pat says, you can set your own hours, just so long as it's twenty a day. Susan was determined, after years of those tiny little soaps at the "Big H" hotels, to use big fat bars. But guests got nervous, against all reason, about using a bar someone else had sudsed with, so Susan had to give in. And Mary never did get to serve a breakfast of warm, homemade fruit pies in bowls with cream; too many people said it just wouldn't fly.

But we're our own bosses, much of our work we do for fun, and we're building something for the future. That's the spirit of innkeeping.

A Closer Look

WHAT IS A
BED-AND-BREAKFAST INN?

Country inns, guesthouses, bed and breakfast — it's getting downright complicated to choose an escape to a simpler era. And with Nevada casinos advertising "bed, breakfast, and blackjack" on freeway billboards, somebody has to get serious about saying what's what. As a prospective innkeeper, you need a particularly clear vision of the nature of your future business.

Staying at inns is an exciting new way to travel in many parts of the United States today, but the origins of these hostelries are historic, based on the traditions of New England and Europe. Country inns, indigenous to New England, provided food and lodging to travelers and locals, and were often a focal point for a community. George Washington slept there.

Bed-and-breakfast establishments (B&B's) in the British Isles and tourist homes and guesthouses in the United States were historically the projects of widows or wives who supplemented the family income by renting out spare rooms as children grew up and moved away.

Accommodations in the United States today include both country inns and home B&B's, as well as that unique American invention, the bed-and-breakfast inn.

INNS These are generally small, owner-operated businesses that provide the primary financial support of the owner. Inns advertise, have business licenses, produce their own brochures, comply with government ordinances, and pay "bed" and sales taxes. Usually the owners have spent a great deal of personal time and money renovating and have a strong emotional, as well as financial, commitment to the inn. Owner-innkeepers tend to be people who "like people," and have often made major lifestyle changes to create the business. In the East, such inns have often been operating for decades, but the loving, personal care remains.

Within the inns category, bed-and-breakfast inns are distinct from country inns. Bed-and-breakfast inns serve breakfast only, and only to overnight guests. Country inns usually serve at least one meal in addition to breakfast, and operate as restaurants as well as lodging houses. Modified American plan (MAP) inns serve dinner to overnight guests only, and the cost of dinner and breakfast are included in the room rate.

Innkeeper associations around the country have defined bed-and-breakfast inns as historically or architecturally interesting structures used primarily for the business of providing overnight lodging. Hospitality and personal attention to guests are priorities. Rooms are all decorated differently, a common room is open to guests at least during evening and breakfast hours, and, naturally, breakfast is served.

Bed-and-breakfast inns typically have from four to twenty-four guest rooms, and are usually owner-operated; a staff may assist the innkeepers in attending to the inn, and necessary provisions are made for guest safety while staff or owners are out. Housekeeping, food preparation and service, decoration, and hospitality are topnotch. Inns must have certifica-

2

tion from appropriate governmental agencies and adequate commercial insurance, and pay taxes as required. Appropriate and reasonable security and safety provisions should be made, including smoke alarms, fire extinguishers, front-door locks, and lighting. Consistent as to quality (ideally), each inn is nevertheless unique in its policies, procedures, price ranges, and so on.

BED-AND-BREAKFAST HOMES On the other hand, bed-and-breakfast homes offer a spare room or two to travelers. The hosts are interested primarily in meeting new people and making a little extra money while continuing their present employment or retirement. The rooms are fresh and tidy, and the best linens may be used, but the operation is not a full-time business that could be sold to a new owner. These homes are usually not licensed or inspected by the local government. They vary a great deal and can be a fascinating, economical glimpse at another person's home and way of life. Prices are often lower than inn rates.

BED-AND-BREAKFAST HOTELS These are larger establishments—twenty-plus rooms—often owned by investors who hire employees to run them as businesses that imitate the "inn" experience. The motivation is primarily financial, but these operations also attract investors who are interested in historic preservation and renovation.

From the point of view of the traveler, each of these accommodations meets different needs. People who visit the home B&B usually want to experience the area they're visiting and meet "real" people in their homes. They also want budget accommodations and are willing to put up with the idiosyncracies of the lives of the family whose home they share.

Visitors to a bed-and-breakfast inn generally are looking for a special traveling experience and a strong dose of romance, history, or elegance. They expect a consistency of experience from one inn to another, but they also enjoy the variety of inn buildings, furnishings, breakfasts, and amenities. They hope to spend some time with an owner-innkeeper.

Country inn guests are often attracted primarily by the reputation of the kitchen, but they too look for romance, history, and elegance, in a setting that may also have resort qualities. They want plenty to do within easy range of the dining room.

Country inn: Old Rittenhouse Inn, Bayfield, Wisconsin. Mary and Jerry Phillips opened the Old Rittenhouse Inn in 1976, on the shores of Lake Superior. They started with four rooms and a fifty-four-seat restaurant in a three-story 1890s mansion; they recently purchased two more historic buildings, bringing their total rooms to twenty-two.

During their May to November season, the Phillips serve breakfast and dinner daily to the public as well as their own overnight guests; the restaurant is also open all year to the public on weekends. They like to cook, but they opened the restaurant out of necessity, to help fill the rooms. Their advice to prospective innkeepers today: "Locate near a good restaurant if you can — a restaurant is a lot of work."

B&B hotel guests generally expect the service and privacy of a hotel in the setting of an inn. They may want someone to carry their bags, but they also want individual attention from someone who plays a host role.

There are no hard lines here; each style of accommodation is as individual as its provider.

STATE OF THE ART

The entrepreneurial spirit is burgeoning in the United States, and bed-and-breakfast inns are among the brightest blossoms. People are reevaluating their goals, values, and lifestyles, and opening their own businesses in a reach for freedom and a greater sense of control over their destinies.

As author John Naisbett says so well in *Megatrends*, people are "re-turning" to smaller businesses, face-to-face contact, and a sense of connectedness, and away from anonymity and isolation. In many ways, prospective innkeepers are seeking, as are inn guests, a way out of the plastic, sterile, mass hotel environment into something personal and welcoming.

Innkeeping is a dream business that many today are choosing to make a reality. It's an entrepreneurial opportunity people can tackle . . . and make a success.

SUCCESS

What constitutes success in the bed-and-breakfast industry today? Guests often ask innkeepers how they can possibly make a living. The answer, of

---

B&B Inn: The Mainstay, Cape May, New Jersey. Innkeepers Tom and Sue Carroll fell in love with historic Cape May when they were there during Tom's Coast Guard service. In 1971, just as Victoriana was catching on, they paid $38,000 for an enormous old Victorian with nine bathrooms, furniture, and fixtures. After five years there, they sold the place to move to their dream house, which they opened as The Mainstay. In addition to its own six guest rooms, the Mainstay now includes a cottage next door — six more rooms — connected to the main house by a common garden and walkway. Like many innkeepers starting out, Tom had an outside job and Sue continued to teach for the first year.

The Carrolls made a deliberate choice to serve breakfast only, because there are plenty of good restaurants in their area. In addition, Tom says, "I think very few inns do a really outstanding job in both meals and rooms. The common rooms often get lost in the dinner shuffle. On the other hand, in New England, where an inn can be the town center, the full-service country inn is a good concept."

LODGING

JEN·ANN '85

course, depends entirely on how you define "living." A surprisingly high number of innkeepers say that if they can afford the travel, the antiques, the books, or wines they want, they feel successful. Part of the reason financial success is so ambiguous is that inns must have live-in innkeepers, most of whom are owners. As a result, the business often provides shelter, food, and sometimes even clothing, if the inn's image requires you to look more or less like George and Martha Washington. All you need (and all you get) is an allowance.

Beyond the concrete indicators, like an ability to pay the bills, success also means that innkeeping works for you. It's a lifestyle as much as a business.

URBAN OR RURAL?

Where are inns located? We expect them on Cape Cod and in California's Napa Valley, but inns can also be found today in Arrow Rock, Missouri, Park City, Utah, and five minutes from Disneyland.

Where does it make sense to locate a new inn?

The "Review of Studies on Bed and Breakfast Homes and Inns," presented by Pat Hardy at the 1989 Annual Travel Review Conference, says "small rural properties have difficulty holding their own in colder climates. Without a larger number of rooms to capitalize on the seasonality of business, [these] operators will have difficulty recouping their financial and time investment — especially if they are not located at high tourist destinations."

City trends are somewhat different, according to the review. "San Francisco has numerous high rate/high occupancy inns, while most major cities have only been able to spawn a few inns that often cannot command as high a price as their tourist destination counterparts."

B&B Home: The home of Mr. and Mrs. O overlooks the Pacific and the Santa Ynez Mountains. The O's are retired, and their children have grown up and moved to their own homes. Through Bed & Breakfast International, a homestay reservation service based in Kensington, California, the O's provide accommodations to overnight guests in two rooms that open on to the patio. Room rates are set by Bed & Breakfast International, which takes a 20-percent booking fee.

Mrs. O says, "We really enjoy the people who come, but we wouldn't do bed and breakfast if we weren't paid for it; the income augments our retirement money. During the summer, we had guests most weekends; between September and Christmas, we had no one. We don't turn down hopeful guests without a reason, but we do take trips and have parties, limiting availability somewhat. All our bookings come through the reservation service; we don't have a brochure, and only one of our neighbors knows we provide bed and breakfast."

There's a trend in city inns toward providing more amenities specifically aimed at attracting business travelers: telephones in guest rooms, a television lounge, earlier breakfast hours, and facilities for small meetings.

From an occupancy perspective, the best location for a new inn is probably in an area where people expect inns, but where they haven't reached a saturation point. Being a pioneer and jumping on a loaded bandwagon can be equally hazardous.

Finally, there must be attractions or activities for guests at or near the inn. Few people will travel simply to stay in a nice inn if there is no other reason to go to the area.

GUEST EXPECTATIONS INCREASE COMPETITION

Inn guests are sophisticated creatures, and to a great extent innkeepers foster that sophistication. The B&B tradition may have begun in the simple, private homes of Britons who needed a bit of extra income, but in the United States the bed-and-breakfast inn guest wants more. Inns compete for guests, with antique furnishings, hot tubs, and Godiva chocolates.

Once optional, private baths are now *de rigueur*. But if the inn next door puts in a swimming pool, it won't necessarily diminish your business. If you provide high-quality, caring, professional accommodations, if your inn, while retaining its uniqueness, is comparable in quality and services to other establishments in the area, and if your guests appear to depart satisfied and send their friends to you, you've no doubt met and probably exceeded their expectations.

Basically the inn guest has come to appreciate a different mode of travel, the "inn experience." Once "hooked," inn guests consider themselves part of a travel elite, discoverers of a cherished place, a secret unknown to the mainstream. Fostering this feeling is important.

The longer an inn is in business, the more likely the innkeepers will hire staff, take vacations, and even move off the premises. This is important for the innkeepers, but guests often don't like it; they tend to want to see the owner. It's a real challenge to establish an ambience that can be maintained to the satisfaction of the guests without the innkeeper doing the impossible: being everywhere, all the time.

TRENDS

Where is the inn industry going? The answer depends on who you ask, what you read, and where you look. It's still a new industry in many ways, but one clear thing is the public interest in inns, reflected in their prominent coverage in national media from *Newsweek* and the *Wall Street Journal* to *Vogue*.

Inns are no longer just an economy option for travelers. In fact, room prices for some inns are in the luxury range, as are the features provided.

Innkeepers provide many extras to guests at no extra cost. These may include refrigerator use; sitting room, porch, or patio for social interaction; fresh flowers; puzzles and games; and even bicycles. Inns routinely offer complimentary wine, fruit, candy, cookies, hors d'oeuvres, social

AVERAGE ROOM PRICE FOR 1988 BY GEOGRAPHY

	Destination or Coastal Resort	Rural	Urban	Wine Country	Overall Average
Extra space/ privacy	$108.10	$ 91.10	$ 91.50	$ 83.83	$ 96.99
Fireplace	$131.10	$ 99.09	$ 81.10	$118.44	$123.96
Jacuzzi	$155.13	$ 93.17	$ 0.00	$106.70	$136.57
Private bath	$109.38	$ 75.81	$ 82.51	$ 92.00	$ 95.24
View	$117.93	$ 69.99	$ 70.42	$ 97.71	$ 98.90
Basic room, no features	$ 72.31	$ 49.78	$ 50.10	$ 80.00	$ 57.60
2 or more features	$116.48	$ 78.66	$ 96.86	$ 98.87	$103.96
3 or more features	$144.99	$ 97.88	$110.00	$112.18	$132.06

Source: 1988 PAI I Bed & Breakfast/Country Inn Industry Survey & Analysis.

hours, or afternoon tea. Concierge floors, special greeters who welcome guests at the door, training programs that encourage line and front desk staff people to talk to guests, all-suite hotels, social hours, and stocked refrigerators are all hotel responses to guest demand for services typically found at inns.

Do inns take business away from hotels? Probably not, because the total number of inn rooms is small. Although more and more people try and then continue to choose inns, the majority of travelers do not. The lack of televisions and telephones in rooms, along with concerns about omnipresent innkeepers, discourage some travelers.

Nevertheless, the profile of the inn guest might cause some concern among hoteliers. The upper-middle class couple, twenty-five to fifty-five years of age, with expensive tastes and in search of something different, are the typical inn guests. Age limitations on children send some people back to hotels; other parents view inns as a way to escape from the kids for a weekend.

Finding lodging is not always simple for inn goers. Travel agents are often not used, although access to inn booking information has recently become available to them through their computer systems. Purchased guidebooks are the major referral source for inns, along with word of mouth. Major travel-series guides like those published by the American Automobile Association and Mobil Oil Corporation now include inns.

When asked why they choose inns, travelers say hospitality, location, private baths, and full breakfasts attract them to one inn rather than another.

Bed-and-breakfast travel is growing exponentially. Once an area "gets the idea," the number of properties can quintuple in a year. Then, as economic reality sets in, the local inn industry begins to stabilize.

The longer the life of an inn, the greater its success. Average room rates increase with longevity, and in many areas, inn travel is not budget travel, with rates exceeding $100 a night. Smaller rural properties have a tough time; inns need more rooms to capitalize on short seasons. Observations of New England and California inns indicate that expansion in the number of rooms per property occurs with success.

Studies of industry trends are somewhat confused by the interchangeable use of the term "bed and breakfast" for both small inns and homestays. Bed and breakfast is here to stay, but we will be better off if we add the clarification of "inn" or "home" after the term. The traveler, travel industry, researchers, and writers will all benefit if the distinction is clearly made.

Finally, the inn business has reached a level of maturity where inns change hands. Like other small businesses, approximately 20 percent of the inns are on the market at any one time.

Nowhere are there any signs that financing inns or running them will become less work. It is a time- and energy-consuming business, but the rewards are many and customer demand is still growing. Innkeepers tend to see a bright future for the industry.

SUPPORT SERVICES

A number of innkeeping support industries and service providers also expect a bright future. It is possible today, for example, to buy commercial insurance packages developed exclusively for bed-and-breakfast inns, from brokers who make insuring innkeepers and answering their insurance questions almost a full-time career.

California and Washington were the first states with regional inn associations, but now these organizations can be found in more than one third of the states. The industry also has its own trade newsletter (first published in 1982), a national consumer organization, an international trade association for innkeepers, at least six inn-traveler publications plus two glossy magazines, some one hundred guidebooks specifically published on bed-and-breakfast and country inns, local legislation, inn realtors and consultants, and more than one hundred vendors regularly serving and catering to the small-lodging property marketplace. Seminars for aspiring innkeepers are widely available in areas where inns are found.

The state of the art? Based on sheer growth, variety, and vigor, the prognosis is excellent.

WHO MAKES A GOOD INNKEEPER?

You like to cook, you're great with people, you start tingling when you're a block away from an antique shop, and you slipcover all your own furniture. Putting all that to work is part of the reason you want to have an inn. Every one of those skills will come in handy, along with a number of others.

Innkeeping is also serious business, requiring energy, responsibility, and leadership for success. It's a lifestyle change for anyone. For some, the change fits like a glove; for others, it's like a mitten—warm, toasty, and clumsy.

LIFESTYLE CHANGES

There is a timeless quality to innkeeping. The work never seems to be done, interrupted by the phone, sporadic eating patterns, late-night arrivals, a water heater that burns out when the inn is full, a travel writer who arrives unannounced when the septic tank is being pumped.

On the other hand, there are opportunities to sit down and enjoy pieces of the day most nine-to-fivers don't have: a late breakfast in the garden on a slow weekday, an early afternoon nap, the bargain matinee, evening wine with interesting guests.

Your whole idea of how to use time is changed. When you have a moment of peace and quiet, should you grab a needed nap or skim the newspaper for a crash course in current events? Time off tends to be in snatches: the concept of a "weekend" grows increasingly foreign; "quitting time" disappears.

Then there's the financial side. No more regular paychecks. Buying a car or a boat becomes a different kind of decision when you depend on the inclinations of the public for your income. Can-we-pay-the-mortgage panic can become a monthly event, along with juggling creditor priorities. In the meantime you'll be describing to wealthy guests the charms of nearby expensive restaurants.

In some situations you may be able to try those restaurants, with the inn picking up the tab, because making restaurant recommendations is part of the innkeeper's job. (Consult with your accountant on this.) You also need to "shop" the competition to keep up with changes in the inn business, so your business pays for inn visits or you exchange nights with other innkeepers. If you live on the premises—and someone must—the expense of a separate home is eliminated. A warm, resident innkeeper is expected by guests. Your presence isn't your gift to the business. The business pays by providing housing and some meals.

All the usual employee benefits can be yours: perhaps health and life insurance; car mileage allowance or repairs and gasoline; car leasing; wages for your children who perform inn tasks. Business expenses like these are not taxable profit. So, instead of a large paycheck, you will more likely receive a small allowance to supplement the essentials of life that the inn provides.

IF YOU'RE NEW IN TOWN

It takes almost anybody a year or two to establish a new social base and to make close friends. Meanwhile, you'll be more or less lonely, during the years when you'll most need moral support. Complicating this is the intensity of the involvement and the unorthodox hours the inn will demand, making meeting and getting to know people even more difficult than normal.

A *single woman's business: "I used to be married to a man who looks just like a sea captain and, for a time, we actually had a tuna boat and went all over—New Zealand, the Cook Islands, and so on. I've always been involved in businesses where I had a lot of freedom and dealt with people on a one-to-one basis. When my marriage ended and I was faced with an enormous life change, I needed to figure out a creative way to avoid ending up like a lion in a cage.*

"When you've been liberated by someone else's choice, you suddenly find you must be self-reliant in a new way. I was coddled like many women are, but once on my own, I've discovered that this house fits all my needs. It's a business, a legitimate tax shelter, and a nucleus for old friends and a lifestyle I love.

"It was on a visit to Jericho once that I had an insight that probably inspired me to trying innkeeping. I happened to think about the importance of the "harlot" who saved Joshua by letting him down over the wall. She wasn't really a harlot, but an innkeeper, one among a number of innkeepers who have made decisions of great historical consequence, for good and bad. The harlot of Jericho wasn't the only influence on my innkeeping career; Master-piece Theater's Duchess of Duke Street was right in there. I entertain 'angels unaware' and just people who have their traveling shoes."
—Beverly Nesbitt, Toll House Inn, Boonville, California

STATUS

Carol Beazley of the Beazley House in Napa, California, says this guest query puts it in a nutshell: "Is this all you do?" It's a shock to many new innkeepers to be viewed as part-time dabblers, hosts who accept fees. Any businessperson operating out of the home experiences this to some degree, and the British B&B model of renting a spare bedroom is the mental image many guests still have of the bed-and-breakfast inn.

To test for yourself whether the innkeeping profession is for you, fill out the following inventory as honestly as you can, checking the answer that best reflects your reaction. Have your partners fill it out too, for themselves and for you. Use it as a tool to evaluate how well you'll succeed as innkeepers, individually and as a team.

How do you feel about people?
____ I like people. I enjoy talking with a variety of people and can get along with just about anybody.

_____ I enjoy people in general but don't consider myself primarily a "social animal." I need private time.

_____ Generally, I prefer my own company to that of most others.

What was your parents' and/or your own childhood entrepreneurial experience?

_____ One or both of my parents or a close relative ran his or her own business, and I helped.

_____ I ran my own business before I was eighteen years old.

_____ I've been doing it now for five years or more.

_____ My parents and/or I have usually worked for someone else.

How persistent are you?

_____ I can name five projects I've worked on where I was most tenacious in getting the job done.

_____ I stick to things for a while, but when I've had it, that's it. I usually finish what I start if it goes well.

_____ I'm not sure persistence is the answer. If I start something and then discover it doesn't appear possible, I'll give it up. Why beat your brains out?

How well do you face facts?

_____ I enjoy the decision-making process of learning from the event and changing my behavior accordingly.

_____ I believe that the way I have decided to do things is generally right and need to be shown a better way before I change.

_____ My experience has taught me that the way I do things is right, and I shouldn't question that.

How well do you minimize your risks?

_____ Although I see myself as a risk taker, I always have a backup plan if I fail. I'm open to new ideas but cautiously plan when to stop risking.

_____ I have an optimistic streak that leads me to play hunches. Planning usually just slows me down. I *can* make a budget, but usually I don't plan enough for expenses.

_____ I thrive on risk taking. If you listen to the naysayers, you'll never get anywhere.

What is your hands-on quotient?

_____ I enjoy learning by doing. I have no difficulty cleaning toilets, repairing things, and doing what needs to be done.

_____ I don't mind doing the everyday things, but it's really not valuable for me as owner to get involved in room cleaning or doing the books.

_____ It is not my plan to do this kind of physical work. My skills will be better utilized elsewhere.

How do you feel about business?

_____ I love the challenge of long-range planning, endless daily decisions, and organizing to keep a step ahead of the "other guy."

_____ I do get bored with repetitive problems, demands, and struggles of
a business.

_____ Innkeeping is my escape from business.

Do you have the energy?

_____ I have worked in a setting demanding eighteen hours a day of my
time, seven days a week, and I thrived on it. I do, however, enjoy
time off if I can arrange it.

_____ I have worked in a setting demanding eighteen hours, seven days a
week. I did fine as long as I got regularly scheduled time off.

_____ I really need my weekend time to rejuvenate when I work forty to
sixty hours a week.

_____ I have no interest in working more than forty hours a week.

How do you feel about providing service to others?

_____ I'm excited about providing my guests with a wonderful experience
and look forward to going out of my way to make that possible.

_____ I believe that what we'll have to offer is plenty, and we'll deal as best
we can with guest demands.

_____ I do not intend to serve anyone. A nice room and breakfast is better
than our guests get elsewhere, and I think they'll be pleased with it.

What is your level of acceptance of people?

_____ I enjoy giving people of all kinds (including those with different
moral standards, religion, lifestyle, politics, race, ethnicity, and so
on) a wonderful experience. Everyone has a right to a pleasant time.

_____ My basic philosophy is "live and let live," and I can accept people of
all kinds.

_____ I have some difficulty with people different from myself, and would
feel uncomfortable having them in my home.

How do you handle pressure?

_____ I perform well under pressure. When time demands seem impossible, I enjoy the challenge.

_____ If I have reassurance and assistance from someone else, I do well
under pressure.

_____ I dislike working under pressure and usually organize my life so I'm
not faced with undue stress.

Your sense of humor?

_____ Even when things are not going well, I always can find something to
laugh about.

_____ I tend to be somewhat serious about life but try to laugh when
things are tough.

_____ What's to laugh about? Joking only complicates an already bad
situation.

Flexibility

_____ I can move smoothly from one task to another without complete
"closure" and not feel bothered.

_____ I prefer to complete one task before moving to another.

_____ Interruptions drive me crazy.

How do you handle conflict?

_____ I can usually find a way to talk to someone with whom I have a conflict without alienating that person.

_____ Though I dislike conflict and my stomach gets nervous, I go ahead and sometimes disagree with another person in a situation where I know that person will end up being unhappy with me.

_____ I hit head-on and let the "chips fall where they may," even if it makes the other person unhappy.

_____ I avoid conflict.

Like marriage and parenting, innkeeping has to be experienced. It can't be adequately described. But if you're willing to attend to the experience of innkeepers who are old hands, and evaluate honestly your own feelings about the behavior the job demands, you'll minimize the surprises when you hang out your own sign. Consider the comments below as you review your completed worksheet.

PEOPLE

Successful innkeepers like people. There is no quality more important. The innkeeper's appreciation and enjoyment of every guest is what keeps visitors coming back.

Innkeepers tend to begin with a feeling of "I like people night and day," and gradually become protective of their private and family time and space the longer they're in business.

ENTREPRENEURIAL BACKGROUND

Michael Phillips and Salli Rasberry, authors of *Honest Business,* point out that most people who successfully start and run small businesses either had parents or close relatives with a business, or had significant business experience themselves before age eighteen. "The children of taxi drivers, greasy spoon restaurateurs, and dentists have a very good chance of succeeding in business," they say. "Children of teachers, bureaucrats, and soldiers don't. A child who worked in her father's drugstore selling sodas, or in his mother's bookkeeping office doing ledgers, has a good grasp of how business works and can respond, intuitively, to business advice. All the unspoken, invisible issues of business are subtly communicated to children, and no amount of schooling can fully take the place of that process."

PERSISTENCE

This quality will be important in every area of your life as an innkeeper. It's the difference between merely "hanging in there" and "keeping on trucking." As Phillips and Rasberry put it, it's "being willing to keep trying something long after your energy is used up, long after your enthusiasm has waned and certainly long after other people have lost interest in helping you. The people who can't make it in business are the ones who give up easily or divert their attention from the long, hard parts to do the easier, more glamorous parts." It's facing life with an awareness that change comes slowly and wisdom is gained in the process.

FACING THE FACTS

Innkeepers cannot be shifting with the breeze; it takes too much energy to change your mind and your policies every day of the week. On the other hand, you must be open enough to examine the consequences of your decisions and directions, willing to learn from the evidence, and able to change in response to it. Sometimes the necessary changes will go deep; some dear principle on which you based your inn image may not work.

One innkeeper, for example, had decided to charge high prices to get the kind of clientele she wanted. When times were slow, she planned to provide special services rather than cut prices. It was all part of a quality image. But during 1982, when the recession strangled not only her business but also that of the fine hotels and restaurants in her area, she decided to follow their lead and begin offering reduced prices and mid-week specials. She faced the facts and acted.

MINIMIZING THE RISKS

We all hear stories about the business person who takes a gamble and reaps millions; it's enough to make you believe success requires the abandon of a gambler. But studies of successful business people usually reveal not a gambler, but a cautious casino owner who minimizes risks in several ways.

Developing backup plans and alternative solutions is a common strategy of successful people. Innkeepers need to be open to and seek new ideas, but they must plan carefully for their implementation, setting benchmarks for pulling back from risks too great.

HANDS-ON QUOTIENT

Innkeeping requires many and varied skills, from plumbing and cooking to bookkeeping and gardening. Using all these is for many innkeepers a highlight of the business. Actually doing a task forces you to understand the ins and outs of it. If you've cleaned rooms for a year and then hire staff, you know how long the job should take and you notice the details. You have an advantage over the innkeeper who starts right out with a staff to clean rooms.

On the other hand, having and imposing your firm idea of the "right" way to do things may slow you down on delegating tasks to others and taking hold of new important areas. Your hands-on skill may conflict with your management skill.

BUSINESS ATTITUDE

Prospective innkeepers frequently explain their interest in the career change as a way to escape to a quiet country life, avoid the competitive rat race of business, and get back to the earth. In fact, owning this kind of small business brings a deluge of mundane problems and repetitive tasks such as preparing breakfasts, doing dishes, painting, and repairing. After the first year, some aspects of innkeeping get boring. You'll be tempted to make unnecessary changes for excitement's sake.

Enjoying the challenge of providing a quality stay for every guest is crucial. You must delight in a smooth operation — accurate confirmations, prompt follow-up on mail, regular maintenance. You must thrive on a near-total commitment to the needs of your business. Persisting through the trials and tribulations is easier when you enjoy the business side of innkeeping.

ENERGY

People who consider themselves dynamos get winded operating an inn. It's not only the quantity of energy necessary, it's also a restructuring of when it must be expended. Weekends and evenings are no longer time off; weekdays and afternoons more likely are. At the same time, those spare moments when guests don't demand your attention are the times you'll fill with repairs, inventory, advertising, promotion, and confirming and taking reservations. The less your start-up capital, the more you'll do yourself, and the less leisure you'll experience.

SERVICE

Phillips and Rasberry define service as "the conscious act of offering our talents, resources, and support to other people." This *is* innkeeping, and you can tell how well it's done almost the moment you enter an inn. It doesn't mean you have to become a bellhop or offer room service. It's an attitude that puts a special stay for a guest at the top of the priority list.

ACCEPTING PEOPLE

All kinds of people visit inns, and almost all of them probably offend someone. Unmarried couples, mixed-race couples, gay couples, single women or men traveling alone, older men with younger women and vice versa, the unsociable and the gossips, drinkers, smokers, Jews, Arabs, born-again Christians, Buddhists, bratty kids, macho males. In some areas, such as smoking and drinking, you can set limits at your inn. In others you cannot. Beware of opening an inn if you are uncomfortable with people different from you.

PRESSURE

The idyllic image of unhurried, pastoral calm is for the guests, not the innkeepers. There is always some deadline to meet: breakfast at nine, rooms cleaned by two, tea at five.

The greatest pressure is often financial: how to pay too many bills, increase income, renegotiate swing loans or credit lines, make refunds, pay staff, pay for necessary repairs and a new washing machine. An innkeeper makes a supermom look like a duffer.

SENSE OF HUMOR

Being an innkeeper is fun—and you'll make it that way. The longer you're in business, the less the disasters feel like *your fault*, and the more humorous the problems seem. Laughing at problems removes them from that anxious area in your stomach to a warmer place in the heart.

A healthy sense of humor helps avoid burnout. At the same time, when situations you could once have laughed off start looking serious and like just more bad news, a red light should go on: time for a day off. Make it a habit to ask yourself, "What's funny here?"

FLEXIBILITY

If being in the center of everything happening at once sounds like fun to you, so will innkeeping. If wearing many hats is your style, innkeeping is too. If you can shift gears quickly without stripping them, innkeeping is the career vehicle you've yearned for. And if you can break briefly from a heated argument to book a room with grace, you've got what it takes.

CONFLICT

You will have to handle disagreements with staff and guests, and it's disillusioning. Someday, some couple will take one look at the room they've reserved and ask for their money back. Some staff person will rearrange your carefully planned parlor. Unfortunately, perfection, like beauty, is in the eye of the beholder. Here's where your sense of humor and flexibility receive a good workout.

Getting Your
Act Together

PREPARING FOR INNKEEPING

Here's the next step in evaluating your innkeeping potential: a checklist of skills, with comments on how they're likely to be applied in a bed-and-breakfast inn. Some of them you already have, some you've always wanted to learn, and others you wouldn't touch with a ten-foot pole. Give the skills you already have a star, the ones you want to learn a plus, and the others a zero. Your partner should do the same. Then evaluate your combined inventory.

SKILLS CHECKLIST

Financial
- Bookkeeping and accounting: Balancing a checkbook is just the beginning. You'll also need to balance your books — and know when they're balanced. You must understand how to track the deposits you receive and the checks you write, and how to set up your books so they'll yield the information you want and need.
- Developing and monitoring a budget: You must know how to predict the future, so you'll know when you can expand or hire additional staff. The plan must be reviewed frequently, and changes must be made when the projections aren't panning out.
- Understanding financial statements: Good financial statements provide information on the equity you've built up, your return on investment, depreciation, cash flow, and problem areas. They need to be set up so they'll tell you what you want to know, and you need to know how to read them.
- Tax benefits and planning: Understanding the tax structure and what it means in your particular situation is critical. How does your tax bracket affect decisions about whether your spouse should continue present employment for a while? What are the benefits of holding the inn as one spouse's separate property? Are the cash benefits of renovating a historical structure sufficient to offset the expense of it?

Marketing
In an area like accounting, novices tend to recognize their need for help and gladly pay for it. In the marketing field, however, beginners more often feel they can do it themselves. Be careful; you may need more help than you realize. Getting your inn off to a slow start can be expensive in lost revenues.

- Graphic design and layout: You'll want brochures and stationery, and possibly advertisements, postcards, confirmation forms, gift certificates, and so on. The necessary skills range from an eye for design to the ability to create a functional reservation form that only you and your staff will see.
- Copywriting: Maybe you'll want to write your own brochure and regular media releases.

- Promotion methods: What kinds of things do people do to promote businesses? How will you promote the inn?
- Telephone skills: Are you comfortable talking on the phone, and is your voice pleasant and warm? Turning calls for booked Saturday nights into midweek reservations depends a lot on phone skills.
- Media relations: How do you get the kinds of stories you frequently see in magazines, newspapers, and on television about great inns to visit?
- Photography: Good photographs are a must for courting the media. Sometimes writers send their own photographers, but your good shots enable you to present your inn in the best light. This is especially helpful if there's a tornado in progress when the writer's photographer arrives.
- Organization of special events: From your first open house to fund raisers that benefit a favorite charity and your inn simultaneously, confidence in carrying off a lulu of a party is a real asset.

Property
You may be a crack decorator, but can you fix a toilet? Read on.

- Understanding basic building terminology and process: You will need to work with contractors and subcontractors; you may even end up being an owner-builder.
- Basic maintenance skills: From changing a washer to touching up enamel, these skills will save you a lot of money.
- Landscaping, both planting and design: Which plants stay alive in your area? What lasts in a bouquet? What landscape design will lure passersby to your door?
- Decorating: Do you know how inviting a cool blue-and-white color scheme is in a snowstorm? Not very. Can you make a silk purse out of a sow's ear? You'll probably need to.

Food Services
- Menu creation: Color, temperature, and taste combinations must be more than the sum of the parts.
- Health department standards: Also known as Botulism 101. Protecting the public health and safety is your responsibility.
- Serving food to a group: There are techniques for getting it all on the table, hot or cold. Do you have them mastered?
- Kitchen setup and organization: If you do this wrong, you'll be annoyed by it every time you make a pot of coffee.

GETTING WHAT YOU NEED

Now that you know the skills you want to acquire, start soon. There are numerous resources available.

Classes
Check the community college catalog, adult education flyers, professional

organization workshops, and lecture series for classes and seminars in your interest areas.

Friends
Some of your friends are undoubtedly pros in areas where you need help. Contact them for advice, possibly for instruction, and perhaps as hired consultants. This can be sticky, since you won't want to take advantage of the friendship to get for free something they make a business of selling. If you're careful and courteous about how you handle the situation, working with friends can be fun.

Consultants
If you have a good general grasp of an area, but need specific answers to important questions, consider working with a consultant. A good consultant can help you design systems you'll live with a long time. Working with someone on this short-term basis can be a good way to test whether you would work well together for the long term. If your consultant talks slowly and you talk fast, work sessions will be uncomfortable and probably not very productive.

Libraries and Bookstores
People in many other businesses need much of the same information prospective innkeepers need. Books written especially for the small business can help a great deal. See Resources for specific suggestions.

Practice
Maybe you could do great layouts and write fine media releases with a little practice. Give it a shot, if it interests you. Ask friends to look over your product and give you frank feedback. To check how clearly your effort communicates, ask a friend to review it and then explain back to you what it says.

Observation
Keep your eyes open for the ways others handle areas with which you'll need to deal. For example, keep a file of inn brochures and advertisements. Observe a wider field, too: How do other businesses promote? What kinds of signs attract attention and still retain a "feel" you like? What can you tell about selling by analyzing television commercials?

Volunteering
Get some on-the-job experience in budgeting, say, by working with a nonprofit group. Volunteer to organize the Boy Scouts fund raiser or to do the publicity for the women's center calendar.

Work Experience
While you're planning your inn, you may be able to work at a job that will help in your ultimate objective. If you're a retail clerk, maybe you can work in a decorator's shop. If you're a graphic designer, maybe you can take on some design work for a local inn.

Apprenticeship Innkeeping
All the research in the world can't fully prepare you for the actual experience of innkeeping. Some workshops arrange for the participants to take

over an inn for a weekend. It can be a wonderful experience or a horrible one, giving you in either case a real taste of what may be ahead.

RESEARCHING YOUR MARKET AND SITE SELECTION

If you've bought the inn concept but not the inn, this section will help you make a good choice. If you've already found the perfect inn or place to create one, this information will help you review its pros and cons, which you'll want to include in your business plan, explained in the chapter on financial planning.

RESEARCHING YOUR MARKET

To understand the milieu in which your inn will function, you need to research the travel field in general, as well as the bed-and-breakfast industry. Use these questions as a guide:

- What are the trends?
- What is the profile (economic position, family status, interests) of the bed-and-breakfast traveler?
- Why do people travel?
- What is the overall economic health of the travel industry in general and of the bed-and-breakfast business in particular?
- What kinds of competitive influences are there in the travel accommodations market?
- Do people travel to some areas more than to others?
- How do the policies, laws, and codes of state and national governments affect local travel?
- How do people make travel arrangements?

Be creative in finding the answers. Try these avenues:

- Watch for sales trends as you travel. Are travelers being offered unusual services or bargain prices?
- Subscribe to travel magazines and read travel ads. You can get a sense of the health of an industry and a destination by evaluating the desperation of the ads and the number and kind of "specials."
- Attend industry meetings, seminars, and training sessions.
- Interview industry people as you travel. Ask innkeepers, hotel managers, and travel agents the market questions given here.
- Talk to your librarian. Find out what's new on the shelves.
- Subscribe to hospitality industry publications.

MEETING YOUR PERSONAL NEEDS

Like everyone else, people considering new careers as innkeepers have distinct likes and dislikes about where to live. Many are city-bred and intend to stay that way; for others, heaven is the desert — or the mountains, or the sea. Don't get so excited about a particular property that you ignore these personal parameters. The first criterion for selecting your site is that the environment meets the needs of you, your family, and your innkeeping partners.

Look next at recreational, social, educational, and employment needs. Does one of you intend to continue to work while another runs the inn? This naturally limits your site to areas with desirable employment opportunities. What about schools for your children? You may dream of living in the desert, but if your child is training for Olympic ice-skating events, your options will be severely limited. Whether your favorite pastime is miniature golf or amateur theater, be sure you choose a place where you can pursue it.

You can save time and money by establishing and agreeing on some basic search guidelines with the other members of the new inn family or families. The guidelines could read something like this:

- Ten to fifteen miles from the ocean, for cool climate and love of the sea.
- A city population of 40,000 to 75,000, to satisfy needs for community involvement, good educational system, and cultural events.
- Not more than a day's drive to parents and grandparents.
- Employment opportunities in the computer field.

Starting from a framework like this — and it can have many more selection criteria — use a map to begin choosing possible locations. You can gather a tremendous amount of information even before you leave home, by contacting the local chambers of commerce, subscribing to area newspapers, and doing library research.

Then the fun begins. Vacation trips become business trips. (Ask your accountant about tax writeoffs for these exploratory forays.) Areas you may simply have passed through on the way to somewhere else will become important stopping places. Towns, cities, historical monuments, and scenery suddenly look different.

Not many people can start from scratch to decide where to live. Enjoy it!

---

*P*amela Hall O'Connor of Hall House chose a location in the town where she lived: Kalamazoo, Michigan. Her husband didn't want to leave his job there, and, with its four colleges and universities and an active convention and visitors bureau, Kalamazoo fit their profile for an inn location that would be busy all week long in an area with a lively cultural life. Choosing the city was easy compared to the two-year search for the perfect property, close to a college, in a quiet residential neighborhood, and with drive-by traffic.

EVALUATING YOUR SELECTION

Now that you've found a place that meets *your* needs, you need to decide whether anyone else would like to spend time there. If not, you won't have any customers.

WHO WILL BE YOUR CUSTOMERS?

The type of customer you attract is an important factor in the image and size of your inn, what the best location is, the room prices, and the amenities offered. So naturally your first task is to discover which type of visitor comes to your area: tourist, business person, or traveler. A "tourist" comes to the area as a destination and normally stays at least two or three days. A "traveler" stops in the area on the way to somewhere else. A "business person" comes on a specific mission, perhaps to sell a product or attend a meeting.

Most major cities attract all three kinds of visitors. Seaside villages attract chiefly tourists. Towns along freeways attract travelers. Different sets of features tend to attract each category of prospective guests, so review the following questions carefully.

Tourists
- Are you close to a large city? Americans enjoy mini vacations three or four times a year. In general they drive no more than three hours each way for a two- or three-day vacation.
- Are there enough tourist attractions to encourage people to stay more than a day? Are there good restaurants, historical sites, museums, zoos, gardens, amusement parks, unique shopping areas, cultural events, or beautiful scenery?
- Is there a "season" and if so, is it long enough to support the property? If snow sports are the main tourist attraction, are there also visitors in the spring, summer, and fall?
- Is there good public transportation into the area, by airplane, bus, or train?

Travelers
- Is your location near a highway or freeway? Are the on and off ramps convenient to drivers who hate to lose even ten minutes' driving time? Will your location be visible from the freeway?
- Is your area a logical overnight stopping point? Portland, for example, is a good stop between San Francisco and Seattle.
- Are there already signs on the freeway encouraging travelers to stop and eat, buy gasoline, or sleep?

Business People
- Is there a significant large industry in the area?
- Is your location a state capital or county seat, which attracts government agencies?

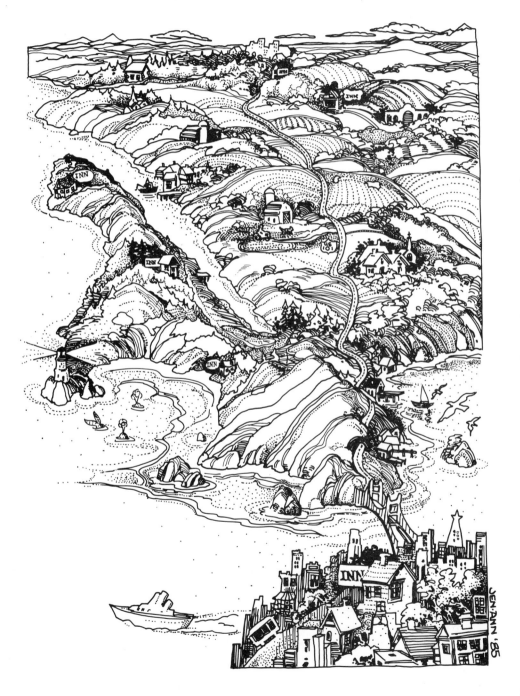

25

• Is it a central shopping area for the surrounding population? Such locations tend to attract sales people and distributors, who can be regular customers.

In most areas you will deal with some guests from all three groups, but there may be many more from one category than from another. Consider your personal preferences about the type of guest that would be most interesting. If you've spent much of your life in the corporate world, you may prefer to play host to business people — or you may strongly prefer not to! If you're most comfortable with casual encounters, travelers would be best. If you enjoy knowing people on a more intimate, one-to-one level, tourists who stay awhile and return often would be good guests. Your daily life as an innkeeper will be significantly affected by the guests you choose to attract.

RESEARCHING YOUR SPECIFIC LOCATION

This is where you apply your general field research to the specific area you are considering for your inn. This information will help you in big and little decisions about ambience, breakfast, pricing, promotion, amenities, location, specific property, and so on. Don't skip this research step. Questions to ask include:

• What is the nature of the overnight guest in the area? Consider age, economic status, children, interests and activities, purpose of visit.
• What is the occupancy level of nonconference hotels/motels and inns?
• What is special about the inns in the area?
• What is lacking in existing inns? How would you make your inn unique?
• What is the season? Are there off-season prices?
• Where do guests come from?
• What hostelries have opened and/or gone out of business in the last two or three years?
• How many inns are there in the area? How long have they been in existence?
• What role does the government or chamber of commerce take in supporting tourism?
• What kind of recreational and cultural activities are there in the area?
• What is the restaurant scene like?
• What new commercial or recreational developments are planned?
• What special events bring travelers to the area?

HOW TO FIND OUT THE ANSWERS: A RESOURCE LIST

The sources below will have answers to the above questions. The more sources you consult, the broader and more accurate perspective you'll have on a location.
• Chamber of commerce or visitor bureau: tourist materials; research materials on the area; in-depth discussion with tourism director.
• Brochures and rate sheets of lodging establishments.

- Local reference librarian.
- Local elected officials.
- Local Service Corps of Retired Executives (SCORE) consultant of the Small Business Administration (SBA).
- Stay in local lodgings, especially inns or the most obvious competition.
- Subscribe to a local newspaper. Read the ads to see what the best hotels stress and when they offer specials. Take a business or travel reporter to lunch and talk about the general health of the economy and the prospects for a new inn.
- Talk to experienced innkeepers in adjacent areas. They may be more willing to speak candidly about what works in your area than innkeepers located right there.
- Talk to new and longtime innkeepers in the immediate neighborhood.

EVALUATING EXISTING INNS

How do you determine whether the bed-and-breakfast inns in an area are prosperous? Some innkeepers don't keep good records and won't be able to answer questions concretely; others are naturally hesitant about sharing such information. Here are clues to look for:

- Do they require minimum stays? This often indicates that an establishment can afford to be selective.
- Have existing inns expanded? When, how much, and in what way: more rooms, additional services, more baths?
- Are price ranges at the area's inns similar? If they are uniformly high, innkeepers may be prospering; if low, competition may be intense.
- How do "deals" and amenities affect prices? Do prices vary based on mid-week stays, fireplaces, private baths, bed sizes?
- When did prices last increase?
- Does the inn support the innkeepers financially? Is one partner working outside? Are there other apparent sources of income, such as retirement pensions?
- Is there a supportive innkeeper association in the area?
- What do innkeepers see as trends?
- What kind of media coverage have area inns received?
- What are the impressions of inn staffs?

HOW TO TALK TO INNKEEPERS

Most innkeepers are helpful and will be happy to talk with you, but they're also busy, and your questions aren't the only ones they get. To make your time together most productive, plan to book a room and stay at the inn on a weekday or off-season when the innkeeper will not be too busy. Identify yourself as a prospective innkeeper and make an appointment to talk. Offer to pay a consulting fee.

Don't ask directly about occupancy rates. For some innkeepers, this is as touchy as inquiring about their salary level. Other innkeepers will offer the information. If not, ask what a new innkeeper could expect in occupancy for the first year or how long it takes for area inns to become financially successful. Another approach would be to ask what kind of occupancy other inns in the area are experiencing.

Treat the innkeeper as an expert consultant, even if you don't like the inn or the way business is done there. Innkeepers don't owe you time and information just because they've succeeded or just because you've booked a room.

Be willing to share your plans and ideas with innkeepers in the area. Don't be secretive; remember, you're getting a great deal of help from them, and you may want to join the local innkeeper association.

After you've done the research, sit down and put it all together: the industry, your personal needs, the realities of the area. You can't move a river: If people come to your area to hike or ski, capitalize on it; don't try to open their eyes to the joys of flyfishing. Build on the mood, energy, environment, neighborhood, and facilities that exist. Create a great inn that fits.

INN LOCATION WITHIN A SELECTED AREA

Once you've selected the general area for your inn, your first stop there will be the local building and zoning department. Most cities and towns will have such a department. In rural areas, county offices serve this function. The telephone book should help you locate the office. If you have trouble, telephone a local contractor or architect, who should be happy to point you in the right direction.

If there are already bed-and-breakfast inns in the area, you may wish to talk with some of the owners about their experience before contacting building officials. Your progress with local officials will be smoother if other inns have pioneered the concept there. In virgin territory, you may be dealing with people who don't even know what a B&B is, and your first task will be education. Carrying selected inn books under your arm can help you demonstrate that inns are an established tradition, one that will not be a threat to the community.

Most communities are divided into specific zones, such as:
RESIDENTIAL R-1 zones designed for one single-family dwelling per lot.
MULTIPLE RESIDENTIAL R2, R3, R4, and so on, specifying the number of residential units permitted per lot, i.e., R3 would allow a three-unit apartment building.
COMMERCIAL For manufacturing, offices, retail stores.
AGRICULTURAL For farms only.
PROFESSIONAL For doctors' or attorneys' offices, for example.
TOURIST SERVING For restaurants and motels.

Many communities have rigid restrictions separating residential and business uses. For most Americans, the largest investment in life is a home, and they will fight fiercely to protect the neighborhood from any kind of business use. Permission to operate a bed-and-breakfast inn in a purely residential area would, in most communities, require a variance or a conditional-use permit. Before one is given, all neighbors have an opportunity to express an opinion at a hearing, and local officials determine whether or not to allow the infringement. This can be a highly volatile situation. It is prudent to bear in mind during this process that these folks are going to be your neighbors for many years and can greatly affect the success or failure of your inn.

As a rule of thumb, a street of all upper-income, single-family residences, with no visible apartment buildings, service stations, professional offices, or retail stores, is not a good place to look for a potential inn. Many bed-and-breakfast inns are located in older areas where large homes have been converted into apartments, and a mix of single-family residences and multiple housing exists. These areas are usually closer to downtown and stores and restaurants. While you're exploring, you might try driving or walking the blocks immediately adjacent to this central area.

In addition to zoning restrictions, many cities also have master plans that reserve particular areas for retail outlets, professional offices, tourist-serving businesses, and so on. This information should be readily available from local officials.

An ideal neighborhood will have interesting old houses (or vacant lots suitable for building) zoned for multiple residential use in an area that includes motels and restaurants. Finding such a spot can greatly reduce the time and money involved in getting necessary approvals.

As bed-and-breakfast inns become increasingly popular, you can more often find an established one for sale. The following location guidelines for buying a building to convert to an inn apply also to buying an existing inn. Even with an established property, it is important to look ahead to when you may wish to expand. Consider these factors:

Location within the Community
- Close, but not too close, to restaurants, shops, and similar businesses.
- A "safe" area, i.e., one with a low crime rate.
- Falls within the service area for police and fire departments, emergency vehicle services, and hospital facilities.
- Convenient to highways.
- Roads and utilities are developed.

The Lot
- Large enough for off-street parking for guests and owners.
- Room to expand.
- Outdoor living area for guests that includes a variety of amenities, such as a garden, croquet field, barbecue, swimming pool, spa; a separate outdoor area for the innkeepers.

The owners of the Old Monterey Inn, one of the first in California's Monterey-Carmel area, spent many hours talking with all their neighbors, explaining the concept, their plans, and related pros and cons before proceeding with any legal requirements. Their diligence and patience have paid off, and their inn has operated for years in a climate of goodwill.

- Acceptable adjoining properties, with privacy, fences, landscaping, sound insulation, animals, children, and air pollution all well explored.

The Building
- Charm, character, curb appeal, historical significance.
- Structural soundness.
- Resale value.
- Size and number of bedrooms; dining room, parlor, and kitchen areas.
- Number of bathrooms or convertible closets.
- Private innkeeper quarters and storage.
- Inn storage areas and laundry facilities.
- Utilities, water, and sewage systems.
- Ventilation, natural light, protection from sun, wind, snow.
- Cost and future availability of energy: gas, electricity, water, solar.

Of course, no one can say you should consider only properties that meet certain very specific standards, like private baths for every guest room or certifiable historic status. Your decisions will relate to many other factors, including the type of inn you wish to have, the community you've chosen, and your budget. The guidelines above are designed to help you evaluate your first, second, and third choice inn locations against each other. Appendix 1 is a sample worksheet on which you can record impressions.

FOR BETTER, FOR WORSE: CHOOSING A LEGAL STRUCTURE

Exploring the question of legal structure is a mental giant step for anyone who has been mostly an employee, especially of a large corporation or organization. These institutions are so complex that most of us don't even think about their legal structures, let alone understand them. But for the entrepreneur, choosing a legal structure is one of the most important decisions.

There is a strong temptation to seal your business agreements with partners or investors with simple handshakes. Don't do it. It rarely makes good sense and can lead to legal, financial, and emotional chaos. The best of friends can and do part ways, leaving in their wake angry words, depleted bank accounts, and ruined businesses. Treat the planning of your business structure with the same care, respect, and professionalism you'll bring to your guests.

Your first step should be getting acquainted with the options. In addition to the information in this chapter, you might also explore the resources of your local library or consult Small Business Administration publications. Then you'll want to evaluate your own personal situation in light of the options, and finally, consult an attorney who specializes in property law. The more you know before you see him or her, the briefer your meeting and less expensive your legal fees will be. You'll also want to involve a certified public accountant (CPA).

Legal language and descriptions tend to be too complicated to be clear to lay persons. The information that follows has been written for simplicity, so not every possible situation is mentioned and explained. The idea is to get you thinking of things you'll need to discuss with your attorney and potential partners, and to give you some idea of the complexities involved.

There are three principal business structures that can be used for operating an inn: the single proprietorship, the partnership, and the corporation. Each has certain general advantages and disadvantages, but each must also be weighed in the light of your specific situation, plans for the future, and personal needs.

THE SINGLE PROPRIETORSHIP

The single proprietorship is basically a business owned and operated by one person or a married couple. To establish a single proprietorship, you need only obtain necessary licenses and hang up your sign. Because it's simple, it's the most widespread form of small business organization.

Advantages of the Single Proprietorship

- This structure requires little or no governmental approval and is usually less expensive to set up than a partnership or corporation.
- Sole ownership of profits.
- Control of the operation and decision making is all yours, which makes for greater flexibility.
- Relative freedom from government control and special taxation.

Disadvantages

- You are responsible for the full amount of business debts, even exceeding your total investment and extending to all your assets, including your house and car.
- The enterprise faces a potentially unstable business life, as it may be crippled or terminated upon your illness or death.
- Less available capital, ordinarily, than other business structures.
- Relative difficulty in obtaining loans.
- Viewpoint and experience of management is limited—to your own!

The sole proprietorship may be a good way to begin. Later, when you're rich and successful, you can consider forming a partnership or corporation.

THE PARTNERSHIP

The Uniform Partnership Act, adopted by many states, defines a partnership as "an association of two or more persons to carry on as co-owners of a business for profit." Though not specifically required by the act, written articles of partnership are usually drawn up, outlining the contributions of the partners to the business, whether material or managerial, and generally delineating their roles in management and sharing of profits and losses. Partnership agreements typically contain these articles:

- Name, purpose, domicile.
- Duration of agreement.
- Performance by partners, i.e., job descriptions of active partners.
- Kind of partners, whether general, limited, etc.
- Contributions of partners, both up front and later on.
- Business expenses, specifically how they are handled.
- Authority and rights, i.e., who's responsible for what and what rights they have.
- Separate debts, i.e., a clarification of individual debts of partners as opposed to partnership debts.
- Method of general record keeping and accounting.
- Division of profits and losses.
- Draws and/or salaries.
- Procedure for dissolution following the death of a partner.
- Release of debts.
- Sale of partnership interests.
- Arbitration.
- Additions, alterations, or modifications of agreement.
- Settlement of disputes.
- Required and prohibited acts.
- Absence and disability.

Partnerships have specified characteristics that distinguish them from other forms of business organization: limited life span; unlimited liability of at least one partner; co-ownership of assets; mutual agency, in which either partner can act for the business; share in management; and share in partnership profits.

Kinds of Partners

Partners can be "ostensible" or secret and several variations in between. The kind of partner most inns deal with, in addition to an active partner, is a limited partner. To the extent the law allows, limited partners risk only an agreed-upon investment, so long as they do not participate in the management and control of the business. In essence, limited partners are investors without a vote on how you do business.

Advantages of the Partnership

- Legal formalities and expenses are less than for corporations.
- Partners are motivated by direct sharing of profits.
- More capital and a better range of skills are available than in a single proprietorship.
- More flexibility in the decision-making process than in a corporation.
- Less government control and special taxation than in a corporation.

Disadvantages

- Less flexible than a single proprietorship.
- Unlimited liability of at least one partner.

- Elimination of any partner dissolves the partnership, though you can create a new one.
- Long-term financing is harder to get than for a corporation, but easier than for a proprietorship.
- The inn is bound by the acts of just one partner who acts as the agent.
- Buying out a partner may be difficult, unless that possibility has been specifically arranged for in the written agreement.

THE CORPORATION

The corporation is by far the most complex of the three business structures, so only its general characteristics will be discussed here.

As defined by Chief Justice Marshall in 1819, a corporation is "an artificial being, invisible, intangible, and existing only in contemplation of the law." In other words, a corporation is a distinct legal entity, separate from the individual who owns it.

Forming a Corporation

Inn corporations usually are formed by the authority of some state government. The procedure is, first, that subscriptions to capital stock must be taken (in other words, investors must buy shares), and then a tentative organization is created. Finally, approval must be obtained from the secretary of state, in the form of a charter for the corporation that states its powers and limitations.

Advantages of the Corporation

- Limits stockholder's liability to a fixed amount, usually the amount of investment.
- Ownership is readily transferable.
- Because it is a legal entity, separate from the individual, it is stable and relatively permanent. For example, in case of illness or death of a principal (officer), the corporation goes on.
- Relative ease of securing capital in large amounts and from many investors.
- Capital may be acquired by issuing stocks and long-term bonds.
- Getting financing from lending institutions is relatively easy because you can take advantage of corporate assets and often personal assets of stockholders and principals as guarantors. (Personal guarantees are often required by lenders.)
- Centralized control is secured when owners delegate authority to hired managers, who are often also owners.
- The expertise and skill of more than one individual.

Disadvantages

- More legal requirements and limitations than proprietorships or partnerships.
- Minority stockholders are sometimes exploited.
- Extensive government regulations and burdensome local, state, and federal reports.
- Indirect reward (less incentive) if manager does not share in profits.

- Considerable expense in formation of corporation.
- Numerous and sometimes excessive taxes: the corporation itself is taxed, and profits are taxed again as income to shareholders.

SUBCHAPTER S CORPORATIONS

The shareholders of a corporation may elect to make it a subchapter S corporation. For tax purposes, this structure is more like a partnership, but shareholders retain the "corporate shield" with respect to liability. Subchapter S corporations are relatively new, and the rules governing them are continuing to evolve; consult your attorney for current details.

APPLYING THE OPTIONS
TO YOUR OWN SITUATION

Now that you have some general sense of structural opportunities, these questions should help you narrow your choice. (Note that these questions are framed in terms of "I," but apply as well to couples and partners.)

- Do I want anyone else involved in owning this inn? For many, the inn is home. Owning it with someone else may not feel right. On the other hand, during the last ten years many young couples without inns have used partnerships as a means of financing the purchase of a personal residence.
- Do I have significant assets that will not be part of this venture that I need to protect? If you're putting all your life savings and assets into the inn, you won't have to worry about this. On the other hand, if you or your working partner have other substantial assets, you would be wise to choose a legal structure that offers protection for them.
- Do I want to share the management of the inn with someone else? Many prospective innkeepers have come from large, formal organizations. An important goal for them is being their own boss, with no one to tell them what to do. Even if you are "boss," having several partners or shareholders will infringe to varying degrees on your freedom to do things your way. On the other hand, some prospective innkeepers feel strong in one area but weak in another, and consider a partner with complementary skills and experience an essential part of the new venture.
- Do I have enough assets and cash to do it alone? The down payment is just the beginning. Do you have enough to pay for remodeling, furnishing, stocking, and staffing the inn until it is open and revenue covers basic expenses? Can you qualify for loans on your own?
- Do I want full responsibility for start-up, day-to-day operations, and management of the inn? Partners and shareholders can provide a wealth of skills, but that may not matter much to you if you prefer to operate alone.
- Will I be a full-time innkeeper, or will innkeeping be secondary to my full-time employment? Naturally, if you plan to keep working outside the inn, someone else will have to cook breakfast and make beds, as well as supervise remodeling, building, decorating, and general start-up. That someone else may work harder for less money if he or she owns a piece of the action.

- Do I need a tax loss or will the potential tax benefits of the inn be wasted on me? The restoration of older buildings, plus the normal depreciation factors of buildings and furnishing used for income, will usually result in tax losses during the first years of operation. They may be applied against current income, past income taxes paid, or future income. The loss can be considerable and very attractive to potential investors.
- Will I be selling my personal residence or income property to get cash for the new inn? If you sell a personal residence and want to defer the gain (profit made on the sale) to avoid paying a tax, this may affect your choice of legal structure. If you sell income property, there are rigid Internal Revenue Service (IRS) rulings for tax-free exchange from one type of income property to another. Either of these transactions requires the counsel of a CPA or tax attorney, preferably before you sell existing property.
- Is the inn your final goal or a stepping-stone? If your inn project is a way to make money so you can move on to another career or a work-free retirement, the legal ramifications of the eventual sale of the business will vary according to its structure. Plan now for your particular situation.

In general, as you can see, the major considerations for your legal structure are personal net worth, need for capital, personal lifestyle and skills, and goals and estate plans. These all involve personal decisions for you before you see an attorney or CPA, who can help you accommodate and implement them wisely.

GETTING DOWN TO CASES

Prospective innkeepers range from housewives and do-it-yourself folk to corporate types who hire their attorneys to check out the options first. The real-life examples that follow illustrate the way different factors interact to affect people's decisions about inn business structures.

The Couple Preparing for Retirement
Mary and Harry J wish to sell the family home in Los Angeles and move to a quiet, seaside town in northern California to run a small bed-and-breakfast inn. Mary and Harry are in their late fifties, have raised three children, and now have four grandchildren. Harry was in the restaurant business; Mary was a teacher. Their basic assets are their home, Harry's small restaurant, Mary's pension, and $22,000 in cash, stocks, and bonds. Harry knows the ins and outs of running a small business and is a skilled handyman. Mary is looking forward to cooking, running a large household, and entertaining guests.

Using the four general considerations just outlined, let's see if we can determine which legal structure is best for the J's.

PERSONAL NET WORTH Their home, purchased twenty years ago, has appreciated from $40,000 to $175,000, a profit of $135,000. For sellers under fifty-five years of age, this profit would be taxable as capital gains. However, there is a one-time exclusion of gain on personal residences if you are over fifty-five, so Harry and Mary have, as a start, $135,000 tax-free. In addition, Harry plans to sell his small restaurant (an income-producing property) for $65,000, which *may* qualify for a tax-free exchange if handled properly. Mary and Harry have roughly $220,000 in cash as seed money for the new venture.

NEED FOR CAPITAL Assuming they buy a property for $200,000 or less, in reasonably good shape, put 20 percent down ($40,000), and spend no more than $100,000 on remodeling, furnishing, and start-up costs, they could have $80,000 to cover the first several years' negative income flow with no further investment necessary.

PERSONAL LIFESTYLE AND SKILLS The J's believe that together they have the necessary skills to run their own business. Mary and Harry recognize their need to hire competent professional help in bookkeeping, accounting, legal matters, and such. They have a large family and will wish to close the inn during holidays for family visits. They enjoy traveling, so may not want to run the inn themselves twelve months a year. Outside investors might infringe on these plans.

ESTATE PLANNING AND GOALS Owning and running the inn is their ultimate goal, so we do not need to consider the long-range effects of selling in several years. The major consideration here appears to be estate planning. Mary and Harry will not need outside investors, will not have extensive outside assets to protect, do have the necessary management skills to go it alone, and want the freedom to run the inn as they please and when they please. Any of the three legal entities would accommodate them, assuming that they would choose a partnership or corporation that would be closely held and family centered. One form, however, may be more advantageous than another from an inheritance standpoint.

The Colleagues or Friends

Two young women, Lynn and Yvonne, have worked together for several years in a manufacturing business. They have spent many happy vacations at bed-and-breakfast inns and want to pursue innkeeping as a possible career change. Neither owns a home, but each has saved $25,000. Various wealthy family members have expressed interest in investing in an inn as a tax shelter.

We know immediately that Lynn and Yvonne's personal net worth will not be adequate, and they will need capital. Their capital sources want tax shelters, so their legal structure would probably best be a limited partnership or a subchapter S corporation.

In a limited partnership agreement, the limited partners' liability is limited to the amount of their investment as long as they do not participate in the management and control of the enterprise or in the conduct of the business. The rules are quite rigid, so the limited partners must be willing to let the general partner(s) run the show without interference.

In addition, there must be at least one working partner who has the financial reserves and the willingness to assume unlimited liability for business debts. If all these points can be worked out, the tax shelter advantages of this form of ownership can be very attractive, particularly because tax losses can be distributed unevenly. For example, in the first year 90 percent of the losses can go to 10 percent of the investors, as agreed upon in advance.

In an S corporation, the stockholders have limited liability, usually equal to the amount of their investment, but the tax losses are directly proportional to the percentages of shares owned. For example, if Lynn owns 50 percent of the stock, she will get 50 percent of the tax loss. She may not give it to other stockholders.

Lynn and Yvonne have some basic decisions to make. In addition to capital needs, they may also need a partner or stockholder who knows how to run a small business. It may be that one or both must keep their jobs for a while for financial reasons.

You can see that it's complicated. Planning and professional help are very important here for the future of the new enterprise. And innkeepers choose all kinds of variations on the options: some lease their inns instead of buying; some form limited partnerships for the first several years, then change to subchapter S corporations; some join with investors to buy and remodel property, then lease it back to a separate legal entity for management purposes.

There are many different ways to approach the structural end of your inn business, but all of them require good counsel and careful decision making.

PLAYING POLITICS: WHO WANTS WHAT?

One of your first jobs in dealing with government is discovering which of the various levels will have a hand in your business, and then finding out what each of these wants of you. The local chamber of commerce or a citizens' service office at city hall or the civic center usually provides materials describing the federal, state, and local rules and regulations that apply.

Here are lists of the basic requirements at various levels. There may be more — the list seems to grow — or there may be less, depending on the area.

FEDERAL REGULATIONS

Identification Number, I.R.S. Form SS.4

You'll be required to identify yourself on tax forms and licenses. All employers, partnerships, and corporations must have a federal employer tax identification number. If you are a sole proprietor without employees, you can simply use your own social security number. Whichever number you use, it will go on the payroll tax return forms the IRS automatically mails quarterly and at year end, which you must complete even if you have no employees.

Self-Employment Tax

For employees, social security is deducted from paychecks. When you're self-employed, you must pay the government directly. This involves a separate form and is a tax in addition to federal income tax. You may owe no income tax, but still be liable for self-employment tax. When employers and employees share the cost of social security, each pays about half the total. Since no employer will supplement your contribution, it will amount to somewhat more than the half you would have contributed as an employee. Check with your accountant and the local IRS office for details.

STATE REGULATIONS

Sales Tax Permits

In states that require sales taxes, almost all businesses need to obtain a sales tax permit from the state. Sales taxes must be collected on the breakfast portion of room charges, gift items, books, and so on. The taxes are collected from guests and remitted to the tax collector, usually monthly or quarterly. Some local governments also require sales taxes.

State Employer Tax Identification Number

If you have employees, you will need to pay unemployment insurance taxes, which are collected by your state employment service office. You'll be issued a state employer number that you'll need to complete the required quarterly and year-end payroll tax reporting forms. The forms will be sent to you automatically.

CITY AND COUNTY REQUIREMENTS

Fictitious Business Name

When a business operates with any name other than the operator's own, the "fictitious" name must be filed with the county clerk and published in a public newspaper for a required period of time. (Corporations, which are registered with the state, are exempt from this requirement.) There's a small fee for the fictitious business name statement, as well as a small fee to the newspaper for publishing it. This procedure also involves a check against the names of existing businesses in your area to avoid duplication. Name publication also informs the public of your business intentions. Banks require a copy of this statement before opening a business checking account for you.

When Donna Gustafson opened Chatsworth Bed and Breakfast in St. Paul, Minnesota, there were no rules. She went directly to the Planning and Zoning Commission anyway, and kept them informed every step of the way. Ultimately the commission used her experience and her advice in developing a bed-and-breakfast ordinance. Donna has found that local politicians are afraid of the unknown, and that innkeepers' willingness to educate them is most helpful.

Building and Zoning Department

This department, in some areas called the building and safety department, protects the community from haphazard growth and from inferior, unsafe buildings. For example, it:

- Enforces city or county regulations and permitted uses of property in specific areas. Would you want a bar or gas station next to your home?
- Approves structures for safety and compliance with local building codes. Some allowances may be made for historic buildings in areas where meeting codes would endanger the building's historic value.
- Approves remodeling plans to meet local setback requirements, height limitations, landscape design, and building codes. This involves initial plan check and sign off by inspectors at different stages of construction, such as framing, rough electrical, rough plumbing, drywall, finish, and roofing.

Department of Public Works

A good name for this department would be street and sidewalks department. It enforces regulations that affect traffic patterns, safety for pedestrians, and flow of bicycles and vehicles. Some of their concerns are:

- Off-street parking: For example, this department may require one space per guest room, plus two for owners. Some jurisdictions require that parking areas be paved, striped, and have bumper guards. A rule of thumb on space requirements is that a car should be able to exit after one backup motion. In general, diagonal parking is allowed only if the driveway is one-way.
- Width of driveway, curb cut (many cities use remodeling as an opportunity to modernize curbs), and condition of sidewalk.

Fire Department

Fire departments' requirements vary from community to community, but usually include the following to protect the public from fire.

- Exits: Requirements are more rigid for buildings with more than two stories. These may, for example, include two legal exits, steel door jambs, and one-hour fire doors.
- Smoke detectors: Some building codes require electric detectors; others allow battery-operated ones. Ask where they should be located.
- Ability of fire hose to reach all structures on property.
- Commercial fire extinguishers on each floor and in kitchen.

Planning Commission

This commission approves or disapproves requests for modifications, special-use permits, variances, conditional-use permits, and rezoning. Any of these exceptions to the rule may be applied for if your project does not meet zoning or building codes.

Review Boards

- Architectural review: Many communities have standards, color schemes, or themes with which all new projects or exterior remodels must be consistent.

- Sign reviews: Height, size, colors, and lighting may be subject to review.
- Landmark review: If you would like your inn to be classified a historic landmark, this review board must approve remodeling plans.
- Environmental review: This process requires you to prove that your project will not damage the environment. It can be expensive and involve questions of drainage, air quality, and even visual damage. Find out early if you're subject to it.

Board of Health
This is an inspecting and licensing board charged with protecting the public. License is renewable for an annual fee when standards, which usually relate to the following, are met.

- Kitchen and bathrooms: General condition and cleanliness of kitchen, such as washable wall and floor surfaces and absence of cracks around cupboards that would allow rodents and bugs to enter. Facilities for either high-heat or chemical sterilization of dishes, including either a commercial dishwasher or three-bin commercial sink with drainboards. Adequate ventilation and exhaust over stove. One option may be a commercial convection oven (exhaust self-contained). Stove approval may not be necessary if only continental breakfast service is to be offered. Employee bathroom equipped with liquid soap, paper towels, and automatic door closure.
- Spas and swimming pools: There are specific requirements for tub and deck materials, grab bar, water-depth marker, and chemicals. Filter, heaters, and other mechanical and electrical equipment must meet commercial-use standards.

Business License
Most cities require a license and fee to do business. The fee is usually annual and based on projected gross income. This agency may also collect local bed taxes, which are added to room prices.

Assessor's Office
Local property taxes are based on purchase price and reassessment of improvements. In addition, there may be an annual business tax on furniture and equipment, and some local governments also have a sales tax ordinance separate from the state one.

Good intentions are not enough. The first step toward being a law-abiding business owner is discovering the laws.

LOCAL GOVERNMENT AND YOU

"Button, button, who's got the button?" Few things are as frustrating as the fourth trip to the building and zoning department to retrieve signed preliminary plans and building permits, only to discover that public works hasn't signed off yet on the parking, or the fire department took your plans last week and won't have them back until tomorrow. Meanwhile, your crew is waiting another week to get started.

Aggravating? Yes. Exaggerated? No. Few wheels turn as slowly as those of government, or of any other bureaucracy, for that matter. The people and systems that hold the future of your business in their hands have flaws, foibles, and limitations. On the other hand, you may run into individuals and even entire departments that will go out of their way to be helpful and downright expeditious.

Bed and breakfast is still so new that few communities know what to do with it. Existing zoning categories don't seem appropriate, and health regulations don't quite fit. As a result, innkeepers inadvertently create a lot of work and brand-new problems even for people with a great deal of experience. Some bureaucrats enjoy the challenge, others do not, and the effect individuals have on the process is enormous: no department is the same to two different innkeepers, and no bureaucrat responds, interprets, and implements policy exactly the same as the others.

Every business faces this, but many of us innkeepers expect a warmer greeting than we get. We think we improve our neighborhoods, encourage tourist dollars, increase tax revenues, and provide unquestionably outstanding quality. Apparently, every new business person feels this way.

Prospective innkeepers also need to be aware of the social and political ramifications of their plans. In Santa Barbara, California, for example, there's a critical shortage of affordable housing. Therefore, when some well-meaning entrepreneur seeks approval to renovate a run-down Victorian presently housing six families, numerous legitimate concerns are raised. Such a situation immediately puts the prospective innkeeper in an adversarial position, at odds with the community and its governing bodies before plans are even submitted.

You can often avoid this unfortunate position. Spend some time becoming familiar with and understanding the needs of the community, especially if you are a newcomer. Newcomers start out on the defensive. People tend to be territorial and protective, and to resent outsiders "coming in and taking over." You need someone on your side who knows the ropes.

Respected architects and contractors representing you with governing agencies can smooth the way simply because they have proven themselves with quality past performances.

In addition, any contacts you may have with longtime residents can be very beneficial. A phone call from such an ally to the mayor or city councillor can smooth the way for permit approvals. In any corporation, school district, or other bureaucracy, some people accomplish their goals with ease. You need these people on your side.

Here are some tips on the positive way to deal with codes, regulations, and inspections:

- Avoid adversarial positions.
- Sit down and talk.
- Get the experts involved to talk with each other.
- Know the regulations yourself, but listen carefully to the ones that most interest your inspector.
- Believe that modifications can happen.
- Expect everything to take time.

- Provide all the information you can, but *only when it's requested.*
- Don't try to get away with things.
- Go to the top gently, when problems seem insurmountable.

Finally, be there for the inspections; accompany the inspector around the site.

PREVENTIVE MAINTENANCE IN THE POLITICAL REALM

In many areas, bed-and-breakfast inns are operating under little or no legal authority, somewhere in the definitional crack between boarding houses and hotels. How long this will be allowed to continue is anybody's guess. Even inns that meet strict kitchen standards for serving breakfast and other meals are constantly subject to political changes that may affect them: sprinkler-systems requirements, earthquake-safety modifications,

---

During the chaos of remodeling at the Glenborough Inn, JoAnn Bell somehow never realized that the spa would need permits and health department approval separate from those for the other areas of the inn. She found out, expensively.

All the spa equipment was sitting in the driveway the day the health department made the initial kitchen inspection. Next day, a department supervisor called and informed JoAnn that a nonpermitted spa was a violation of the code. Panic!

She discovered that it was still possible to meet the standards, but additional equipment would be required, including an automatic chlorinator, an additional filter, gauges, special floor surface, and so on, amounting to an additional $3,000. After a rather heated discussion with her contractor, who pleaded total ignorance of any need for permit or special equipment, JoAnn continued to pursue her options, which seemed to become less clear the longer she looked. In California, spas are regulated under the state code on swimming pools. Obviously, however, spas and pools differ dramatically in gallonage, use capacity, diving boards, and so on. Finally, the light dawned. Why not get the health inspector and the equipment supplier together to figure out what was needed for compliance?

JoAnn pursued this course, and also spent time herself poring over regulations with the supervisor, discussing the issues, and studying the diagrams. And waiting. Eventually, a solution was worked out, equipment installed, floor area enlarged, and floor surface altered.

Inspection day came, bringing an inspector she'd never seen before. "There's a problem," he said. With tears in her eyes, gripping the gate for support, JoAnn choked out, "What's wrong?" "Oh, you just need to spring-load this door so the latch will close automatically."

Compliance at last!

handicapped-access ordinances, and off-street-parking proposals, for example.

For political problems as for forest fires, prevention is the best cure. These problems often occur because somebody is angry with somebody else; on the other hand, they are often avoided because people don't want to cause their friends trouble. You can prevent problems by making friends.

At the most basic level, be a good neighbor. Be alert to problems your inn may cause the residents in the neighborhood and try to solve them. Figure out ways your inn can benefit your community: hold neighborhood meetings there, initiate a neighborhood crime-watch program, or work together on disaster-preparedness planning. Share some cuttings from your geraniums. Have a coffee klatch. Be a friend.

On the larger community level, be visibly involved in issues of concern in your town or city. Donate accommodations for the public television station fund-raiser auction, hold benefit teas for a local charity, or cook the Shrove Tuesday pancake supper for the parish. Try to position yourselves as innkeepers in the best light in the eyes of your community and the media—before you have reason to need public support on a political issue. You'll not only be building goodwill, you may also get some helpful free publicity.

Know Your Officials
Make a point of getting to know the people who represent you on the city council, the county board of supervisors, the state legislature, maybe even the United States Congress. And be sure they know who you are. Invite them to an open house. Ask them to speak briefly at an innkeepers association meeting, then follow up their remarks with a question-and-answer session. This will give you a chance to demonstrate your political interest and awareness and to present yourselves to political figures—who are always running for office—as a constituency to be reckoned with. Do

---

*S*herry and Wally Lossing had a lot to celebrate on May 1, 1982: they were married that day, and had received a use permit for Livingston Mansion, their inn-to-be in Jacksonville, Oregon, just two days before. Unfortunately, shortly after they began restoration work, forty-one neighbors signed a petition against their bed-and-breakfast plans.

Sherry says, "We appealed the decision. We got all the necessary checks on fire safety, water, septic system, and so on, and showed we met all the county regulations. In the end, the county said the neighbors had no case to make against us. But we were actually under surveillance at one point, just in case we had been sneaking in guests illegally.

"I've lived in this area for many years. The townspeople were actually anxious for us to have the inn. But we're in an outlying neighborhood where outsiders come to build homes, and they wanted to keep it to themselves."

some research before you become directly involved with an elected official so you will know the issues of prime interest to him or her. Take a look at where the official's support is weak and try to figure out ways you can benefit him or her by providing some good publicity or helping polish an image.

Find out your officials' positions on issues likely to affect you: development, economic growth, local control of local issues, historic preservation, and conservation, for example. Get involved in issues they care about, whether they affect you directly or not: If you're available to help your officials on their issues, you're in a good position to ask them for help on your issues.

What Are the Candidate's Needs?
Every elected official is a candidate all the time. No matter how idealistic and dedicated officials may be, they can't be effective unless they can get elected. Election is the bottom line, and in all your dealings with political people, don't forget it. You need to understand and be able to communicate how your issues can make political mileage.

For example, let's say Councillor Doe is a staunch supporter of preserving coastal access and has been taking a beating as a result: the development community is scaring the voters with stories about economic decline. If you want support in opposing an ordinance that threatens to put your inn out of business, you might approach Doe armed with data on the positive economic impact the inns have had in your area, not only on your own businesses, but also on the local restaurants and merchants. You might suggest organizing a press conference at one of the inns to give Doe a showcase for presenting her version of economic development: using existing buildings to bring in tourism without putting the additional strain on taxpayers of paying for the new streets and educational and fire-fighting facilities that new construction usually requires.

Never approach a legislator for assistance without having a good case to make on how helping you will help him or her.

Say Thanks Loud
When you get help from an official, be noisy about it. Write a letter of thanks and send copies to your local newspapers. If your local chamber of commerce has a newsletter, write an article about the help you got and send copies of it to the legislator's office, for constituents to see when they drop in. The help you receive may merit an award. This gives you the chance to stage a media event, presenting your legislator with something like an oversized key to the inns of your area or a handmade quilted wall hanging naming him or her the "Innsightful Legislator of the Year." Do something that will make clear to the official who helped you out, and to others who might, that helping you pays off. The publicity opportunities here are limitless, for the legislator and for you and your inn.

The political game is complicated, but you neglect it at your own risk. Plan a preventive maintenance stategy now. If you need political solutions to problems, do your homework and get help from the friends you've made. Never, ever forget that all officials are candidates and that you get the most earnest assistance from people who stand to gain from being helpful.

BUTCHER, BAKER, CANDLESTICK MAKER: SELECTING YOUR SUPPORT PEOPLE

There are so many "professionals" in the marketplace today, it is difficult to know *if* you need them, *when* you need them, and *how* to choose them.

Naturally you'll want to work with people who are competent in their fields. Ask friends and other professionals for recommendations, and consult local business publications. You can begin to evaluate competence on the basis of the professionalism with which initial contacts are handled. Are they on time for appointments? Do they provide reports on the outcome of meetings? Are the documents they prepare clear and attractive? Can you get in touch with them conveniently?

Once you've narrowed your choices, ask your candidates for references from local businesses; then check them out. Before you make your final decision, there's one last aspect to consider, and it's one of the most important.

Take an honest look at how you feel about your candidates. Comfort and trust must characterize your relationship with all the people you hire. Don't allow yourself to feel inferior to them because they know something you don't. Remember, they all work for you; you pay them to provide services to you and your inn. Of course you don't understand the intricacies of accounting; that's exactly why you hire an accountant. Good professionals won't encourage your feelings of inadequacy. They'll work

---

The State of Maine seems to have an ideal system for regulating bed-and-breakfast inns. And since the inns and the law have been around for a long time, it must be working. According to Susan Chetwynd of The Chetwynd House in Kennebunkport, she is subject to unannounced annual inspections of rooms, bedding, bathrooms, kitchen, and water heater, but she doesn't have to meet any special equipment requirements. In 1989 Susan paid $27.50 for the annual license for her six-room B&B; the rate varies with the number of rooms. Country inns, those serving more meals than breakfast, must meet regular restaurant standards.

The Maine plan makes a lot of sense. Bed-and-breakfast inns are a new animal in many areas of the country, and making them fit into existing, inappropriate categories, as many states have done so far, results in some cases in the kinds of rules that have earned government a lousy reputation.

with you, spend enough time with you to meet your needs, and give reasonable answers to your questions, no matter how naive they may sound to them. Choose support people with whose pace you are comfortable. You shouldn't feel like you're racing your engines or struggling to keep up during your meetings.

What are reasonable fees? You can find out by shopping. Ask about prevailing rates in the field. The range can be very wide, and the highest-priced professionals may not necessarily be the best. Make your choice based on the balance of comfort, trust, expertise, and price that feels right to you.

ACCOUNTANT AND BOOKKEEPER

Tales are told of the business owner who hauls three shoeboxes to the accountant every year on April 14. Accountants worth their salt would probably smile politely and hand the boxes right back. Your inn is a business. Whether it's a corporation, a partnership, or a sole proprietorship, well-organized financial records are imperative. The Glenborough Inn's accountant was chosen long before the doors opened, because, as JoAnn puts it, "we were spending a lot of money, and I had no idea where or how to account for it.

"We started out with a very basic accounting system and chart of accounts. My fantasy was that I could do the bookkeeping, and it turned out to be a real fantasy. Early in our second year of business, our accountant suggested very gently that I might consider the services of a reliable bookkeeper she could recommend. I got the hint: My bookkeeping skills are nil, and the money I hoped to save by doing my own bookkeeping was being spent to correct my poor efforts."

At most inns, it's unlikely that the innkeeper will be able to avoid every financial task. The financial accounting jobs are usually shared like this:

Innkeeper
- Writes all checks, including payroll.
- Assigns expenses to appropriate ledger categories, e.g., utilities, advertising, and laundry.
- Receives and records income.
- Makes all bank deposits.
- Prepares monthly bed-tax return.
- Prepares quarterly sales-tax return.

Bookkeeper
- Posts to general ledger (lists expenditures in appropriate categories, e.g., utilities, advertising, and laundry).
- Reconciles bank statements.
- Prepares quarterly payroll-tax returns.
- Readies all information for business income taxes for the accountant.

Certified Public Accountant
- Prepares the business income tax return.
- Prepares any other necessary tax-related information.

• Consults with innkeeper or bookkeeper as necessary.
• Prepares business financial statements as needed.

ATTORNEYS

An attorney's skill is invaluable, and the fees reflect it! But buying a few hours' consultation at the right time can help prevent real heartache and grave financial repercussions. Negotiating contracts, deeds, and leases, and choosing the appropriate legal entity for your inn are examples of areas where you probably need legal advice.

In any case, do your homework before you call. With a little research, you may be able to answer some legal questions yourself. At the very least, you can clarify your problem so it's easier, faster, and therefore cheaper to resolve. Find out whether your attorney bills for every minute or will answer occasional telephone questions for free. Many attorneys are very cooperative in responding to telephone queries about whether a particular situation genuinely warrants their attention. It's something like calling your doctor to find out if an aspirin will do the job, instead of paying for an office visit to get the same advice.

INSURANCE

Surely one of the most difficult expenditures to make is one that does not apparently pay off at all, until and unless some minor or major catastrophe strikes. If that loss occurs, you will want and need the immediate, caring attention of an efficient, prompt, and fair claims service.

Choosing the right insurance agent, whatever the details of the policy, requires the same kind of analysis you use in choosing other support people. (Getting the right coverage is a complex subject that's dealt with in depth later in this book.)

Insurance is complicated; agents should not only be willing and able to answer your questions about policies, they should also spend time outlining your coverage and clarifying what it will mean in case of a loss.

As your business grows and changes, your policy should too. Even if nothing else changes, inflation can erode your coverage. Your provider should maintain a regular schedule of contact with you, probably annual, to make necessary updates.

Insurance agents make money on insurance renewals, so keeping you happy is important to them. If you're not pleased with the service you get, take your business elsewhere.

BANKERS

"Know more about your business than anyone else does," a banker will tell you. No matter how large or small your operation, bankers don't like to be told you'll have to check with your accountant when they ask a question. They want to know you're in charge. They'll expect you to understand your cash flow and be able to discuss financial projections intelligently. (And if you've chosen your other support people with care, you'll be prepared for your banker!)

Just like anybody else, bankers lend money in situations where they feel comfortable. So choose your bank and your banker with care. Find someone interested in small business, and build a relationship based on professionalism. Don't hesitate to ask about special services: a business credit card, a line of credit, payroll services, and so on. But recognize at the same time that the more banking needs you handle through one bank, the more valuable a customer you are. As a result, it can pay to concentrate your banking business instead of giving it in pieces to the least expensive provider of each banking service.

Is it possible to go it alone? Certainly you can operate your business without bookkeeper, accountant, or attorney, and without real relationships with an insurance agent or banker. But that approach will require a great deal of time and a high degree of skill. Except in a few areas where you are undeniably a pro, you're wisest to put your talents to work choosing terrific support people and using them well.

Go or No Go?
Financial Planning

Which comes first, the chicken or the egg? The inn structure or the business plan? In other words, do you develop a business plan and base your inn search on it, or do you find a promising inn and then develop a business plan?

It's a dilemma. You'll find that material already covered on inn location, image, marketing, and so on will be required for your business plan. At the same time, other financial material, which the plan also requires, will be developed as you move through this section. There is an inevitable moving back and forth.

In addition, until you are ready to compare possible inn properties and make detailed budget projections, this section may be heavy going. It's okay to speed through the first time; you'll be back, and you'll find the detailed explanations and charts extremely useful when you get down to specifics.

One final word of caution: attorneys and CPAs make full-time careers in matters of finance, with good reason: Reporting, taxation, and financing questions are complex and continually changing. The information that follows is accurate and current, but prepared by innkeepers, not financial professionals. Use it as a guide to issues and an introduction to questions you'll be handling with professional assistance.

YOUR BUSINESS PLAN

At the beginning, getting the inn building in shape seems like the primary hurdle. But just as you wouldn't renovate an inn structure without a full set of plans and cost estimates, you shouldn't move ahead on your business without a comprehensive plan for its "construction."

The Small Business Administration indicates that businesses with plans have a far higher success rate. If you've been working your way through this book, you've already developed much of the information for your business plan, in your head, your lists, and your files. Writing the plan will make all those pieces fall into place. It's also a check to see if you've considered everything and whether your plans can be made clear and compelling to others.

In addition, your business plan has other beneficial uses:

- Financing: Your plan is crucial in approaching banks, friends, and prospective partners for money. It's your "application."
- Communication tool: The plan is an efficient, effective summary of your business concept to share with your attorney, insurance agent, accountant, partners, and directors. They'll understand your ideas for the future better when you present them in such an organized format.
- Organization medium: Writing and developing the plan gives you practice in thinking and making decisions based on a business approach, not just a dream.
- Focus: A business plan can be the inn's "bible" to which you turn when nothing seems to be going right; it acts as a reminder of why you're in this

Before remodeling. See page 72 for "after."

business anyway. It can help keep you on track when another great idea—making widgets on the side, maybe, or adding a restaurant—threatens to sidetrack you.

- Base from which to flex: It's not a hard-and-fast rule book, it's a framework. "Rolling with the punches" is different from reeling from one crisis to another, and a plan helps to keep everything, including change, in perspective.

A plan that can do this much for you should be done well. It will represent your inn, so make it look professional: typed, reproduced on high-quality paper, and kept in a neat folder or binding. Copies should be numbered and dated. Keep a log of those who have the plan; it's privileged information.

Developing a plan requires time to think, and think creatively. Getting away from interruptions and routine daily pressures to work on it can be the start of a good management practice. Managers need perspective. In innkeeping, it's difficult but crucial to be far enough away to gain that perspective. Start here.

WHAT GOES INTO THE PLAN?

Naturally, plans differ in outline as well as in content, but here's a good model.

Introduction
- Title page with date, writer's name, inn name.
- Table of contents.
- Overview or summary of what plan will cover.

Description of the Business
- The type of B&B you will provide.
- Auxiliary services offered, if any.
- Description of physical structure.
- Location.
- Legal structure, i.e., partnership, corporation, sole proprietorship.
- History of business if it is an existing inn.

Marketing
DETERMINING SALES POTENTIAL Include the information you've gathered on site selection, researching your market, and so on, including specifically:
- Who will be your customers (age, family, occupation)?
- Who is your competition (inns, hotels, B&B services)?
- What are the visitors statistics and accommodations occupancy rates in the area?
- What makes your inn competitive in that market?
- How will your location affect your market?
HOW WILL YOU ATTRACT GUESTS? Include here information on inn ambience, initial and ongoing marketing, plus pricing structure and policies and procedures.

Personnel

Your own résumé(s) and business histories/accomplishments. The bank and others will want to know what qualifies you to be an innkeeper. If you have little business experience or no hotel/inn experience, you may want to include the background(s) of your outside consultants.

• Names and histories/résumé(s) of your board of directors, if you have one.
• How will work be arranged? Will you do it all or hire staff? When? How many? To do what? It may be helpful to include a simple chart of responsibilities describing who will deal with the bookkeeper, supervise cleaning staff, and so on, to clarify roles and structure.

Consultants and Outside Resources

Successful businesses are not opened all alone, and the resources you have can help you get others. Include here all the people you can think of who have helped or will help you in your business: architect, attorney, contractor, accountant, promotion professional, consultants, insurance agent, decorator, and innkeepers and innkeeper associations.

Commitments

These are arrangements already made: building in escrow or leased, furniture already available or promised, arrangements made with antique dealers, innkeeping class scheduled to be taken, and inn association promise of referrals.

Financial Information

Many of your readers will turn to the financial figures first. For them and for your own peace of mind, develop this section carefully and honestly. Try to follow these guidelines. First, estimate expenses high and income low. This is no time for optimism. Be as pessimistic as you can bear to be, so you build in contingency plans. You will feel much better about a low December if you've planned for it than if you unexpectedly need $2,000 you haven't set aside. If you've allocated $2,000 for the expected deficit, you'll have the satisfaction of knowing you're at least good at planning!

Second, go over your figures in detail with someone who will ask hard questions, like why you expect your gas bills to be identical in summer and winter. Talk to more than one knowledgeable person, and preferably someone familiar with hotel or inn operations.

These figures might be developed with an accountant, but there are very substantial advantages to doing them yourself. You'll be making presentations to bankers and investors, as well as making decisions based on these numbers. If you develop them, you'll know them. If your financial situation is a mystery at this stage, you'll be totally lost once you're in operation.

Try not to let sensitivity about finances get in your way. Like most people, innkeepers tend to take on the good old American value of secrecy about money. This can not only make it difficult to disclose finances, but also to develop them honestly. Remember, the inn is not *you*. It's created by you, but it is not you. If it should need repairs or overhaul, it won't mean you're a loser.

WHAT TO INCLUDE IN THE FINANCIAL SECTION

In brief, the financial section should be divided into seven pieces: a summary of financial needs and your plan to meet them, your personal financial statement, the projected personal benefit income, projected occupancy rate, a cash flow projection month by month, a balance sheet (if buying an existing inn) and a pro forma (estimated or projected profit/ loss statement), and an itemization of start-up costs.

PROJECTED FINANCIAL NEEDS

Five-Room Inn, Tourist Town, USA

Start-up costs		$211,000
Renovation/furnishings	125,000	
Down payment	50,000	
Working capital*	30,000	
Closing costs	3,000	
Moving costs	3,000	
First three years' deficit projection		48,926
First trust deed on building		
Purchase price $250,000		
less down payment		200,000
Total projected financial needs		$459,926

*Includes office supplies, legal and professional fees, utility deposits, licenses and permits, advertising and promotional materials, owner's draw and expenses during renovation, and petty cash

PLAN TO MEET FINANCIAL NEEDS

Capital supplied by partners		$234,185
Cash from sale of present home	127,925	
Savings and stock	47,250	
Partner No. 2 continues present employment 18 months	59,010	
Capital needs from bank or investors		216,000
Mortgage on building	200,000	
Loan from Mom (deferred interest)	16,000	
Additional financial needs from bank		
Cash flow credit line collateralized on money-market account for 1 year, then uncollateralized		10,000

Summary of Financial Needs

This section summarizes the financial plan that will be developed in the pages that follow. Don't get stuck here trying to figure out the source of the figures. That will become clear as you read on. The summary is based on a hypothetical turn-of-the-century residence. It is in good condition, has two bathrooms, and costs $250,000. It could provide five guest rooms in addition to innkeeper quarters. The summary for this property begins with a list of financial needs and dollar amounts, followed by a list of financial resources.

The following section includes descriptions of other financial reports that most business plans contain. Two other pieces, your personal financial statement and personal benefit income, are described here.

Your Personal Financial Statement

Readers of your business plan who might provide loans or business support are interested in your ability to repay a loan or your collateral assets as represented by your financial situation. Potential investors will also want to evaluate your stake in the business.

The sample financial statement in Appendix 2 includes categories specifically relevant to the inn business. It's an excellent information tool for you, whether or not you plan to seek outside funding. If you do need a bank loan, a form like this will be required, along with your last three years' personal tax returns. Financial statements include a current listing of assets and liabilities, including all real estate, stocks, bonds, insurance, loans, pension funds, personal property, and fixed expenses (child's college, alimony). You can also include here assets like the value of antique furnishings you'll use in the inn.

Personal Benefit Income

Owners who live on the inn premises and are involved in daily inn operations receive related benefits of significant value. A projected breakdown of this information can help explain to bankers why you'll be able to pay back a requested loan even without a large salary.

For each category, enter your previous yearly costs, exclusive of inn

	Past Experience	In an Inn
Housing		
Utilities		
Gardening service		
Food		
Insurance		
Auto expenses		
Travel and entertainment		
Home repairs		
Cleaning service		
Miscellaneous supplies		
(toilet paper, soap, etc.)		
Total		

expenses, in column two. In some areas, the inn will cover your personal costs completely; in others, partially. For example, travel to other inns to keep up with the market is a justifiable expense, but a Caribbean cruise isn't. Eating breakfast breads with the guests is a justifiable expense, but a filet mignon dinner for twelve at a bed-and-breakfast inn is not.

With additional financial pieces that you'll develop as you go through the next chapters, you'll have a complete business plan. The plan is an important step in the organizing of your thoughts and your finances. Done well, it will be a valuable resource that you and your potential investors and assistants will use for planning, evaluation, and decision making.

EVALUATING THE OPPORTUNITIES

You've found a lovely, turn-of-the-century residence that hasn't seen a coat of paint for thirty years, but the lines are good and you know a Queen Anne when you see one. How do you evaluate whether it will pay for itself as an inn? And if you've found more than one attractive property, how do you choose among them?

There are four areas of projections to compare: start-up costs, including purchase and renovation financing; operating expenses; income, based on room rates and occupancy levels; and cash flow. In the following pages we'll look at each in detail, then put them all together for comparison in a property evaluation worksheet.

START-UP COSTS

Let's begin with the question of cash up front, i.e., start-up costs. These are divided into several major categories: building acquisition, renovation and decorating, and the typical start-up costs for any business. Remember to estimate high.

Building Acquisition Costs

How you account for building acquisition costs varies with how you plan to acquire the inn. If you already own it, list it in the asset section of your business plan. If you plan to lease, the costs of first and last months' rent and security deposits must be included, as well as any fees involved in negotiating the arrangement. If you plan to buy, the down payment, closing costs, points, and so on need to be included.

Typical acquisition costs in California houses to convert to inns range from $35,000 to $75,000 per guest room; they're usually lower in the East and Midwest. Generally speaking, wherever you go property values will be higher in cosmopolitan and tourist areas than in rural or small town areas.

Say you can buy an attractive structure for $250,000, with six bedrooms and two baths. Typical renovation and furnishings costs in California are $20,000 to $40,000 per guest room. Acquisition and renovation costs are keyed to number of guest rooms, but the figures are guides to total acquisition and renovation costs, inclusive of common room, kitchen, and the like. After reserving one bedroom and one bath for innkeeper quarters, there are five guest rooms left. The acquisition cost of each, therefore, is $50,000.

Renovating and Furnishing

Since the acquisition costs are moderate on the scale, which should indicate that the house is in reasonable condition, let's estimate renovation and furnishing costs on the low end, at $25,000 per room, or $125,000 for the hypothetical five guest rooms. The $125,000 will break down into costs for bathrooms (created out of closet space, with no additional square footage), furnishings, painting, landscaping, and so on. To cross-check your estimate, figure $5,000 per room for furnishings, small equipment, linens, wall coverings, drapes, carpeting, and so on, for guest rooms and common areas. This estimate will be lower if you already have a houseful of antiques, linens, and crystal.

RENOVATION AND FURNISHINGS COST ESTIMATE

Parlor/living room	$ 5,000
Dining room	5,000
Kitchen	5,000
5 guest rooms at $5,000 each	25,000
Add 4 bathrooms, ($4,000 to $10,000 each)	25,000
Paving/landscaping	15,000
Exterior painting	10,000
Electrical work	10,000
General plumbing (i.e., new sewer, gas, and water lines)	5,000
Carpentry, drywall, etc.	20,000
Total	$125,000

If your detailed breakdown is higher than your renovation/furnishings estimate using the $20,000 to $40,000 guide, use the detailed total for planning purposes.

You can see that it's easy to spend $125,000 renovating and furnishing a house even if it is apparently in good condition. Your inn now has five guest rooms, five baths, and innkeeper quarters, and has cost you $375,000, which includes the acquisition cost plus the renovations.

Start-up Working Capital

Working capital covers living costs during the renovation period, in this case an estimated six months, when the inn will generate no income, and during the first few months of operation. It also includes:

• Office supplies (letterhead paper, envelopes, typewriter, etc.).
• Deposits for utilities.

- Legal and professional fees (for drawing up incorporation papers or partnership agreement, setting up books, etc.).
- Licenses and permits.
- Advertising for opening, including ads, brochures, logo, business cards.
- Mortgage or lease on building during renovation, prior to opening to guests.
- Owner's draw during renovation, prior to opening.
- Operating cash (also called petty cash, probably not to exceed $100).

Your realtor can figure your mortgage payments, or you can buy a comprehensive mortgage payment table at an office supply if you want to experiment with different mortgage rates and years of payback. (The longer the mortgage, the lower the monthly payment.)

In our example, financing $200,000 ($250,000 purchase price less $50,000 down payment) for 30 years at 12 percent fixed will cost about $2,057 a month. For six months estimated renovation time, the mortgage alone will cost $12,342 and other start-up costs $17,658.

SAMPLE START-UP COST PROJECTIONS*

Down Payment	$ 50,000
Closing costs	3,000
Moving costs	3,000
Renovation/furnishing	125,000
Working capital	30,000
Initial costs	$211,000

*Assumes the down payment is 20 percent of $250,000, or $50,000.

These initial costs are high, but remember, they include a home *and* a business opportunity. We'll look next at projecting operating expenses and income, i.e., developing a budget.

DEVELOPING A BUDGET

Your budget is a listing of all projected expenses and income; it's what you expect to happen financially. You can develop it initially based on the figures and percentages presented here, but after six months to a year of operation, you can use your own real figures and project them into the next year. Comparing actual expenditures with your projections, you can discover expenses to cut, expansion possibilities, slow times that need to be promoted, and problem areas.

The related income and expense statement includes the same categories of income and expense, but describes at the end of a period, such as year-end, what actually happened. It also includes noncash transactions, depreciation, and amortization, and becomes your official financial statement for tax purposes.

In 1988 coauthors Pat Hardy and JoAnn Bell, as editor and publisher of *innkeeping* newsletter, sponsored the first comprehensive survey and analysis of income, expense, and return on investment for bed-and-breakfast and country inns throughout the United States. The following expense categories are consistent with their study. They are recommended for all innkeepers, so that in the years to come we will always be comparing apples and apples.

SAMPLE CHART OF ACCOUNTS

Revenue Accounts

• Room revenue	Room rental, excluding sales and bed taxes
• Food and beverage revenue	Meals, catering, liquor, etc.
• Other revenue	Weddings, entertainment, conferences, books, souvenirs, etc.; does not include room rental

Operating Expense Accounts

• Food	All food and liquor for the inn
• Room and housekeeping supplies	Supply items such as soap, toilet paper, light bulbs, cleaning supplies, laundry soap, notions, toiletries, etc.
• Hourly or part-time employees	All wages and payroll taxes such as FICA, worker's compensation, etc.
• Food and beverage employees	All wages and payroll taxes as above for full-time and part-time food and beverage employees, if the inn serves meals other than breakfast
• Utilities	Trash pick up, gas, electric, water, etc.
• Towels and linens	Purchase price of towels, linens, blankets, pillows, bathrobes, etc.
• Marketing, advertising, and promotion	Brochures, magazine and newspaper ads, printing, direct-mail lists, etc.
• Travel commissions and bank charges	Agent commissions, referral services, credit card discount fees
• Office supplies and postage	Paper, tape, pens, letterhead, etc.
• Telephone	Telephone and related expenses
• Travel and entertainment	Travel-related expenses and business entertainment
• Dues and subscriptions	Dues to associations and subscriptions to services, magazines, etc.
• Auto expenses	Automobile gasoline, repair and maintenance, car leasing

continued on next page

• Maintenance, repairs, and fixtures	Materials for maintenance and repair; include miscellaneous purchases under $300 for appliances, fixtures, furniture, etc.
• Outside services	Fees for outside services such as gardening, maintenance, laundry, etc.
• Insurance	Nonpayroll insurance such as fire, theft, auto, liability, etc.
• Legal and accounting fees	Fees for legal and accounting services
• Business and property taxes and fees	Property taxes and business fee, excluding sales and bed tax and income tax
• Interest and/or lease expenses	Interest paid on all types of business-related loans, excluding mortgages
• Salaried or permanent employees	All wages and payroll taxes such as FICA, worker's compensation, etc.; does not include owners
• Owners' wages or draw	Money actually taken out of the business by the owner(s)
• Other expenses	All expense items that do not belong to any other fixed or variable account

In addition to the categories listed, you may wish to add a category for rent or lease payments. This is appropriate where the inn or outbuildings are leased.

Using these categories, we will do a sample budget for a hypothetical five-room inn.

Of course, not every chart of accounts category is included in every budget or income and expense statement; only the categories that are useful to your particular situation should be included. Most prospective innkeepers underestimate expenses other than mortgages. The percentages shown in our sample budget are based on a composite of several inns in Santa Barbara and the *innkeeping* newsletter survey. Use them as a guideline.

PROJECTING EXPENSES

Category	% of Total Expenses*
Food	9
Room and housekeeping supplies	4
Hourly/part-time employees and payroll taxes	7.5
Utilities	6
Towels and linens	1.5
Marketing, advertising, and promotion	8
Travel commissions and bank charges	2.5

continued on next page

Category	% of Total Expenses*
Office supplies and postage	2
Telephone	2
Travel and entertainment	2
Dues and subscriptions	1
Auto expenses	2
Maintenance, repairs, and fixtures	4
Outside services	4
Insurance	5
Legal and accounting fees	1
Business and property taxes and fees	3.5
Interest and/or lease expenses	30
Salaried or permanent employees	5
	100

*Does not include salary or draw for owner(s), capital purchases and payments, and depreciation.

The *innkeeping* newsletter survey showed the following total annual expenses per guest room (without salary for owner(s), capital purchases, or depreciation) for 1988: five-room inn, $15,000; seven-room inn, $13,500; and ten-room inn, $11,000.

Adjust these figures for your number of rooms and locale. It would be very helpful to obtain expense percentages from established inns in your area. Geography, climate, mortgage interest rate, and type of food service all affect the percentages.

Back to our calculation: The expenses for our five-room inn should be about $75,000 (five rooms at $15,000 each). Plug this number into the "total expenses" slot, take your various percentages, and then apply the "reality test" to them. In other words, look at each item and see if it's reasonable in your particular circumstances. Make adjustments where necessary. And remember, always project expenses high and income low. The percentages will not be accurate in every instance. For example, we know our mortgage payment for the five-room inn is $2,057 per month, or $24,684 annually. According to the industry standard percentage calculation, the interest expense should only be about $18,000. This reflects higher acquisition costs, hence higher mortgage. Simply adjust the figure in the "reality" column.

PROJECTING EXPENSES FOR THE FIVE-ROOM INN*

Standard Percentages Of Expenses	Expenses Category	Annual Expenses Using Standard Percentages	Adjustments For Reality	Comments
9	Food	$ 6,750	$ 6,750	
4	Room and housekeeping supplies	3,000	3,000	

continued on next page

Standard Percentages Of Expenses	Expenses Category	Annual Expenses Using Standard Percentages	Adjustments For Reality	Comments
7.5	Hourly or part-time employees and payroll taxes	5,625	7,200	Need $600 per month for cleaning help and breakfast service, so one partner can work part
6	Utilities	4,500	3,900	Will hold expenses to $325 per month.
1.5	Towels and linens	1,125	1,125	
8	Marketing, advertising, and promotion	6,000	7,200	More advertising the first year.
2.5	Travel commissions and bank charges	1,875	1,875	
2	Office supplies and postage	1,500	1,500	
2	Telephone	1,500	1,500	
2	Travel and entertainment	1,500	1,500	
1	Dues and subscriptions	750	750	
2	Auto expenses	1,500	1,500	
4	Maintenance, repairs, and fixtures	3,000	3,000	
4	Outside services	3,000	3,000	
5	Insurance	3,750	2,750	Health insurance provided by outside employment of one partner.
1	Legal and accounting fees	750	750	
3.5	Business and property taxes and fees	2,625	2,625	
30	Interest and/or lease expense	22,500	24,684	Mortgage $2,057 per month (for simplicity, the entire mortgage is treated as interest)
5	Salaried or permanent employees	3,750	3,750	Absolutely necessary for innkeeper sanity.
100%		$75,000	$78,359	

*Does not include salary or draw for owner(s), capital purchases and payments, and depreciation.

PROJECTING INCOME

Now that you have a beginning handle on expenses, let's work on projecting income.

Income includes all revenues from the operation of the business, plus other revenue such as interest earned on bank accounts. Typical operations income includes room rents, food sales, gift and book sales, and other services such as rental of the inn for weddings, meetings, and so on. It is wise to keep revenue sources separate so you can evaluate their profitability. For inns, income is primarily the product of room rate multiplied by the number of rooms rented.

ROOM RENTS Most bed-and-breakfast inns include breakfast in the room rate. As a rule of thumb, innkeepers set their standard room rate higher than an inexpensive motel to keep out those looking for the "cheapest"; comparable to a good full-service hotel or motel; and lower than the local resort with golf course. Rate reductions may be made off-season, midweek (if this is a slow period), or for commercial customers who stay frequently and for several days at a time. Tourist towns tend to be slower midweek; city inns see little difference weekdays to weekends.

OCCUPANCY Occupancy means percentage of available rooms actually rented. For example, a 5-room inn, during a thirty-day month, has 150 available rooms, or 5 rooms multiplied by thirty days. If half the rooms are rented each day of the month, the occupancy rate is 50 percent. The following formula may be used to compute the monthly occupancy rate:

Monthly occupancy rate (%) =
# of rooms rented ÷ # of rooms × # of days

Using this formula, you can project occupancy rates. By combining projected occupancy and projected room rates, you can project income.

To see this formula at work we will use the example of a property in a weekend and summer tourist town. The research indicates that the inn should be full weekends year-round and all week during June, July, and August. The going room rate for weekends/summer is $85 per night for rooms with private bath.

# of rooms rented winter weekends: 5 rooms × 80 days = 400
# of rooms rented summer weeks: 5 rooms × 92 days = 460
Total: 860 rooms rented annually
# of rooms available: 5 rooms × 365 days = 1,825
860 ÷ 1,825 = 47% (rounded) annual occupancy rate

To project annual income:

# of rooms × # days × room rate = maximum income at
    100% occupancy
5 × 365 × $85 = $155, 125 (maximum income at 100%)
47% of $155,125 = $72,909
or
860 rooms @ $85 = $73,100 (difference due to rounding)

Local chambers of commerce or tourist bureaus can usually give you annual occupancy figures for existing hotels, motels, and inns. Large hotels that do convention business should be taken out of the sample, if possible. A prudent projection is 50 percent of the area occupancy rate for a new inn in its first year of business. The longer you're in business, the closer you'll come to the area rate.

Use the suggested guideline of half the area occupancy rate for first-year inn operation and assume an increase of 10 percent per year until area standard occupancy is reached. (An exceptional advertising program or terrific referral system with existing hotels or inns could make this low, but it's not likely.)

Cash Flow Analysis

For our sample inn, with five rooms with baths, we'll compile the budget information developed so far into a simple cash flow analysis.

CASH FLOW ANALYSIS
AREA OCCUPANCY: 60%

	Year 1	Year 2	Year 3
	30%	40%	50%
Income	$46,538	$62,050	$77,563
Expense	[78,359]	[78,359]	[78,359]
Cash Flow	[31,821]	[16,309]	[796]

For simplicity's sake, we have held both room prices and expenses constant, even though both would rise. As you can see, there is a considerable negative cash flow for the first three years. Any banker will want to know where the cash to make it up is coming from. Let's recap our financial needs.

	Start-up	Year 1	Year 2	Year 3
Down payment	$ 50,000			
Closing costs	3,000			
Moving costs	3,000			
Renovation/furnishing	125,000			
Working capital	30,000			
Negative cash flow		[31,821]	[16,309]	[796]
Total Needs [$259,926]	[$211,000]	[31,821]	[16,309]	[796]

Now we'll combine all this financial information in a property evaluation form (see Appendix 3 for blank forms).

WORKSHEET: PROPERTY EVALUATION

Address: **Five-Room Inn**
Tourist Town, USA   All amounts and percentages are estimates.

Area occupancy rate **60** %

Number of guest rooms:
original house **5**
proposed addition _____

Area room rate:
private bath $ **85**

Number of guest bathrooms:
original house **1**
proposed addition **4**

continued on next page

A. Financial Needs: Purchase/Renovation Phase

Purchase: Total price **250,000**

Mortgage(s) **200,000** **1st, 12% fixed, 30 yrs.**

GUIDE

$35,000–$75,000 per guest room

Down payment **50,000**	**50,000**	Usual is 20–25% of price
Closing costs, loan fees, etc.	**3,000**	Get realtor or banker estimate
Moving costs	**3,000**	
Working capital	**30,000**	Expenses from purchase period

(**6** month renovation)

Renovation and furnishings **125,000** Estimate $20,000 (good condition) to $40,000 per guest room in original house

Additional guest rooms: construction **N/A** Estimate new construction at $60–$125 per sq. ft. (room 200–250 sq. ft.)

Additional bathrooms: construction **N/A** Estimate $5,000–$10,000 each

Additional guest rooms: furnishings **N/A** Estimate $5,000 per room

Other _____

TOTAL **$ 211,000**

B. Income

5 rooms × 365 days ×

average room rate $ **85** = income @ 100% occupancy $ **155,125**

1st year projection:

50% of area rate **30** % = **30** % × 100% occupancy = $ **46,538**

2nd year projection:

1st year **30** % + 10% = **40** % × 100% occupancy = $ **62,050**

3rd year projection:

2nd year **40** % + 10% = **50** % × 100% occupancy = $ **77,563**

C. Expenses

innkeeping Newsletter Survey:

Five-room inn: $15,000

Seven-room inn: $13,500

Ten-room inn: $11,000

Use detailed expense percentages shown in E and adjust accordingly **$78,359**

D. Cash Flow Projection

	1st Year	2nd Year	3rd Year
Income (B)	$ **46,538**	$ **62,050**	$ **77,563**
Expenses (C)	**⟨78,359⟩**	**⟨78,359⟩**	**⟨78,359⟩**
+ or − Cash flow	**⟨31,521⟩**	**⟨16,309⟩**	**⟨796⟩**

To break even:

Expenses = $ **78,359** = **50.5** % occupancy needed

Income @ 100% = $ **155,125**

continued on next page

E. Detailed Expenses

Standard Percentages Of Expenses	Expenses Category	Annual Expenses Using Standard Percentages	Adjustments For Reality	Comments
9	Food	6,750	6,750	
4	Room and house-keeping supplies	3,000	3,000	Need $600 per month for cleaning help and breakfast service so one partner can work part-time.
7.5	Hourly or part-time employees and payroll taxes	5,625	7,200	
6	Utilities	4,500	3,900	Will hold expenses to $325 per month.
1.5	Towels and linens	1,125	1,125	
8	Marketing, adver-tising, and promotion	6,000	7,200	More advertising the first year.
2.5	Travel commis-sions and bank charges	1,875	1,875	
2	Office supplies and postage	1,500	1,500	
2	Telephone	1,500	1,500	
2	Travel and entertainment	1,500	1,500	
1	Dues and subscriptions	750	750	
2	Auto expenses	1,500	1,500	
4	Maintenance, repairs, and fixtures	3,000	3,000	
4	Outside services	3,000	3,000	Health Insurance provided by outside employment of one partner.
5	Insurance	3,750	2,750	
1	Legal and accounting fees	750	750	
3.5	Business and property taxes and fees	2,625	2,625	
30	Interest and/or lease expense	22,500	24,684	Mortgage $2,057/mo.
5	Salaried or permanent employees	3,750	3,750	Absolutely necessary for innkeeper sanity.
100%	Total	75,000	78,359	

The break-even percentage at the bottom of the property evaluation worksheet is the figure important to the question of cash flow. If you do not break even, you must continue to put cash into the business. If your break-even occupancy level is too high, you will have a constant cash struggle. In this example, the 50 percent occupancy needed to break even is a difficult goal, since the area rate is 60 percent.

The five-room inn property is relatively inexpensive at $250,000, but it has room for just five guest rooms and bathrooms. Let's say, for example, that in addition to the five-room property, you're also looking at a turn-of-the-century residence in good condition that could provide seven guest rooms in addition to innkeeper quarters. The cost is $275,000, $25,000 more than our first example house, but this property has potential for several more expensive rooms with balconies. Here is a second example, using the larger property.

The partners have put into the projected five-room inn $234,185 from sale of home, savings, and one partner continuing to work outside

---

WORKSHEET: PROPERTY EVALUATION

Address: **Seven-Room Inn**
Tourist Town, USA All amounts and percentages are estimates.

Area occupancy rate **60** %

Area room rate:
private bath $ **95**

Number of guest rooms:
original house **7**
proposed addition _____
Number of guest bathrooms:
original house **3**
proposed addition **4**
  back to back

A. Financial Needs: Purchase/Renovation Phase

		GUIDE
Purchase: Total price **275,000**		
Mortgage(s) **220,000** @ 12% for 30 yrs.		$35,000–$75,000 per guest room
Down payment **55,000**	**55,000**	Usual is 20–25% of price
Closing costs, loan fees, etc.	**3,500**	Get realtor or banker estimate
Moving costs	**3,000**	
Working capital	**30,000**	Expenses from purchase period (**6** month renovation)
Renovation and furnishings	**140,000**	Estimate $20,000 (good condition) to $40,000 per guest room in original house
Additional guest rooms: construction	**N/A**	Estimate new construction at $60–$125 per sq. ft. (room 200–250 sq. ft.)
Additional bathrooms: construction	**N/A**	Estimate $5,000–$10,000 each
Additional guest rooms: furnishings	**N/A**	Estimate $5,000 per room
Other _____		
TOTAL	**231,500**	

continued on next page

B. Income

__7__ rooms × 365 days ×

average room rate $ __95__   =   income @ 100% occupancy $__242,725__

1st year projection:

50% of area rate __60__ %   = __30__ % × 100% occupancy = $ __72,818__

2nd year projection:

1st year __30__ % + 10% = __40__ % × 100% occupancy = $__97,090__

3rd year projection:

2nd year __40__ % + 10% = __50__ % × 100% occupancy = $__121,362__

C. Expenses

innkeeping Newsletter Survey:

Five-room inn: $15,000

Seven-room inn: $13,500

Ten-room inn: $11,000

Use detailed expense percentages shown in E and adjust accordingly $__94,500__

D. Cash Flow Projection

	1st Year	2nd Year	3rd Year
Income (B)	$72,818	$97,090	$121,362
Expenses (C)	(94,500)	(94,500)	(94,500)
+ or − Cash flow	(21,682)	2,590	26,862

To break even:

$$\frac{\text{Expenses}}{\text{Income @ 100\%}} = \frac{\$ \ 94,500}{\$ \ 242,725} = \underline{39} \text{ \% occupancy needed}$$

E. Detailed Expenses

On this property, we are using standard annual expense figures. The $220,000 mortgage for 30 years at 12 percent has a monthly payment of $2,263, or $27,156 per year. Thirty percent of estimated expenses of $94,500 equals $28,350, so the difference leaves us some room to pay interest on a credit line.

the inn for a year and a half. Add to this the $10,000 credit line and the $16,000 borrowed from mom, and the expected cash needs of $259,926 for the first three years are met. Let's take a look at how much more cash would be needed to invest in the seven-room inn.

For a larger initial investment of approximately $20,500 (the

PROJECTED FINANCIAL NEEDS

Down payment	$55,000
Closing costs	3,500
Moving costs	3,000
Renovation/furnishings	140,000
Working capital	30,000
Negative cash flow	21,682 (handled through credit line)
Total	$253,182

difference between $211,000 cash outlay for the five-room inn and $231,500 for the seven-room inn), the buyer now has a more luxurious seven-room inn with much more potential return and a break-even point of 39 percent. Also note that in the third year the five-room inn lost $800, but the seven-room inn made $25,862 in the third year and $2,590 in the second, which more than pays for the difference in the initial cash investment.

We've used small inns for these first examples, even though many inns have twenty rooms and even more. The dream of prospective innkeepers seems most often to be a small inn—a marvelous old residence to fix up, live in, and operate themselves. Also, in many areas of the country, old houses with more than four or five guest rooms are difficult to find.

In reality, innkeepers often start with four or five rooms and, after struggling for several years, build an addition, expand by converting common areas to guest rooms, or buy the property next door. As the examples so far demonstrate clearly, a small bed-and-breakfast inn is not a reasonable way to make a million bucks! In fact, neither example 1 nor 2 shows owner salaries.

It's important to keep the future in mind when you look at property for the present. More rooms mean a more adequate return for all the work you'll be putting in. Would the house next door make a suitable annex? Is there land enough on a nice property to add a structure and additional parking? Is there a carriage house to develop?

Say, for example, the property we used for our seven-room inn is large enough to accommodate another structure and parking for three more rooms. Some of the expenses for a ten-room inn will be very little more than for a five- or seven-room inn; legal and accounting fees, office supplies, and auto expenses are good examples. Other expenses will be somewhat higher, but not proportionately so. An ad can sell ten rooms for the same price as five rooms, but you may need to advertise in more media to fill ten rooms.

As is true everywhere in this financial realm, you must use judgment and knowledge of your own area to calculate expenses and income. The beginning expense percentages on the property evaluation worksheets are basically relationships, not fixed standards. As a general rule you can figure that cash flow will improve as you add rooms, if building costs are not exorbitant.

Example 3 details the effects of adding an addition to the seven-room inn. The inn will then have a total of ten guest rooms with private baths.

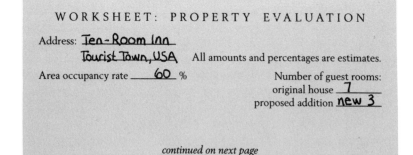

WORKSHEET: PROPERTY EVALUATION

Address: Ten-Room Inn
Tourist Town, USA   All amounts and percentages are estimates.

Area occupancy rate _____60_ %

Number of guest rooms:
original house _7_
proposed addition new 3

continued on next page

Area room rate:
private bath, balconies $ __95__

Number of guest bathrooms:
original house __3__
proposed addition __4 + New 3__

A. Financial Needs: Purchase/Renovation Phase

Purchase: Total price __275,000__ · 12% fixed 30 yrs.   GUIDE
    Mortgage(s) __220,000__ · 2nd, 15% interest only, 5 years
              __95,000__ $35,000–$75,000 per guest room
    Down payment __55,000__   __55,000__ Usual is 20–25% of price
Closing costs, loan fees, etc.   __3,500__ Get realtor or banker estimate
Moving costs   __3,000__
Working capital   __30,000__ Expenses from purchase period
                                     (__6__ month renovation)
Renovation and furnishings   __140,000__ Estimate $20,000 (good condi-
                                     tion) to $40,000 per guest room
                                     in original house

Additional guest rooms:
construction   __56,250__ Estimate new construction at
                                     $60–$125 per sq. ft.
                                     (room 200–250 sq. ft.)

Additional bathrooms:
construction   __15,000__ Estimate $5,000–$10,000 each
Additional guest rooms:
furnishings   __15,000__ Estimate $5,000 per room
Other _____   _____
      TOTAL $ __317,750__ Less $95,000 2nd,
                                      $222,750 cash.

B. Income

__10__ rooms × 365 days ×
average room rate $ __95__ = income @ 100% occupancy $ __346,750__
1st year projection:
  50% of area rate __60__ % = __30__ % × 100% occupancy = $ __104,025__
2nd year projection:
  1st year __30__ % + 10% = __40__ % × 100% occupancy = $ __138,700__
3rd year projection:
  2nd year __40__ % + 10% = __50__ % × 100% occupancy = $ __173,375__

C. Expenses

innkeeping Newsletter Survey:
Five-room inn: $15,000
Seven-room inn: $13,500
Ten-room inn: $11,000
Use detailed expense percentages shown in E and adjust accordingly $ __118,405__

D. Cash Flow Projection

	1st Year	2nd Year	3rd Year
Income (B)	$104,025	$138,700	$173,375
Expenses (C)	⟨118,405⟩	⟨118,405⟩	⟨118,405⟩
+ or – Cash flow	⟨14,380⟩	20,295	54,970

To break even:

Expenses _____ = $ __118,405__ = __34__ % occupancy needed

Income @ 100% $ __346,750__

continued from previous page

E. Detailed Expenses

Using the survey figures to calculate expenses, the total would be $110,000 per year (10 rooms at $11,000). Using the percentage calculation, the mortgage would be 30 percent of $110,000, or $33,000. The actual mortgages will total $41,405, $27,155 on the first and $14,250 on the second, so we will adjust the $110,000 total upward $8,405 to $118,405.

The break-even point for this ten-room inn occurs in the second year, but you will have an additional five-year interest-only second mortgage, which must be dealt with when it comes due. The following chart gives a picture of the investment after cash-flow impacts.

THREE-YEAR INVESTMENT ANALYSIS

	Initial Investment	3-Year Cash Flow	Net Investment After 3 Years
Five rooms @ $85	$211,000	<$49,106>	$259,926
Seven rooms @ $95	231,500	7,770	223,730
Ten rooms @ $95	222,750	60,885	161,865

Big is economically better, but with more than four or five guest rooms, you'll spend more of your time dealing with staff and organizational matters than with guests. Financial projections before you buy help you make comparisons, understand all the options, and then make an educated decision.

OTHER FINANCIAL REPORTS FOR YOUR INN

Balance sheets show the relationship of current assets and liabilities; income and expense statements show the profitability—the bottom line—of your operations. Neither the balance sheet nor the income and expense statement needs to be produced until you're in business, unless you are seeking investors who want tax losses. Your accountant prepares these financial statements based on your general ledger records of all income and expenses of the year.

The balance sheet reflects what you own and owe at a moment in time: "at December 31, 19— —" or at "June 30, 19— —." It consists of a listing of all your assets and all your liabilities. The difference between assets and liabilities is the owner's share of the business, which is added as "equity" and balances the totals.

71

After remodeling. See page 51 for "before."

The income and expense statement, also called a profit and loss statement or p/l, is your formal financial statement for tax purposes. It is particularly important if you are looking for a personal tax shelter or for investors. Like your budget, this document will cover a period of time: "twelve months ending December 31, 19— — ," "three months ending ———," or "month of ———."

In addition to the actual expenses and income reported in the budget or cash-flow analysis, it also includes the noncash expense of depreciation. Depreciation is the "using up" of a building, automobile, furniture, equipment, dishes, linen, and so on. It recognizes the life expectancy of these things and their declining usefulness over the years.

If you buy an older house for an inn, you are buying both land and structure. Property tax bills break out the assessed values of each; you can generally find the ratio on an old tax bill. (Your CPA may not accept the ratio, but will need to justify any new one.) In California coastal cities were land costs are high, the ratio may run as high as two to one, land to buildings. In rural areas or in the East, it may run two to one, buildings to land. You want the building portion to be high, because land is never depreciated, i.e., it doesn't wear out. Depreciation may put your business in a loss position for tax purposes even when you break even.

In addition to buildings, all other assets such as furniture and equipment are depreciated each year on a schedule followed by your CPA. IRS depreciation rules change often; ask your CPA about them.

Other major changes in the budget to make it a profit and loss statement include: moving capital purchases from expenses to assets, which are then depreciated, and moving out of the budget the portion of your mortgage payments that is principal.

The government grants tax credits that can be even more important than tax losses in restoring old buildings, since they come directly off the taxes you owe. Check with your CPA for current legislation on tax credits.

Financial statements are management tools. When you understand them you will be better able to recognize and respond to business problems, and you'll be able to discuss the money side of your business intelligently with anyone.

GETTING THE MONEY

What? You say you don't *have* a couple of hundred thousand dollars to start an inn? Don't despair. Just because our examples call these enormous sums "cash needs" doesn't mean you need cash in your pocket to get started.

WHERE TO LOOK FOR MONEY

Friends and family are possible sources for loans. A caution here: Since you know you will be in a negative cash flow situation for the first few years, delay repayment until a period when your projections show you'll have adequate cash flow. Extend out your projections as long as necessary to reach this point, possibly as many as five or ten years.

Include in a formal promissory note the agreement to defer all interest and principal payments for the first three years, say, when monthly payments of a specified amount will begin, the total to be repaid in full by a specific date.

The Small Business Administration makes business loans, usually collateralized by real property. Offices of the Service Corps of Retired Executives (SCORE) throughout the country can direct you to retired professionals who donate their time to the SBA to help entrepreneurs; they can help you through the notoriously precise, detailed, cumbersome, and lengthy application procedure.

As a rule of thumb, it's unwise to finance short-term needs like working capital with long-term financing (financing for more than a year). The reverse of the maxim is that you *should* finance furniture or building improvements — long-term fixed assets — with long-term loans or liabilities.

Your ability to arrange for a new mortgage will be based on your income at the time, which must be high enough to support the monthly payments. If at the end of three years you are breaking even and have a three-year track record of income, refinancing should not be too difficult.

Financial institutions will ask you two questions: How much money do you need? How are you going to repay it? The more thorough your preparation for the project, documented with a business plan and financial projections, the more impressed a lender will be with your seriousness and your dependability.

BUDGET AND CASH FLOW PROJECTIONS
MONTH BY MONTH

You may want to break out your projections into monthly figures during the process of demonstrating to lenders or investors your ability to plan and repay. You will certainly want to do the monthly projections for your own business planning purposes. It's not enough to have income equal expenses at year-end; you must also plan for paying your property tax in April, for example, even though it's at the end of your absolutely dead season. Copy and complete the format in Appendix 4 for your own projections.

Let's Make A Deal: Buying, Selling, and Leasing An Existing Inn

BUYING AN EXISTING INN

Twenty years ago, if you wanted to be an innkeeper anywhere but in New England, you almost had to start an inn. Not so today. There are plenty of inns around the country, and some of them are for sale.

Like other small, largely owner-operated businesses, inns change hands with some regularity. There is little quantitative measurement of this activity, but a seven-year ownership is the rule of thumb. A limited study by William A. Oates and Associates, an inn consulting firm in Brattleboro, Vermont, tracked eighty-five inns, mostly mature properties with dinner service, over a four-year period. The average length of ownership was seven years, four months, twenty days, and twenty hours!

Start-ups may turn over sooner, often because of cash flow problems. In most cases, though, inns sell for positive reasons: the owners have achieved their original goals, lifestyles and family relationships have changed, or a new challenge has become more attractive. More inns sell because of success than because of failure, and even problem properties can be turned around by a new owner with the necessary reserves of money and energy.

WHY BUY AN EXISTING INN?

There are several advantages to buying an existing inn. In the first place, you will be dealing with a known quantity with a measurable track record of income and expenses, occupancy rates, patterns of seasonality, and sources of business. Of course, what you'll be buying is the future, not the past. The previous performance of the inn will naturally be affected by your new style of operation. You will, however, have a starting point from which you can — and must — do your own projections.

Second, you can easily verify the existence of necessary licenses and permits. Again, do your own investigation. Permit procedures vary considerably from place to place. As the codes change regularly, the mere existence of a permit is not sufficient. Health department licenses are in some areas issued to a location; in other jurisdictions, to individuals. A sale may or may not trigger fire-marshal inspections. If you buy a place that serves alcoholic beverages, you will probably need to apply for a transfer or a new license, and that often involves investigation into your moral character and finances.

A special word of caution: You'll often hear of "grandfathered" conditions or exceptions. This term is used correctly to refer to nonconforming, preexisting uses in regard to zoning. It's often used incorrectly in relation to health, safety, parking, and fire codes. Waiver of conformance to codes may occur through forbearance, persuasion, or ignorance, but none of those have legal standing, and new ownership may be a signal for the authorities to act. Still, the existence of current licenses and permits does indicate the likelihood of their continuation. Before purchase, make that a certainty.

A third important advantage is that you will be in business the day the sale closes. An income flow, however meager, is strong psychological support, and real guests activate the learning curve in a hurry.

Fourth, you'll start out with market recognition. A 1988 *innkeeping* newsletter survey indicates that repeat guests and their referrals of friends account for about 48 percent of the business of mature inns. An additional 23 percent comes from inn guidebooks and newsletters. Neither of these categories, amounting together to 71 percent of a mature inn's business, is available to a start-up inn. Most people underestimate the time it takes to build a critical mass of guests sufficient to ensure a strong repeat business. Most guests try a variety of inns. Those who do return normally do not come frequently. The average inn guest, according to a *Yellow Brick Road* newsletter survey, visits an inn once every eighteen months.

A critical recognition factor for inns is inclusion in inn guidebooks. Many of the best guides are, like the inns they review, reaching maturity. They are full, and inclusion of a new inn in a future edition will wait upon the exclusion of another. Even when new editions are published, travelers are slow to replace their travel-worn but note-enhanced previous editions.

A fifth reason to buy an existing inn is that, contrary to popular wisdom, you can often put together a better financing package. Since you can describe the business more completely and most major renovations are already in place, financing needs are more clearly definable. A relatively mature inn will have a demonstrable cash flow to convince lending institutions of your ability to repay a loan. Finally, the selling owner will often wish to, or at least recognize the need to, participate in the financing in the form of a second mortgage or second deed of trust.

The final advantage is the availability of transition help: ongoing, hands-on advice and assistance from the original owner, for a time you specify in the contract, often two weeks to a month. This can help ease transition jitters, though success, of course, is in your hands alone.

As you can see, there are many good reasons to consider buying an existing inn. It's even possible, in some locations, that current zoning and other restrictions may prohibit development of new inns, limiting you to the purchase of an existing inn—and that's not bad!

Are there reasons *not* to buy an existing inn? It does limit you to the inns that exist and to those that are for sale. And you may face difficult price negotiations with owners who have an inflated idea of the value of their business.

Nevertheless, done right, buying an existing inn can provide a quicker and, in the long run, better economic return with less risk.

FINDING AN INN FOR SALE

The best inn you can buy probably isn't for sale—but you can still buy it. What do we mean? Just this: It's highly improbable that you will drive up to the inn of your dreams and find a For Sale sign in the front garden. But it's still possible that the owners might be interested in hearing your proposition, even if they hadn't thought about selling.

That's one reason why the best places to find an inn for sale are innkeeper publications. Write an ad describing the inn you hope to find, and it's just possible that an innkeeper will decide to sell it to you. Among the inn industry publications that have classifieds are *innkeeping, Innquest,* and *Inn Review* newsletters, and *Innsider* magazine. (See Resources)

You can also check the business opportunities section of the *Wall Street Journal* and of the local and major metropolitan newspapers in your target area. Business and real-estate consultants who specialize in the inn field are beginning to show up around the country.

If you've targeted one or two specific areas where your inn should be located, contact local innkeepers by mail or telephone for their advice on what might be for sale.

Whichever of these methods you choose, you'll be taken most seriously if you have a clear picture of what you want. Use the checklist below to "build" your model inn.

Number of rooms
Nature of innkeeper quarters
Monthly income necessary for personal needs
Type of breakfast (sit-down, formal, in bed — affect space needs)
Ambience and decor
Geographical requirements (weather, beach, city, rural, etc.)
Amount of renovation you want and can afford
Architectural style
Special features (pool, acreage, etc.)
Services to provide (dinners, baked goods — affect kitchen requirements)
Extent of your involvement in the inn operation.

VALUATION

How do you know what an inn is worth? Well, it's a complicated question.

Size is a factor. Michael Yovino-Young of Berkeley, California, who has specialized in inn appraisals for more than ten years, says, "Small inns, under six or seven rooms, are perceived as highly personal businesses, with revenue vulnerable to the whims and abilities of a particular owner-innkeeper. Thus the ability of the inn to sustain income from year to year is judged to be at risk." A small inn is sometimes perceived to be worth its real-estate value as a residence, and not much more.

Age is a factor. Bill Oates, inn-acquisition consultant from Brattleboro, Vermont, says, "Rarely is there any business value to an inn until it is at least three years old. There are exceptions for certain very high tourist areas where the number of inns is too small for the existing market."

But the truly critical factor for any potential buyer is whether the property makes economic sense for him or her. The most practical approach to determining this is to do a return-on-investment calculation.

To figure this, take the upfront cash you will have to invest, plus a figure for the value of your time in running the inn, including the time spent during any renovation. Divide this into your projected net profit, including your salary and the value of your personal benefit income. The resulting figure is the rate of return on your investment.

For example, say you buy an existing inn for a $125,000 down payment and spend an additional $30,000 on renovation and furnishing. You project a net profit of $12,000 the first year, plus $18,000 in personal benefit income, including your living quarters. To determine the return on your total initial capital investment, divide $30,000 (net profit plus personal benefit income) by $155,000 (down payment plus renovation costs); the .19 answer translates to a 19 percent return on investment.

In some very desirable areas of the country, property values are so high that this kind of simple return-on-investment calculation is discouraging. But there are other factors you need to consider.

First, buying an inn and becoming an innkeeper are, to some degree, emotional decisions. If being an innkeeper is what you really want to do, it may be worth it to you, in effect, to buy yourself an innkeeping job.

The second factor is property value. When we buy homes, we don't expect any yearly return on our investment, but we do look forward to reaping a gain when we finally sell. This same opportunity should exist with an inn.

And finally, in those cases where an innkeeper has substantial income in addition to that from the inn, the inn can provide considerable tax deductions, allowing the innkeeper to keep more of that other income in his or her pocket.

You need to feel good about all the money and time you'll put into your inn, so if you're going to make less on your investment than you would in U.S. Treasury bills, think again. If the figures only look good when you donate all your labor, think about how much you're paying to buy yourself a volunteer position.

On the other hand, keep in mind that it's not the total value of the inn that is used for this calculation. It's the actual out-of-pocket cash — and that makes the rate of return look better.

These are the practical considerations involved in making a decision on an inn's value to you. By contrast, here is inn appraiser Michael Yovino-Young's glossary of terms appraisers and banks use to explore inn value.

PRICE PER GUEST ROOM UNIT: An all-inclusive index that includes the component values of the real estate, personal property including fixtures and equipment, and intangible assets of the business, such as goodwill. This index normally ranges quite widely even in one community, based on quantitative and qualitative differences among inns, and the appraiser's judgment.

PRICE PER SQUARE FOOT OF GROSS FINISHED BUILDING AREA (GBA): This index relates the total purchase price to a unit amount based on the total size of the inn building, excluding basements and attics that are not living space. It is all-inclusive and incorporates real estate, personal property, and intangible assets.

GROSS ANNUAL RENT MULTIPLIER (GRM): This is income-based and time-honored in real-estate transactions. It is the purchase price as a multiple of the annual gross income or revenue that the inn generates.

OVERALL RATES OF RETURN (OAR): This is the relationship of the net operating income (before depreciation or debt payments) expressed as a percentage return or profit on the total purchase price. For example, an $800,000 inn that produces a net operating income of $82,000 per year has a 10.25 percent OAR. This index makes no distinction between equity capital and debt.

COST APPROACH: In the absence of any other possible approach, say when there are no sales of inns in the area and no income data to analyze, an appraiser may be forced to rely on replacement cost or reproduction cost methods.

The cost approach is essentially a real-estate value. What are typical ratios of real-estate values to other assets of a going concern? Based on a Yovino-Young sample of more than sixty inns appraised since 1983, the ratios vary as follows: real estate, 85 to 93 percent; personal property, 7 to 15 percent; and other intangible assets, 0 to 5 percent.

Placing a value on a business, particularly on an inn business, is not

INN VALUATION: A COMPARATIVE WORKSHEET

Value Components of an Inn
  Land and site improvements
  Building improvements
  Personal property, furniture, fixtures, equipment, etc.
  Intangible assets, goodwill, covenant not to compete, etc.
  Sum total of all the above equals one approach to an estimate of the value
  of the inn as a functioning, operating business.
Market Comparison Indices for the Appraisal of Inns
  Gross price/value per guest room unit
  Gross annual revenue multiplier
  Net income as a return on total investment (including borrowed capital)
Major Influences on the Value of an Inn
  Supply of inns and competitive lodging facilities in a localized competitive
  area
  Demand for transient lodging from visitors, tourists, business travelers
  Actual share of local lodging business versus competition's share, comparison of room rates, occupancy rates, amenities offered (private baths, fireplaces, spa, etc.)
  Quality of income history over recent past years and relationship of gross
  and net income characteristics to the asking or agreed purchase price
Possible Influences on the Purchase Price (as Viewed by the Appraiser)
  Special terms of financing, usually offered by the seller
  Major upside potential for increasing income and net profit: adding rooms,
  baths, and special features; increasing room rates and occupancy ratio;
  reducing expenses; etc.

an exact science. There is no one way to do it. But there is one certainty: Sellers will always want more than buyers want to pay. That's not surprising. Sellers have conceived and nourished a property and business, perhaps since its inception. They're almost like parents. How do you place a fair value on something this personal? This part of your inn-search process may be the most difficult and exasperating. Owners tend to value their inns on the basis of what they've put into them, rather than on what a new owner can get out.

Hire your own value consultant or appraiser if you're uncomfortable with the price being asked. Listing agents for inns are not always well informed about the inn business and lack the resources to gather market data on comparable properties.

A word of caution: Don't commit yourself to an expensive appraisal — and they can cost $5,000 to $10,000 — before you consult with your lender. Lenders usually have their own lists of approved appraisers and will not act upon reports from others.

Your appraiser or consultant should look at the inn for quality of location, the facilities themselves, and the consistency and reliability of the income history. Your adviser should also be able to inform you about the inn's desirability from the viewpoint of local institutional lenders. Unbiased answers to these and other practical questions are usually worth the cost of hiring independent experts.

ACHIEVING FINANCIAL GROWTH

How can you project the income effect of positive changes in the inn? Very carefully! Consider the ideas below, and make educated cost projections of the expense to implement them — don't ignore the cost of lost income if you need to close for remodeling — and the additional income from new rooms, more expensive rooms, higher occupancy, and additional sales and services. Be specific, and don't spend money you don't expect to get back in higher income.

Increase number of rooms

Increase room rates

Increase occupancy

Decrease expenses

Upgrade quality

Add capital improvements

    Hot tub

    Swimming pool

    Private baths

    Fireplaces

    Curb appeal

Increase profit centers

    Retail sales

    Additional food service

Wine and beer license
Special promotions
Marketing changes
Expand markets
Small group/conference site
Business travelers
Seniors
Foreign travelers
Travel agent-generated business
Bicycle groups

NEGOTIATING FOR PURCHASE

As a prospective buyer, you can't expect a seller to reveal detailed financial data until you have demonstrated that you are a qualified buyer. You are entitled to summary financial information, however, which may include gross receipts, net operating income, and occupancy percentages for the most recent year. On the basis of this data, you will be expected to make an initial offer. This often includes price, terms, management contract, covenant not to compete, disclosure requirements, and contingencies.

At this point, you will also want to specify the detailed material you will need to review during the escrow period. Naturally, it's essential to protect your interests with contingencies that make the offer invalid if the comprehensive data you receive later fails to support the summary. Now the negotiation begins.

This stage is always touchy, and you'll want to use your consultant or broker in the process. The cardinal rule of negotiation is to determine

---

Specific Inn Assets that Increase (Or Decrease) Inn Value
Larger rooms
Private baths
Spacious common areas
Legal kitchen
Furnishings
Fireplaces
Owner quarters
Jacuzzis in rooms
Acreage
Improvements
Spa
Extra landscaping or outdoor areas
Expansion potential
Well maintained

what you want and what the other person wants and to try to make it a win-win deal, so each of you gets what you want. Of course, you must decide first what exactly you need as a bottom line. Keep that foremost in your mind as you make decisions during the negotiations.

Remember that this is a process. No major negotiation results in immediate agreement. Everyone feels hurt or insulted at one time or another during the deal making, but going back and forth is a necessary part of the successful agreement.

And often, when you think all the negotiations are finished and the papers are ready to be signed, more demands are forthcoming and the process begins again.

During the negotiating period, try to maintain some distance from the owner and let your consultant or broker do the talking. This can keep the normal animosities and personal feelings separate from the working relationship you will want later. During this time, many things change or come up unexpectedly to cause both parties distress. This is normal, but keep your consultant out front and your bottom line in mind.

Once you have reached agreement, you'll want to see: financial statements for the last three years, business tax returns and schedules for at

---

Goodwill: A wonderful term — amorphous, intangible, nebulous, emotional — that asset sellers love to inflate and buyers love to discount. But what is it?

Inn appraiser Michael Yovino-Young: "Most appraisers will tend to let such intangible assets slide by without specifically attempting to quantify value, anticipating that these will be included in the comparative indices developed in the course of the market study."

Frank Kirkpatrick, How to Find and Buy Your Business in the Country: *"Good will, as far as I'm concerned, is an archaic term. For accountants it's a line to fill in on an assets sheet. It is supposed to have something to do with the reputation of the owner, particularly in terms of customer loyalty."*

Arnold S. Goldstein, The Complete Guide to Buying and Selling a Business: *"Pick up 10 different books and you'll find 10 different definitions. Sellers often use the wrong definition, equating it with a 'going concern' and pointing out that the business has an established history. In many cases it's only a history of heartaches and losses. . . . For you, good will means one thing: the business will make money. . . . If a seller demands a good will payment that puts the total price of the business beyond your acceptable rate of return, pass it up."*

Pat Hardy, co-executive director, Professional Association of Innkeepers International: "My favorite appraisal of goodwill is, the first year, the new owners will profit completely from the former owner's efforts, so figure 100 percent of net. The second year, only 50 percent, and 25 percent the third year, so the goodwill value should be around 1.75 times the net profit of a business."

least the last three years, transient occupancy and sales tax returns for at least the last three years, asset inventory and exclusion list, appraisals of real estate and personal property, promotional materials, inventory of goods for sale, tabulation of marketing efforts, and licenses and permits required.

The Physical Premises

You will want a contractor or person knowledgeable about old buildings to walk through the inn to be sure there are no surprises and that you are planning adequate financial resources for renovation in your business plan.

It is also important to double-check that the inn is licensed, approved, and zoned for all the business being done: number of rooms, bathrooms, pool or Jacuzzi, kitchen, fireplaces, parking, septic. Review the chapter on Playing Politics to be sure the inn is properly covered. If your realtor does not know about the licensing of inns, check with area innkeepers to be sure you have dealt with all normal inn requirements.

Most states have laws requiring the sellers and their agents to disclose all information relating to any significant historical problem the property may have suffered, such as flooding, foundation settlement, fire, windstorm damage, and so on. You are entitled to know these facts and should protect yourself by asking direct questions. If in doubt on any point of concern, ask for a written statement from the sellers.

MAKING THE TRANSITION BETWEEN OWNERS

If all has gone reasonably smoothly prior to closing the sale, your working relationship with the former owners will be off to a good start. Most selling innkeepers have invested a great deal of themselves in what you have just made yours, so they will want to share with you what they know about the business and the quirks of the property.

Of course, you will want to make changes and to approach the inn from a fresh viewpoint. Remember to be kind. Usually the former owners know all the things that are wrong, and had their own reasons for not changing them. Your ideas may not be as revolutionary as you think. If you approach the former owners asking for feedback on your plans, they will probably be able to warn you about pitfalls or suggest places to turn for more information.

To be sure you get all the information you want from the former owners, make a list, using this book as a guideline. Also, encourage the former owners to make a list of what they think you need to know. Be sure to go through both lists thoroughly, writing down the information for future reference.

Staff

Staff transitions are especially touchy in inns, because the personal nature of an inn carries over into the relationships between staff and owners. Staff will usually feel loyal to the former owners, and it will take time for you to win that loyalty. On the other hand, staff people will often have ideas for you that they couldn't get the former owners to try.

A change in ownership is naturally threatening to employees, but regular communication and clear renegotiation of job descriptions and your needs will usually lay the groundwork for a strong relationship. If you want to replace staff, however, make a clean break. (See Staffing chapter.)

Promotion

If the former innkeeper is well liked and has long been an integral part of the inn operation, you may want to ask him or her to write a letter inviting former guests to "come meet the newest members of the Long Lost Inn family." You might make a special-discount offer to former guests when you send the letter, as an extra encouragement for them to come.

New owners are news, so try to get local press coverage about the transition. Your aim will be to highlight yourselves and any new exciting direction you plan to take, such as adding dinner service or restoring the original gardens.

You may wish to foot the bill for a transition party, where the former owners will be guests of honor, and invite local merchants, media, and

---

Santa Barbara has been a bustling inn community since the first inn opened there in 1980. Here's what has happened in the last nine years to the thirteen inns:

- *The first inn opened with four guest rooms and shared baths. The original owners remain, minus one partner who was bought out. The inn purchased a building next door, adding five guest rooms and better innkeeper quarters. They recently added private baths and phones to each room.*
- *Four inns have been sold to new owners, two of them twice. One inn changed its name to project a new image. One was sold for a purpose other than an inn.*
- *In four cases the inns were developed from property already owned by the innkeepers-to-be. One of these went out of business after two years.*
- *The first two inns sold involved original owners who had unrealistic views of the business.*
- *One inn was built for speculation and as a decorating experiment, and has been on the market at a very high price since opening three years ago.*
- *Two inns on the market today have been for sale for two years.*
- *One inn with a leased property sold rather quickly because the price was lower than for inns where the price includes property.*
- *In at least two cases, the selling innkeepers carried part or all of the loan.*

Pat Hardy, co-executive director of the Professional Association of Innkeepers International, sees the Santa Barbara experience as a "microcosm of what's happening with inns nationwide. Losing partners and adding baths are not unusual. It's also interesting that in start-ups, sales early on occur with people who really weren't cut out to be innkeepers — and say so themselves when they leave the business. Finally, here as elsewhere, inns take a long time to sell."

restaurateurs. If they're willing, ask your predecessors to make a formal presentation of a certificate acknowledging you as the only people to whom they would entrust their old place.

What if you want to disassociate yourselves and the inn from the old ownership? Even so, it will be valuable for you to understand what kinds of promotion have worked for the inn in the past, so you can develop new promotional angles along those lines.

A final caution: Do not change the inn name without a lot of thought! If you need to disassociate your inn that completely from its past, be aware that you put yourself in the position almost of a start-up operation from the viewpoint of recognition.

SELLING YOUR INN

Deciding to sell your inn — the very thought is a staggering one. For many innkeepers the inn is not only a business, it's a residence, a role in the community, a dream fulfilled. Selling can leave you with no job, no home, no furniture, and a sense of no status. And what if your partner doesn't want to go? No wonder innkeepers sometimes decide to sell, then change their minds.

To make a decision you can stick with, ask yourselves a few questions:

1. What exactly is it about innkeeping that you want to leave? Make a detailed list. Sometimes the smallest remediable things can change your whole outlook on a lifestyle that has become draining. Many problems can be solved. If guests disturb you by putting doggy bags in your refrigerator late at night, buy a convenient refrigerator for guests. You can have control over your life and your business.

2. Money problems? How can you increase your income? Consider adding rooms or private baths — or simply upping the rates.

3. How realistic are you? Are you expecting too much of the staff, and then always feeling disappointed? Do you feel you deserve more financial return for your effort, when in fact the personal benefit income you receive at the inn would be hard to duplicate in any other job? Have you given the inn time to become profitable?

4. What if you stop innkeeping? What will you do instead, and how will you like it? Can you try it out before committing to it, or interview some-one who does it?

5. What do you get from innkeeping? What will you miss?

Spend at least a week away from the inn and see how your perspective changes. If you look forward to returning except for one gnawing prob-lem, it's probably worth a second try. If you just plain dread going home, it's probably time to sell.

*P*roblem Solving

Before your problems make you sell your inn, take a little time to see if you can solve them — and still keep the inn.

1. Make a list. Be very specific. "Lack of privacy," for example, is too vague. Do your guests want to enter your quarters? Do they want you to make them coffee every time you have a moment to yourself? Do they want ice every Saturday night when you're enjoying your favorite television program?

2. Carefully review your problem list. Are the problems real? Are they your problems, or are you trying to meet someone else's unrealistic expectations?

3. Now brainstorm about how you can solve the big ones. Follow brainstorming rules: Get all the ideas down before you critique them. Here's a problem-solving example:

Every time we sit down on the garden bench, somebody wants something. I'm sick of hiding inside to get peace and quiet.

Possible solutions:

- *Move the bench to someplace private.*
- *Clearly mark and staff a station in the inn where guests know they are to go for help.*
- *Wear a disguise.*
- *Meet guest needs before they can ask, with a refrigerator, ice machine, hot water and coffee, and local entertainment information all easily available.*
- *Sell your inn and buy one with a secluded garden bench.*

PREPARING YOUR INN FOR SALE

Plan on at least a year to sell your inn, even if you're asking a reasonable price. It will also take a great deal of your time: probably ten to twenty hours simply to prepare materials, depending on how accurate and complete your past record keeping has been; and uncounted hours talking with brokers, accountants, and prospective buyers.

Getting ready for the scrutiny of prospective buyers takes preparation. Start by putting yourself in their shoes: What would you want to know? What materials and information would you want to see? Keep in mind that most inns are purchased by people who want and need to make a profit. Help the owner see new ways to increase income. Maybe you didn't have the time, energy, or money to add the extra bath or renovate the barn, but you do know how it can be done; you may even have had plans made. Put together your sales package by trying to project yourself into a new owner's shoes.

Now is the time to step outside your "mother hen" role as owner and to look at your inn objectively as a business. Potential buyers may look askance at your family heirlooms and decor; they'll always think they can do it better. This can be painful, but march boldly into your new role as inn-business salesperson. Be reasonable and open to negotiation, but set parameters for showing the property and screening buyers. And you'll need to continue operating a quality inn during the process. It won't be easy, but you can do it.

Now is the time to walk through every room and inventory exactly what you will take and what you will leave behind. This will help to begin the emotional separation from the inn, as well as make for a clearer negotiation and contract period. You don't want the sale hung up on a fifty-dollar vase the buyer has fallen in love with.

If possible, remove from the rooms items that you will take with you, so buyers have a clear picture of what is for sale.

At this point discuss the ramifications and tax consequences of a sale with your accountant. Timing can make a difference in your ultimate gain; you need to understand different sales options, including holding the mortgage or installment sales, to negotiate terms most effectively.

VALUING YOUR INN

The greatest problem small business owners have when selling is realistically appraising the value of the business itself. It's too much like putting a price on your own children! Be prepared for an appraiser's valuation below your own. This is where your good records are an invaluable asset.

Remember that the new owner must be able to make a living. An established inn offers the opportunity to walk in and start serving breakfast to paying guests, for a profit. Review the material in Buying an Existing Inn to arrive at your selling price.

There is no absolute price etched in stone for your inn. There are, however, a set of possible prices that establish a range of values. They, in turn, are determined by a number of subjective and objective factors suggested here earlier.

Willingness to carry back some of the purchase price in the form of a loan to the purchasers may be essential to selling your inn or getting the price you want. (About eight out of ten inn sales involve some form of seller financing.)

PLANNING THE SALE

Follow the plan below for getting your financial, physical, and organizational house in order.

Financial

If you have been manipulating your books to hide income from the IRS, expect to reap the wages of sin when you decide to sell. Start immediately to issue receipts on all cash sales and record them in your financial system to maximize your income figures. Personal expenses that were inappropriately funneled through the business should be stopped if you wish to show an accurate picture of the inn's financial health.

If you have been doing otherwise, begin now to pay staff people "over the table" for a realistic view of expenses. Also, update your financial statements, profit-and-loss statements, and general bookkeeping.

Collect the data necessary to answer these questions: What is the present and historical financial state of the business? What is the occupancy rate, year-round and monthly over the business lifetime? How many rooms are there, and what are the rates?

Organize all marketing materials—guidebooks in which the inn is listed, press kit, brochure, special package deals you've offered—to give a full picture of the marketing health of the inn.

Gather everything together in an organized format for presentation to a listing broker or potential buyer. The absence of any of this information is likely to turn off your prospects, so clean up your act now.

Physical

Clean up, straighten up, touch up the things on your "To Do Next Year" list. Remember that prospective owners want to see all the often-neglected areas where guests aren't allowed, as well as the guest areas. Walk through the inn with staff and a detail-oriented friend to give you a critical perspective on your to-do list.

Organizational

Are all systems functioning? Do you have a staff manual? Is it up-to-date? Do you have a diagram of water, electrical, and gas-main switches and valves? Is there a current list of repair people and their phone numbers?

Your personnel records should show dates of hiring, salary progression, and vacation agreements, as well as job descriptions and scheduling patterns.

Talk with an attorney familiar with business and real-estate sales, an accountant who can discuss the tax implications of a sale, and lender-approved appraisers who can make a formal valuation of the business.

Timeline

Plan a timeline. Obviously you can't predict when the sale will occur, but you can set goals for accomplishing this list and for organizing your marketing steps. Other things continually press in on an innkeeper's time, so important tasks need to be scheduled if they're ever to be accomplished.

CHOOSING AND WORKING WITH A REALTOR OR CONSULTANT

Before you sign a contract with a realtor or consultant, interview your prospects. Ask questions and get references. Ask innkeepers or friends for recommendations of possible agents, but avoid working with close personal friends or family, unless you are very good at keeping your business life and your personal life separate. Check references carefully and beware of fast talkers, pushy people, and those who guess at answers rather than admitting they don't know.

Remember that not all realtors work with "business opportunities." The gap between evaluating real property and valuing a bed-and-breakfast inn is enormous.

Once you decide on a consultant or realtor, make him or her work hard; your future depends on it. But don't rely solely on your agent's judgment. You will have to do a lot of the work yourself.

Unless your realtor actively markets your inn, it won't sell. If the realtor works in the inn field, you will probably have a more positive experience. All too commonly, however, you will need to open the doors to industry contacts yourself.

The realtor must work well with other realtors, and must present you with a plan for marketing the inn. Although it won't seem fair, since this pro will be well paid when the inn sells, you will often have to push him or her to represent you adequately.

MARKETING THE SALE

Once you're prepared for your new position as inn salesperson, it's time to let prospective buyers know your inn is for sale. Start by having your realtor prepare attractive explanatory materials for enticing buyers and send the information to inn newsletters and instructors of classes for prospective innkeepers to hand out to participants.

Also, look through your guest list to locate people who might be interested in buying an inn and send a flyer along with a brief personal note. Finally, run adds in the *Wall Street Journal* business opportunities section, in major newspapers based in areas your guests live in, and in *innkeeping* newsletter.

Don't put out a For Sale sign unless you have little or no business and are desperate to sell. That sign will be an invitation to every neighbor and innkeeper in town to come and take a look. Continue to maintain and market your inn to guests. The most difficult part of selling, after making the decision to do it, is to keep up the good work. There is no need to tell your regular guests about your plans. It will only make them cautious about referring their friends, and may affect your business. Maintain your high standards of service, cleanliness, and maintenance. You not only need the inn to be an attractive property until the day it is transferred to new owners, but you also need to be able to leave the innkeeping part of your life with a feeling of satisfaction and accomplishment. Congratulations!

LEASING AN INN

Leasing is becoming an increasingly attractive way to own an inn business in an area where property values make it difficult to purchase the real property. It's not unlikely, for example, that an inn purchased five years ago may have appreciated so much that a new owner cannot afford to operate the inn and make the mortgage payments. To achieve a sale, the first owner may need to lease the property and sell the business portion.

NEGOTIATING A LEASE

The following issues should be considered.

GETTING OUT Always check on how you can get out of the lease at the time you are getting into it. The length of the lease should protect your investment long enough for you to see a return, and should allow you time to run the business to a level that would be attractively profitable to a prospective new owner. In some cases you can build in a series of points when the lease can automatically be renewed or ended. Build this in the lease in your favor.

LENGTH OF LEASE Stagger the options; three, ten, or twenty years are possible periods of duration. The three-year option protects you if you decide to get out of the business completely. The longer time periods give you an opportunity to sell at a profit, having established the business to a level attractive to a new owner.

PERCENTAGE OF SALES If you agree to pay the lessor a percentage of sales, be sure that the base amount of the lease is very low. This type of provision makes sense in a retail operation where foot traffic is high, but can be crippling for an inn where the number of rooms and thus the amount of

---

*P*hil Brubaker, Cottage Inn at Lake Tahoe, Tahoe City, California, is a realtor as well as an innkeeper. When he negotiated his arrangement with the owners of the property, he followed his own most important rule: Decide everything in advance.

The owners had already held the property for ten years, and were essentially looking for someone to care for it while it appreciated. Phil and his wife Carol didn't have sufficient resources both to buy a property and to rehabilitate and market it, so they chose a lease situation.

The arrangement involved a twenty-year lease. The innkeepers receive a specific initial increment, out of which they pay debt service on the property. Income above and beyond that increment is shared on a percentage basis with the owners. The lease was built so the innkeepers get a fair profit on their work before they pay the owners.

The property was appraised at the time of the lease, and agreement made that at the time the inn business was sold, the lessors would receive the amount attributable to the inn business. For example, if the property was initially appraised at $500,000, then sold later as an inn where the inn value was assessed at $100,000, the Brubakers would receive that $100,000. The lease also included a clause specifying allowable uses and an arbitration clause.

The Brubakers put in a certain amount of their own capital for renovation, which the owners accepted as an indication of their seriousness. As a result, the innkeepers were not required to pay first, last, and security deposits. The owners and the innkeepers signed the rehabilitation loan, both assuming responsibility for default.

According to Phil, "Pleasant, trustworthy, and agreeable owners made this arrangement possible. They understood the advantage to themselves of a lessor who would make the property more valuable."

business has little flexibility. If you must accept such a provision, design it so as to assure the lessor an amount covering basic costs and a reasonable extra. Then the innkeeper should receive a comfortable profit, with the remainder divided between the lessor and innkeeper.

REPAIRS AND RENOVATION Who pays for what? This part of the lease can get very detailed. One option is for the innkeeper to pay for inside work, and the lessor to pay for outside repairs: roof, trees, paint, driveways, and so on.

Another possibility is for the building owner to pay for renovations that would increase the value of the property, but not for extra baths, carpeting, or health-code work in the kitchen, which would benefit the inn business alone.

OPTION TO BUY If you have any hopes of buying, get this in writing. Try to lock in a sales price, unless housing prices seem to be falling. In most cases your business operation will increase the value of the property, and you don't want to pay the seller for your efforts.

Build into the lease the opportunity for a future buyer to purchase the property at the time the inn business is sold. Structure this clearly, so as not to confuse a live prospect.

TRANSFER OF LEASE You should be able to sell the business to a qualified person and transfer the lease with no unreasonable limitations imposed by the lessor.

SALE OF THE PROPERTY If the property is sold, the new owner must be obligated to honor your lease. If possible, also negotiate that you get a percentage of the profit over the value when you first leased it, especially if you are paying for renovations. You may also want a clause giving you first right to buy the property if it is offered for sale ("right of first refusal").

Special thanks to Bill Oates and Michael Yovino-Young (see Resources) for their invaluable assistance on this chapter.

Getting Inn Shape

When you make your plans about who will do what before the inn opens, be sure to keep in mind that time is money, and this cuts two ways. On the one hand, you can save the cost of hiring people to do the tasks you're willing to take on yourself. On the other hand, every day that you spend getting ready to open means one more day that you have no paying guests.

Say you plan first to do the remodeling, then the decorating, and then the promotion. You're planning on lots of time. Hiring a contractor to do the remodel while you get started on the brochure, or vice versa, can be very cost effective if it gets the inn open a month early.

You can calculate roughly how effective hiring help can be. For example, hiring a public relations firm to prepare a logo, brochure, stationery, signs, and a press kit might get you open four weeks early. Since most of your costs are fixed whether or not you're open — mortgage, insurance, auto — the income you receive from room rents can be applied pretty directly to your costs. You might want to reduce that income figure by the projected costs of food, supplies, and staff, if any. But the basic point is this: since your major costs are constant whether or not you're open, delaying your opening costs you money.

AMBIENCE

Ambience is character, atmosphere, and mood. It's the consistent carrying out of a theme, such as the Victorian Mansion or Ye Olde Ski Lodge. Ambience planned and achieved with clarity during the renovation stage can be a major marketing tool over the lifetime of the inn. But before you even consider the marketability of an image, you need to be sure it fits you. You'll look as silly as an orchid at a hoedown if you wear ski boots in a Victorian mansion.

The classic advice to aspiring authors is, "write what you know," and there's a corollary for aspiring innkeepers: More than anything else, your inn should be your own personal favorite, the place you would most like to stay. It must reflect your personality as well as your fantasy. Design it so it feels true to you.

How do you see yourself? Ask your partner and friends to describe you. Does their view match your own? Do you need lots of private time in the mornings, or do you love to sit down to breakfast with a crowd? Do you prefer that friends call before they drop by, or do you keep a big pot

---

A rlene and Jim Moorehead at Joshua Grindle Inn in Mendocino, California, provide a cozy fire in the parlor every evening for guests to enjoy with their sherry and fruit, a photo album with color pictures taken during the restoration work on the inn, sewing baskets and corkscrews in each room, and a book of restaurant menus with space for guests to write up their own personal opinions. The latter makes fascinating reading! Guests feel very cared for, even when Arlene and Jim are busy or relaxing elsewhere.

of soup bubbling to encourage impromptu gatherings? Everybody needs private time, but do you need more than the average?

Are you formal or casual? Are chats around the fireplace, feet up, your favorite way to spend the evening? Or do you prefer long gowns and tuxedoes in a setting that sparkles with elegance? Do you think a little clutter makes for comfort, or do you tend to empty the ashtray before the cigarette is extinguished? Any of these styles can be a success. The question is which one is for you.

What about your community? Who comes there, and for what purpose? Is it a mountainous, rustic area or a city that hums all night long? The personality as well as the geography of your inn's community must be taken into account.

What's your inn building like? It's difficult to do art nouveau in a Federal-style building. The appearance of the structure is one of the biggest elements of the ambience your guests will experience. Inappropriate decor is an assault on the senses, but the range of acceptable choices is wide.

The look of the inn exterior can enhance the mood, creating a quality that draws passersby to stop and stay. The way you set up your property, for example, can be expansive and open, or you can landscape to provide privacy and intimate corners. The entryway can determine what guests feel in the first thirty seconds outside and inside your door. While they wait for you, do you want them to feel formal or relaxed?

What's your family like? Do you have small children or teenagers? Who will be your helpers? Do you need very separate space and physical privacy? Will you feel comfortable with guests wandering into your quarters during family arguments or while you're trying to reprimand your children? And how will your guests feel about it?

Finally, what's the field like? What are industry expectations? What's your competition doing? You'll get the best idea of the range of what's offered at inns by traveling and staying in them. Some are elegant and expensive, others have a warm family feeling; still others exude an energetic sense of the nearby beach or a romantic, intimate atmosphere and fantastic views.

These areas should help you establish a set of "givens" against which to evaluate image options. Keep in mind that your ambience will be a marketing tool. The more clearly you know what you are, the easier it will be to project that image.

As you visit other inns, analyze how their approaches work or don't work. Adapt ideas you like to fit your own objectives. Visit inns with an open mind and adventurous spirit. Let yourself absorb the unique flavor

---

Comments from travelers: " We loved the pets at Captain Jefferds Inn in Kennebunkport, Maine. They seemed like a needed touch of casualness in that very opulent place. It might have been easy to feel like a bull in a china shop there, but not when there are dogs stretched out on the chintz sofas."

of each establishment, and don't prejudge on the basis of your own great concept. Don't try to make an inn what it isn't. If you prefer a mountain cabin, don't reject a place because it's a formal, city inn. Neither one needs to be "better," but each needs to be special.

The inns you like best may differ tremendously from each other, but probably each of your favorites will communicate a definite something. Try to describe it as a starting point for taking stock of what you want. Don't even think about renovation until your unique ambience is clear to you.

RENOVATING

This is what you've been waiting for: the difficult and expensive task of making a promising structure the inn of your dreams.

And it can be fun! Some innkeepers find after several years of operating an inn that the most fun of all was creating it. If you've done the groundwork in visiting other inns to develop a strong sense of what you like and don't; if you have financing in hand so you can hire adequate help; and if you have allowed adequate time, then you're off to one of the most creative challenges of your life.

Renovating an inn is different from renovating a personal home. At home, we usually do a room at a time at our leisure, sometimes during vacations, often when we've decided to sell. With an inn, you'll do all the rooms at once, with a timetable and an opening date in mind, and you'll be attempting to please many different people, not just yourself and your family.

Depending on the size of the project, hiring assistance can make the difference between a challenge and a nightmare. If the job involves little more than choosing new furnishings, you may want to do it on your own. If you feel safer with the advice of a decorator, but haven't the budget or the inclination to put the whole project in a decorator's hands, you'll find many competent designers who will be happy to act as consultants for an hourly fee.

If you are adding rooms, changing the exterior, or doing anything that will require the approval of the local government building department, you will probably need an architect and a general contractor. General contractors run jobs, bringing in carpenters, plumbers, electricians, roofers, drywallers, and so on at the appropriate times. If you decide to act as owner-builder, you will do the job of the general contractor.

Before you decide what you'll do and what you'll hire people to do, complete your financial projections and get the money. Determine and outline precisely:

- The number of guest rooms necessary to meet your financial needs.
- The number of rooms with private baths.
- The number of shared baths.

- The maximum number of guests that will use the dining and living rooms.
- The personal space needs of the innkeeper.
- The number of cars to be parked on the property.

Sketch out your renovation ideas. You can buy drafting paper and templates for bathroom fixtures and furniture. Play with placement in relation to entrances and windows. Decide whether you want sinks in the guest rooms if your bathrooms are down the hall. Consider ventilation of the rooms and bathrooms. Spend time in each room at various times of the day to check lighting and heat needs.

Use the numerous valuable resources for information on restoring old homes to avoid serious and costly mistakes. (Check Resources at the end of the book).

Once you're clear on what to do, you need to find the people to help you do it. You find competent, reliable, honest decorators, architects, and contractors in much the same way that you find other support people.

- Architects, designers, or contractors can often recommend people for the other jobs.
- Look at older homes, inns, and restaurants that have been successfully renovated and ask owners and managers for their recommendations. If you see homes being renovated, stop and talk with the people working at the site.
- A historical society or landmark committee may also be able to give you names of people who work on older homes. Sometimes, though rarely, a building department will give you names.
- Lumber companies, wholesale hardware stores, and other building supply providers may have recommendations.

Select two or three good prospects for each job area. Call them and briefly describe your project and timetable. If some prospects are not interested, they may be able to recommend others. Set up initial consultations at the site with interested people. Usually there is no charge for this, but don't waste the time of a bidder you have no intention of hiring.

Present your list of jobs and your sketches, but also be attentive to the ideas of these pros. They can often solve in a moment a problem you've grappled with for weeks. Don't be afraid to discuss money. Whether you're buying an hour's consulting time or spending thousands on an architect, get rates and bids.

Comments from travelers: "We stayed in a room with a fireplace where we were given, and only after specially requesting it, three pieces of firewood. Small pieces. We understand that there must be safety concerns in a wonderful old mansion like that one, but the message we got from the whole experience was that we'd got a room that was billed as a fireplace room, when actually the innkeepers would have preferred we not have a fire. It didn't draw, either."

If your project requires an architect, he or she will probably send a draftsperson to measure your house and site as the first step in preparing working drawings. Be sure your architect is familiar with the local building department's requirements for site plans, landscape plans, and so on. Provide the architect with what you consider to be the items to include in renovation costs. Use the sample that follows to draw up your own list. Ask for a preliminary design and cost estimate.

When the preliminary design drawings arrive, study them closely. Go over them with someone who is familiar with all the trades and understands the symbols for plumbing and electrical work. Think through these aspects of the project in the preliminary design phase, not after working drawings have been prepared. Every change costs money.

When the changes in the preliminary design are complete, the architect you have chosen will prepare final drawings for the approval of the building department and any necessary review boards.

If you hire a general contractor, he or she will get involved in this phase. Before you hire a contractor, get bids and call the state licensing board to verify that the contractor's license is in good standing. Read the sample contract in Appendix 5 and use it as a model for your own contract. Add a specification sheet detailing your choice of fixtures and supplies by brand names.

ACTING AS OWNER-BUILDER ON YOUR RENOVATION

If you decide to take this on, prepare to work harder than you ever have. Put all your good clothes away. Here are some specific hints.

• Plan to work every evening and early in the morning scheduling subcontractors and deliveries of supplies.
• After approval of final drawings, order enough copies to get three bids from major subcontractors: framing, plumbing, electrical, drywallers, finish carpenters. When possible, get fixed bids, not time-and-materials contracts. (Time-and-materials contracts mean you pay an agreed hourly wage for the actual number of hours to complete the job plus the cost of materials.) Insist upon products specifications in writing; a written contract, including timing, progress payment schedules, costs for changes, guarantees, and warranties; and so on.

Coauthor Mary Davies opened *Ten Inverness Way, Inverness, California,* with five guest rooms and two shared baths in 1980. By 1986, says Mary, "the handwriting was clearly on the wall that, even out here in the country, travelers prefer private baths." That year she and husband Jon made the decision to convert one of the guest rooms into two private baths, thereby creating an inn with four guest rooms, all with private baths. They raised room rates so nightly income remained steady. "I'm sure we came out ahead financially, because an inn with private baths has a much higher occupancy rate," she says.

- Do not schedule everything at one time. Plumbers do not like stumbling over electricians and painters don't want sawdust in the air. Develop a master schedule for subcontracted work. Understand the order of the work to be done. This is the typical order for an addition: clearing the area and demolition, digging the foundation, laying the foundation, framing, rough plumbing, rough electrical, outside siding, sheet metal, roofing, insulation, doors and windows, drywall, painting, wallpapering, finish plumbing and tile, finish electrical, and finish carpentry.

  Using a large calendar and estimated schedules from your subcontractors, figure the length of the project. Anticipate delays.

- Hire manual laborers for regular cleanup. Arrange for a bin for trash. Rent a chemical toilet for workers, if necessary. Supervise the demolition.

- Get temporary worker's compensation insurance during construction, to cover your manual laborers and anyone else you hire on an hourly basis. Ask all subcontractors to provide certificates of liability insurance and worker's compensation policies; make copies for your files.

  Injuries to employees of one of your subcontractors are your responsibility if your subcontractor does not carry the necessary insurance. Subcontractors who have no employees should show you certificates of business liability coverage. These are a defense for you should they claim they were your employees, as well as a backup for them if a suit arises as a result of their work.

  Note: Both your worker's compensation and business liability insurance companies require you to obtain certificates of insurance from subcontractors. Both are within their rights to charge you premiums for these contractors and their employees if you fail to have the certificates on file.

- Have a truck available; space for stacking lumber and supplies conveniently and safe from theft and water damage; and a ready supply of pinup working lights and heavy-duty extension cords, brooms, hoses, miscellaneous nails, demolition tools, hammers, screwdrivers, and so on.

- Develop a master schedule for ordering materials. Some special-order items like doors, windows, and plumbing fixtures have long lead times. Ready space to store them when they arrive.

- On the one hand, it's awful to live in the house during renovation; on the other hand, it's a good idea to have someone on the site. If you are in the house, store as much furniture as you can away from workers, dust, and dirt. Have a telephone on the site.

- Remove windows, if necessary, and have them reputtied by a reputable glazier. Paint them prior to reinstallation. Before doors, windows, and walls are in place, consider moving in to the structure large items like four-by-ten drywall sheets, one-piece shower units, armoires, and the like, which are sometimes impossible to get in later.

WHAT TO CONSIDER IN INITIAL RENOVATION AND SETUP COSTS

As you plan your renovation and landscaping, keep in mind that you are creating something today that you must be able to maintain tomorrow—

and forever. It's worth a little extra expense for long-lasting paint and a high-quality preparation job. It's worth working with a designer on a low-maintenace landscaping plan. And it's worth selecting appliances and plants that minimize energy and water use. Before you begin making changes, survey the areas listed on the next page and set some priorities.

Outdoors

Parking area cleared, paved, striped
Lights along paths, porches, parking areas
Enlarged sewer, water, gas lines
Sign and light for sign
Timers to turn lights on and off
Landscaping: design, labor, materials
Fencing
Sprinkler system and timer
Outdoor electrical outlets for gardening
   equipment, party appliances
House painted, scraped, blasted, etc.
Roof: reroof, cover old and new material —
   tiles, shakes, shingles — skylights
Rain gutters: plastic, metal, or aluminum
Safe stairs and walkways: access for wheel-
   chairs, crutches, canes
Rekeying exterior door locks, deadbolts
Alarm system
Outdoor barbecue, spa
Handicapped access

Indoors

ELECTRICAL
Shavers, blow dryers (short cords, ground
   fault interruptors)
Reading lamps
Electric blankets
Switch close to door for lamp turn on
Laundry
Cooking
Dishwasher
Vacuum cleaner
Separate circuits for coffee makers, other
   small appliances

Heating, cooling systems
Televisions
Intercom, stereo systems
Smoke detectors
Doorbells

TELEPHONES
Jacks in rooms
Portable phone
Two lines or more, or central console

COMMON ROOMS AND BEDROOMS
Windows and doors, double glazed: easily
   and safely operable, replacement,
   keyed, privacy, screens
Decorating: wallpaper, paint, molding
Floors: carpet cleaning, floor refinishing
Soundproofing and insulation: between
   bedrooms and baths, between bedrooms, between floors, above common
   rooms, insulation for energy conservation (everywhere you can!)
Sinks in room: plumb while walls open,
   even if installation is in the future
Fireplaces: add units, stack units, repair,
   clean and outfit, plumb for gas, permanent screen, heat output improvements,
   such as heatilator, wood stove
Closets: linens close to rooms, cleaning
   supplies close to rooms
Smoke detectors (battery operated
   or AC)

BATHROOMS
Design: stacking or back-to-back saves
   plumbing costs
Tile or modular shower stalls
Shower fixtures, hand held

---

*V*acancy, No: At The Captain Lord Mansion in Kennebunkport, Maine, they use a hospitable alternative to the usually harsh No Vacancy sign. Their sign says The Captain Lord Mansion; a smaller sign below says Vacancy, and one still farther below says No. The No one is removable, of course. It's a convenience to travelers not to have to climb the stairs or the path to find out if there is a room. Also, be sure your guests know whether they're expected to walk right in the front door, ring a bell, or find another entrance.

Tub refinishing or painting
Lighting near mirrors
Grab bars for entering/exiting tub
Soap holders or dispensers
Decisions on bathrooms: private or shared,
 room for shower only, tub only, com-
 bined, toilet and sink
Towel racks in guest rooms or baths
Ventilation: fan, window (frosted glass?)
Heater or heatlamp
Hot-water heater adequate and close wrap
 pipes, circulating pump?
Toilet: seats, commode with pull chain,
 water saver

Sink, tub, and shower fixtures and
 stoppers
Counter space: vanity, antique piece, additional dressing table
Handicapped requirements

LAUNDRY
Elecrical outlets
Gas
Plumbing
Machine space for extra dryer
Laundry chute
Shelf for folding

DUMB WAITER

TELEPHONE LOGISTICS

The telephone is so much the lifeline of an inn that it pays to plan an efficient, functional, handy system.

Phones should be located where you'll spend a lot of time. Since that's
often hard to pinpoint in this business, more and more innkeepers are
using remote phones. They'll go with you up to the guest rooms while
you make the beds and out to the garden when you cut the flowers. If you
take a scaled-down version of the reservation book along as well, you have
all the information you need to provide immediate service.

You will probably want at least two lines. The Glenborough Inn has a
business line and a personal line, and four telephone sets. There is a special gadget that allows both lines to be picked up on any one of the phone
sets, at a price far lower than buying a two-line system from the telephone company. The phone sets are in the office, the parlor, the innkeepers' private quarters, and the kitchen.

The personal phone has a pleasant chime; the business phone rings,
so the innkeepers can tell them apart and answer them appropriately. At
Glenborough, the parlor phone has no bell at all, since many guests are
trying to escape the sound of telephones.

Many inns provide a line especially for guests. If your inn will be
catering to business travelers, you should also consider putting phone
jacks in each guest room and making telephone sets available upon
request. This may require extra lines.

Some inns have a pay phone and even a small dish of change for
guests. One inn installed a pay phone in a Victorian armoire, along with a
light, a stool, plenty of coins, and a sign that says, "Fooled you, didn't I?"

Other inns simply allow guests to use an extension of the inn phone
located in the common area. Even if you prefer to discourage guest use
of the phone, there will be occasions when they will need to use it, so be
sure the phone isn't in the middle of busy traffic areas, like the kitchen or
the registration desk. Inns usually ask guests to make long-distance calls
with their credit cards or by reversing charges. This privilege is rarely
abused, but it can be very expensive when it is.

Consider purchasing special services from the phone company such as call forwarding, which routes calls to you when you have to be away from the inn for a substantial period of time, or to a willing, gracious neighbor you can pay to handle phones from his or her own home. Call waiting is another option; it allows you to make sure callers get a personal contact instead of a busy signal.

Give careful thought to who will be using inn phones, when, where, and for what. Letting the phone system grow like Topsy is much more expensive than figuring out at the outset how many phone jacks you need and having them all installed at once.

WHEN YOU'RE NOT THERE

A warm, skilled person to convey your message, your values, and your style in your absence is the first choice for handling phone calls. The second choice, and only for very brief absences—ten minutes or less while you check in the Joneses—is to take the phone off the hook. Then you can be sure to give the Joneses the attention they deserve. Busy signals within reason probably whet a caller's appetite.

For longer absences, such as an afternoon or an evening, a high-quality answering machine is a good idea. More and more people are getting them, and callers are therefore more likely to feel comfortable leaving messages. Make your outgoing message clear, concise, and warm, but not "cute." Cute is too subjective; not everybody wants to hear an imitation of George Burns singing "Reach Out and Touch Someone."

A machine that takes cassette messages allows you to program one for your basic spiel, and modify another one to use for weekend callers. You might say, "Sorry, but we're completely full for the weekend. We'd love to have you come another time. Please leave your name, address, and telephone number, and let us know if you have a specific date in mind. We'll call you right away if we have an opening for the date; if not, we'll send you our brochure and hope you'll try us again."

Voice-activated machines record caller messages of any length, a good safeguard against losing the last digit of the phone number of a caller who wants to book the whole inn for a week in dark, cold January. If your message tape is limited to twenty or thirty seconds, warn callers about it in *your* message.

Be honest and realistic. One inn tape says the innkeepers are out grocery shopping. It's a warm touch, until you hear it the fifth time in three days!

Some inns use answering services, others never will. One advantage to an answering service is that they can often locate absent innkeepers, and therefore possibly arrange a booking that would otherwise be lost. For example, if a caller has stopped in town on a rainy Thursday afternoon and wants a room *now*, a service could call you even at your bookkeeper's and let you know to get back to the inn or arrange for someone else to do so. Some inns also provide their answering services information on when rooms are available, so they can tell callers, "Yes, there is a room, and I'll have the innkeeper call you between five and seven this evening to confirm your reservation."

Answering services are risky, because staffing varies. A tired operator may not only lose you a booking for a night, but also may discourage a potential guest from calling ever again. An answering machine message is canned, but at least you control the canning.

Return all calls promptly. Even at that, you will lose callers to other inns. But even if they've made other plans for the imminent trip, your courtesy, professionalism, and warmth may persuade them to try your inn next time.

KITCHEN ORGANIZATION

You may have been a good cook for years, but as an innkeeper, you and your kitchen are going professional. Before you can plan an efficient inn kitchen, you need to make some decisions.

- What meals, beverages, and snacks will you serve? Inns variously provide breakfast, lunch, dinner, wine, hors d'oeuvres, bedtime milk and cookies, picnic lunches, high tea.
- How extensive will each meal or snack be? Full or continental? Cold cereal or gourmet? Baked, fried, or microwaved?
- How will you serve? Buffet, sit-down all at once, sit-down over a set period of time, family style, individual plates, room service?
- What service will you use? Stainless or sterling, china or stoneware, plastic or crystal, paper or linen?
- Will guests have a menu choice? Or will you serve one item to all (allowing, naturally, for dietary restrictions)?
- Will you serve large groups such as conferences, weddings, and receptions?
- Where will you serve? In the garden, dining room, fireside, kitchen, breakfast in bed?
- Who will cook, serve, clean up?
- How will your food service choices promote your overall inn image?
- How much will you actually prepare in your kitchen? Will you buy baked goods? A number of fine inns cook nothing on premises, serving only fresh fruit, cheeses, and pastries, for example.

Organize the kitchen for its actual use, paying special attention to the preferences and procedures of the person who'll do most of the cooking. If you're designing a kitchen from scratch or making modifications, a few hours consulting time from a restaurant designer could be well worth the price.

On your own or working with a pro, the second step to a kitchen plan involves listing the centers of use you'll need. For example, a baking center includes baking pans, flours, sugar, measures, and so on, conveniently close at hand. Other centers to consider are:

- Table or tray setup: silverware, dishes, glasses, linens.
- Food preparation: knives, cutting boards, food washing, garbage disposal.
- Coffee and tea: cups, spoons, sugar, lemon, and cream available outside your main work area, if guests are welcome to help themselves.
- Desk: for planning menus, answering phones (convenient but out of the way of traffic), making shopping lists.
- Family eating area.
- Guest eating area.

Some kitchens may need all of these; others will need very few. Kitchen centers often overlap, but do consider effectiveness. Draw a plan and play with it until it works well for you.

The needs of an inn kitchen will be somewhat different from those of a home kitchen so think about these ideas when you plan the renovation:

- Health-department requirements.
- Dishwasher. Portable? Commercial?
- Instant hot-water spout on sink.
- Water purifier on sink spout.
- Extra plugs for electrical appliances.
- Coffee maker directly attached to water supply.
- Garbage disposal.
- Three-bin stainless-steel sink.
- Vented hood with fan over stove.
- Adequate, easy-to-clean counter space.
- Storage: open shelves for frequently used items. Space to store items so that they are all ready to use again: coffee cups, sugar and creamer, and spoons set out for the next morning's service or individual breakfast trays set up; wineglasses on trays for evening hours. Room to store cleaning equipment and items purchased on sale and in volume.
- Adequate refrigerator and freezer space, for inn needs and family needs.
- Restroom for innkeepers and kitchen staff. (Health department requirement in some areas.)
- Good lighting.
- Comfortable colors.
- Adequate hot-water heater.

You've probably noticed a heavy emphasis on function in this chapter, and there's a good reason for it. Experience teaches that brass fixtures show waterspots badly and fragile wineglasses can't be safely popped into the dishwasher. Don't furnish your kitchen with "cute" antiques that aren't functional or supplies that require extra work to maintain. In the inn kitchen, form should follow function.

BREAKFAST IDEAS

The Santa Barbara Innkeepers Guild has discovered that the last thing people at their innkeeping workshops need advice on is breakfast. Everybody seems to have good ideas for what to serve. But innkeepers find that some foods and serving strategies work better than others, and contribute more to the overall image of the inn.

---

*T*he importance of breakfast: "It's my strong feeling that travelers prefer a substantial breakfast. It need not include eggs and meat, but it should include some source of protein. Whatever you serve, it's important to serve plenty of it and make sure the quality is high."
—*Pamela Lanier*, THE COMPLETE GUIDE TO BED & BREAKFASTS

JEN·ANN '85

AN ELEGANT BUFFET AT A QUEEN ANNE VICTORIAN

The setting: An ornate mahogany sideboard. A Delft vase of daffodils. Serving dishes of fine antique china and crystal and a silver coffee service. Guests help themselves, then take plates to tables for two and four in the dining room and sun porch. The tables are set with linen, ornate silver service, antique china and crystal, and nosegays. A discreetly available hostess refills coffee cups and prepares soft-boiled eggs on request.

The food: Three choices of home-baked breads with cream cheese, butter, and jam. Fresh fruit compote of berries, citrus fruit, pineapple. Various domestic and imported cheeses. Crystal pitcher of fresh juice.

A COUNTRY BUFFET

The setting: An antique Hoosier kitchen cabinet displays a help-yourself breakfast, served from antique crockery. The hostess serves hot beverages in country-style mugs from her kitchen counter. Guests carry their matching pottery plates to a heavy oak table set with handwoven placemats, overlooking a stream, and a dried-flower arrangement is the centerpiece.

The food: Bananas in a basket or fresh strawberries to slice over a choice of cereals in crocks — granola, Raisin Bran, Shredded Wheat. Large crockery pitchers of milk and juice. Bagels and English muffins to toast yourself, and bran muffins steaming hot. A bowl of berry yogurt.

FAMILY-STYLE BREAKFAST

The setting: A sunny breakfast room, a large table set with a redchecked tablecloth, bouquets of daisies, simple white china, and stainless-steel flatware.

The food: As sleepy guests appear, they help themselves to a bowl of stewed fruit or homemade applesauce. Hot beverages are served by the innkeeper. When everyone has arrived for the nine o'clock meal, a huge platter of the inn's special scrambled eggs, fortified with everything but the kitchen sink, is served; a warm loaf of homemade whole-wheat bread and a cinnamon nut ring are brought out at the same time. The guests pass the foods while the innkeeper keeps mugs filled. Homemade marmalade and fluffy sweet butter are on the table.

ELEGANT SIT-DOWN BREAKFAST

The setting: A dining room table set with sterling silver, linen napkins, an antique lace tablecloth, crystal juice glasses, and antique china. There's a fire in the dining room fireplace. The innkeeper dresses in a period costume.

The food: First, a salad plate of fresh fruit, perhaps kiwi with brown sugar and sour cream or melon and pineapple. Hot beverages and juice are offered. The second course is spinach frittata, served with a basket of hot breads and muffins in a linen-lined silver bowl to pass. There are crystal and silver bowls of jams and butter.

BREAKFAST IN A BASKET

Delivered to the guest room at a prearranged time is a willow basket of specially designed pottery, heated to keep the decadent French toast (topped with fresh blueberries and sour cream) warm and gooey, and chilled to keep the banana-pineapple fruit bowl fresh. A quart vacuum bottle of hot coffee and a carafe of juice are tucked in under the quilted placemat cover, along with tableware wrapped in napkins and tiny pottery sugar and creamer. Cups are tied to the basket handle with grosgrain ribbon. Guests can enjoy breakfast in their rooms or carry it to the garden or the beach.

CONTINENTAL BREAKFAST IN BED

A tray set with unique embroidered napkins holds a coffee carafe and mugs, freshly squeezed juice in stemmed glasses, and a basket of large, flaky croissants with raspberry jam and butter.

PRACTICAL CONSIDERATIONS

Breakfast is a wonderful opportunity for creativity, but there are unexpected parameters. The first is local government health standards. For inns with only a few guest rooms, it's usually not worth investing in a complete commercial kitchen so you can scramble eggs. Be sure you find out about government restrictions in this area.

The second constraint is timing. Business travelers often want to eat early, by eight o'clock. Vacationers are usually happy if breakfast is available between nine and ten. Guests who must leave very early are sometimes offered coffee and rolls that have been set out the night before by the innkeeper. Too long a range of service time can make more work for the innkeeper and push check-out time back.

---

*M*ike and Suella Wass of the Whitehall Inn, New Hope, Pennsylvania, make breakfast an occasion for their guests that sets the theme for the inn. "We wanted to tap into the new cuisine for breakfast," says Suella, "and to differentiate ourselves from the considerable competition in our area." Their candelight breakfasts are a hit. Silver, china, and classical music set the mood for the convivial nine o'clock gathering of guests and innkeepers. The breakfasts have received rave reviews from the media as well. Here's a typical menu:

Beverages: Variety of custom-blended Whitehall coffees
and freshly squeezed red tangelo juice
Breads: Suella's butter coffee cake and caraway-cheese muffins
Interlude Course: Cheddar cheese and corn spoonbread
Fruit: Baked stuffed pear with caramel sauce
Entrée: Fruit, nut, and cheese crêpe and Bucks County sausages
Dessert: Whitehall chocolates

If you decide to serve everyone at once, on the dot at nine o'clock, remember that this can be a great strain on shared bathroom facilities. Also plan ahead for gentle ways to say "no breakfast" to late arrivers.

If you choose to serve breakfast over a range of time, say from nine to ten, whatever you provide needs to look and taste as good at ten as it did an hour earlier. Those lovely puffy German pancakes sink fast, and they take about twenty minutes to bake, longer than you may want to keep unfed guests waiting in the dining room. Make another choice.

If you are willing to serve breakfast in bed, select foods that will still be warm or cold by the time they're delivered. Think of this kind of breakfast as a buffet. Can the foods be cut with a fork or picked up with the fingers, or are you expecting guests to deal with thick slices of ham on a tray full of china that is balanced on their knees—over your antique quilts, too!

Be bountiful! Croissants and jam can look like a feast when the rolls come by the basketful and the jam is generous. It's much better to raise your rates by a dollar a person and serve more food, than to charge less and scrimp.

If government regulations allow it, baking your own coffee cakes is usually much more economical than buying pastry, and at the same time, it adds a homelike touch. Colette Bailey at the Grey Whale Inn in Fort Bragg, California, is always winning blue ribbons at the fair with her coffee cakes, promoting the inn as a side benefit and providing breakfast guests with a very special treat.

Innkeepers are more likely to get tired of serving the same old thing for breakfast than guests are to tire of eating it. Experimentation is not always greeted with delight. If you want to serve a Guatemalan breakfast with refried beans, you had better make granola available for the more conventional eaters. Also plan to have simple things on hand—wholewheat toast, cereals, yogurt—for vegetarians, diabetics, or others with diet restrictions if your usual menu won't meet their needs.

Within the menu on a given day, plan variety in color, temperature, and taste. Don't serve hot spiced cider, warm dried-fruit compote, and pancakes with syrup at the same meal.

Guests who are willing to try anything in the food line with great goodwill are nevertheless finicky about coffee; you just can't please everyone. The best guide is to serve coffee the way you like it, assuming that means it's fresh, hot, and flavorful. Some inns offer brewed decaf as well as regular coffee; it's becoming increasingly popular. Plan to offer an herbal tea, as well as black tea, and honey and sugar substitutes.

Make your table setting creative and attractive. Garnish the plates with sliced fresh fruit or fresh herbs and flowers from the garden. Make the taste and the look of breakfast another enhancement of the overall image of your inn.

Plan breakfast time so you can enjoy it. A frantic innkeeper makes guests uncomfortable. Don't offer what you won't be happy about delivering. If you hate to cook, don't offer a full breakfast; serve bakery croissants with a flair. Don't offer breakfast in bed in your brochure if you're going to begrudge it to the guest who wants to take you up on it.

Food should be memorable: how it tastes, where it's eaten, how it's served, and who eats with you. All these are memories guests take along, and pass along to others.

MARY'S GUATEMALAN BREAKFAST

For each serving, arrange on plate:

2 fried eggs
2 strips bacon
A nice blob of refried beans (preferably black and homemade), topped with unsweetened whipped cream and teensy shreds of orange peel
A tiny dish of salsa
A warm, rolled, buttered flour tortilla

MARY'S GRANOLA

Mix together:

2-1/2 pounds rolled oats
3/4 pound wheat germ
1 pound unsweetened grated coconut
2 to 3 cups sliced almonds

Mix together:

3 cups firmly packed brown sugar
1-1/2 cups water
1-1/4 cups vegetable oil
3 tablespoons vanilla extract

Combine the 2 mixtures. Transfer to a shallow 11- by 17-inch baking pan. Place pan in a 350°F oven until mixture is golden, stirring every 5 to 10 minutes. The total oven time should be 40 to 50 minutes.

GLENBOROUGH SHIRRED EGGS

This is an easy dish when you have just a few guests or an odd number of them.

1 teaspoon fresh bread crumbs*
2 to 3 slices Swiss cheese
1 slice tomato
1 egg
2 slices fresh mushroom
1 tablespoon heavy cream or half-and-half
Parmesan cheese, as desired

Grease a 1-cup ramekin or custard cup with butter (or spray with a nonstick coating). Sprinkle the bread crumbs over the bottom. Arrange the cheese in the ramekin so that it reaches up the sides of the dish, forming a cup shape. Top the cheese with the tomato slice and break in the egg. Carefully place the mushroom slices on top of the egg and drizzle with cream. Finally, sprinkle with parmesan cheese.

Place ramekin in a preheated 350°F oven and bake for 15 to 20 minutes, or until egg is firm. Makes 1 serving.

*Pat likes to use the crusts left over from making French toast to make the bread crumbs.

PAT'S DECADENT FRENCH TOAST

Put this together the night before, so you can sleep a little later in the morning.

2 tablespoons corn syrup
1 cup firmly packed brown sugar
5 tablespoons margarine or butter
16 slices inexpensive wheat sandwich bread, crusts removed
5 eggs
1-1/2 cups milk
1 teaspoon vanilla extract
About 1/2 cup sour cream
1-1/2 cups strawberries, hulled, or one 10-ounce package frozen unsweetened strawberries, partially thawed

Combine corn syrup, brown sugar, and margarine in a small heavy saucepan and heat, stirring, until bubbly. Pour syrup mixture into a 9- by 13-inch pan. Nestle the bread slices into the syrup, making two layers. Mix together eggs, milk, and vanilla and pour over the bread.

Cover pan and refrigerate overnight. The next morning, remove the pan from the refrigerator and discard the cover. Place pan in a preheated 350°F oven and bake 45 minutes.

To serve, loosen edges of bread from pan sides with the blade of a knife or a thin-bladed spatula. Invert the pan onto a serving plate so that the caramelized portion of the french toast is on top. Divide into serving portions and top each serving with a tablespoon of sour cream and some strawberries. Serve immediately. Serves 8.

NANCY'S SOUR CREAM COFFEE CAKE
Breakfast at the Bath Street Inn

1/4 pound (1/2 cup) butter
1/2 cup vegetable shortening
1-1/2 cups granulated sugar
2 eggs, beaten

1 cup sour cream
1 teaspoon vanilla extract
2 cups less 3 tablespoons all-purpose flour
1 teaspoon baking powder
1/2 teaspoon baking soda

Topping:
1/2 cup finely chopped nuts
2 tablespoons granulated sugar
1/2 teaspoon ground cinnamon
Powdered sugar

In a mixing bowl, cream together butter, shortening, and sugar. Add eggs, sour cream, and vanilla and beat well. Combine flour, baking powder, and baking soda and gradually add to butter mixture, mixing thoroughly. Combine topping ingredients and set aside.

Grease one 9-inch cake pan and pour in one half of the cake batter. Sprinkle one half of the topping mixture over the batter. Add remaining batter to pan, and sprinkle with remaining topping.

Bake cake in a preheated 350°F oven 1 hour, or until a cake tester inserted in the center comes out clean. Remove from the oven and set on counter top. Sift powdered sugar over surface of cake. Cut in wedges to serve. Makes one 9-inch cake.

ROOM PLANNING

Hauling home the perfect armoire only to discover that it doesn't quite fit any of your guest rooms is a disaster. But you can easily avoid it with some careful planning. Since you'll have to keep all this information somewhere (and keeping it all in your head will result in a great deal of crowding), follow the plan below for making the whole purchase and decoration operation run smoothly and economically.

Develop a folder for each room that includes:

- A scaled floor plan for placing furniture (see sample below).
- Swatches of fabric for drapes, upholstery, quilts.
- Carpet swatches.
- Paint chips.
- Wallpaper samples.
- Photos of furniture owned or purchased; use a Polaroid camera. This is especially important when you order furniture to be delivered sometimes months in the future.
- A list of measurements of furniture acquired for the room.
- Photos from magazines that convey something of what you want for the look of the room.
- A room planning sheet (see sample, next page).

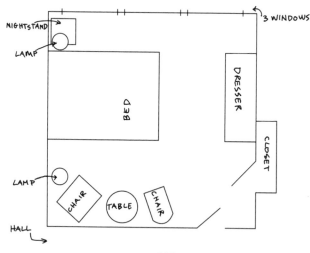

Carry this folder, a tape to measure furniture you may buy, and a small ruler to measure how pieces will fit in your scale plan.

The format that follows can be used in planning your decorating for each room in the inn. A blank sheet is included in Appendix 5 for you to pull out and copy as necessary. The sample reproduces the plan used in decorating one of the rooms at the Glenborough Inn.

ROOM PLANNING WORKSHEET

Room name (or location): **Grand Suite**

Type of room: **Fireplace Suite**

Atmosphere desired: **Elegant, rich, Victorian**

Natural light: **Full afternoon sun, no morning sun**

Colors: **Forest green, peach, rust**

ITEMS TO BE PURCHASED OR INSTALLED

	Budgeted	Spent	Ordered	Installed
Bed Queen-size, canopied reproduction				
Headboard Canopy hand-tied				
Mattress/springs				
Dining Table Round tilt-top				
Light				
Chairs				
1 Straight-back, green needlepoint				
2 Straight-back, Victorian, rust				
3 Armchair, Victorian, tapestry				
Nightstands Half table, cherry				
Table for lamps Grandma's hand-painted				
Bed lights Installed in wall one				
Dresser				
Firewood container				
Armoire				
Desk/dressing table Cherry with mirror				
Mirrors				
Makeup - on dressing table				
Dressing - on armoire				
Heating/air conditioning electric wall heat, fireplace, ceiling fan				
Wall treatment Wallpaper, ceiling painted				
Window treatment green drapes, antique lace sheers				
Floor treatment green w/w carpet				
Bed covering quilt comforter, crocheted coverlet				
Fireplace tools				

continued on next page

continued from previous page

| Linens | _____ |
| Accessories | _____ |

In the format above, make a master list of items needed in more than one room, such as beds, linens, carpeting, draperies, and accessories, which you may be able to purchase in quantity.

LAUNDRY

There are three basic options for getting inn laundry done: do it yourself, send it out, or contract with a linen service, which will supply clean linens from their own stock.

In most areas, a linen service is a last resort. The sheets provided are often worn and mended; the towels tend to be small and the washcloths thin. But if your inn is in a rural area without a laundry, and if water is scarce or laundry space in the inn impossible, you may have to go with a service. Shop them for quality, price, and frequency of delivery. Plan plenty of space to store the clean linens and the bags of dirty ones, in an area accessible to a delivery truck.

Doing your own laundry takes a lot of time, and it's heavy work, with all the folding and lifting involved. Before you decide to take it on yourself, calculate the cost in energy, water, and time, then compare this with the estimates you get from laundries. Remember that working with a laundry has its own time demands, like tracking inventory every week, which must be considered before reaching a final decision.

Before contracting with a laundry, check their references carefully. When you've made your choice, try to find one person at the laundry to be your contact. Reward good service with a small gift at holidays.

If you purchase linens for the inn, the number of sets you'll need depends on how often you want to wash or how often your laundry will deliver. You'll need at least two sets of linens per room, probably more. Light colors spot with mascara and rust from water. Dark towels sometimes show lint. Sheets in prints, rather than solids, show spots less.

Contact hotel linen supply houses in your area and compare their prices with department store sales. Look for quality, price, and consistency of supply. Will you be able to get more washcloths in this same red next January? Linen supply houses sometimes carry products you won't be able to locate elsewhere, such as heavy feltlike mattress pads that last for years. You may be required to order a minimum of half a dozen or more of each item.

If you decide to do laundry at the inn, design your work area carefully. Plan for storage of dirty things as well as clean ones. You'll need a heavy-duty washer, at least one dryer, shelves for supplies such as soap and fabric softener, space for folding, adequate light, and baskets. Locate the area convenient to kitchen and office.

And make the space attractive. You'll spend a lot of time there.

SHOPPING: MAKING THE LIST, CHECKING IT TWICE

Shopping for your inn is one of the fun parts, but there's so much to buy that it's easy to forget essential things—until a guest asks for them.

The best way to make your list is to go through an imaginary day at the inn, beginning with check-in time. Start with the entry: Where will it be? Is there a desk for holding your cash box, room keys, reservation forms, and guest registry book? Are those items on your list?

Is there enough seating in the common room for all your guests at once, and do you need it? Where will they set a drink? Do you need coasters? What will you serve drinks in? How will you keep the drinks warm or cold? Will you serve only one beverage, or will any beverage you serve work appropriately in the glassware on your list?

That's the merest beginning of making your list! Now, in your mind, follow your guests to their rooms, then to the bathroom, to outdoor seating areas, and to breakfast. If you'll serve several menus, picture serving each one, and list what you'll need.

Here's a long list of things to think about when choosing specific items, as well as items you might forget!

- Smaller plates make food look more bountiful.
- Consider how the color of your china will look with the food and with your guest room (if you'll serve breakfast in bed) or dining room decor.
- Containers for ice cubes and for chilling bottles.
- Glasses and openers for beverages guests bring themselves.
- Spares of big things: bedspreads, tablecloths, mattress pads, shower curtains. You will need these for emergency replacements without having to wait for the laundry to finish.
- Outdoor furniture in inviting spots.
- Fancy dispensers for liquid hand soaps; they look good longer than the containers the market sells.
- Bud vases for when flowers are sparse, bigger vases and bowls for midsummer.
- Adaptable tissue box covers so you can buy tissues in the cheaper, less-attractive packages.
- Attractive baskets in all sizes for clutter: menus from local restaurants, other inns' brochures, matches, kindling, coffee filters, plants in from the garden for a week of show, cleaning supplies.
- Large canisters for baking ingredients.
- A powerful vacuum cleaner lightweight enough for quick cleanups.
- A battery-powered hand vacuum for smaller, even quicker cleanups, such as vacuuming up a line of ants.
- Cleaning supplies that are multipurpose, for efficient storage and carrying.
- China, flatware, and glassware in patterns that you'll be able to replace when broken.

- Or wonderful old mismatches of china, flatware, and glassware to use in gay profusion!
- Thermos-type servers to keep hot beverages hot.
- Trays for serving beverages in the evening, taking breakfast to rooms, and for guests who make a special request for a tray even if it's not your normal serving plan.
- Flashlights, candles, and other emergency equipment.
- First-aid kit.
- Kitchen things: skillets large enough, potholders you won't be ashamed to use to carry a warm plate to a guest, a lemon zester for making neat garnishes, one of those tools that will core and slice an apple in one push, and food and serving things for people who won't be able to eat your regular menu.

A mere beginning!

SOMETHING OLD, SOMETHING NEW: A COMPENDIUM OF DECORATING IDEAS

What a guest sees in an inn reflects planning that began long before that moment, often even before the inn was selected. If your dream inn is a Victorian with large airy rooms, you may have problems finding it, since Victorian homes in reality tend toward small, dark bedrooms and larger, also dark parlors.

Once you've chosen a structure compatible with your dreams, you must take care during renovation to ensure that electrical outlets are in the right places, that beds and other furniture will fit between doors and windows, that the floors — whether you're refinishing hardwood or underlaying uneven floors for carpet — will fit with the whole decorating scheme, and that fixtures for bathrooms and hardware for cabinetry complement the rest of the decor.

Remember that you can't be all things to all people. Mary says she was excited at first about decorating at Ten Inverness Way, but then she became "catatonic," as she puts it, because she was trying to decorate for some unknown public. "I finally realized that can't be done well," Mary says, "and decided to decorate as I would for my family. It turns out the public likes it, too!"

Be clear and firm about what you want, but temper it with the reality of what people will "buy." If your taste runs to black walls and ominous furniture, you should probably either rethink your taste or go all out for a "haunted" image. Listen to the suggestions of others, and there will be many, but measure them against your own instincts.

To assist you in making the myriad decisions ahead, here's a collection of ideas gleaned from the experience and research of innkeepers.

BEDS

- Where possible, use queen- or king-size beds. King beds that can be converted to twins provide valuable flexibility in spite of occasional complaints from king bed users about the bump where the beds have been joined.
- A daybed in a spacious room can be made up to accommodate an extra person.
- Antique, handcarved, and reproduction head- and footboards are impressive focal points.
- Footboards can almost double the cost, but not the effectiveness of the look. When you buy bed frames, get them without footboards, or use the footboards as heads for other beds.
- Very tall people can be comfortable in double beds, but not with their feet through the slats of a footboard. Leave it off for tall folks.
- Old doors with beautiful wood can be transformed into headboards.
- An interesting focal point in lieu of a headboard can be achieved by using a large antique map, a large picture or groups of pictures, or by draping the wall.
- Forming corners of drapes around the head of the bed creates a cozy feeling and economical canopy effect.
- Antique double headboards can be attached to double or queen beds; two antique twin-bed headboards can make one king-size headboard.
- Firm, comfortable, quiet beds are an investment in guest happiness.
- Sturdy cotton ticking on mattresses helps your sheets stay tight and smooth, unlike brocade covers.
- Pillows can be part of the room's accents: shams on bed pillows, small crocheted covers on throw pillows.
- One king-size sheet can be made into two pillow shams and a dust ruffle.
- Dust ruffles are a country look and hide bedsprings, but they do make it more difficult to make the bed. Invest in ruffles that fit well.
- Or cover the bedsprings with a coordinated, fitted sheet instead of using a ruffle.
- Guests will sleep, sit, and put suitcases on your bedspreads; choose them with this in mind.
- Have a spare bedspread or two for spills and other emergencies.

BATHS

- Most Americans prefer shower baths to tub bathing—except at inns, where they frequently request the room with a tub. Use tubs where you can, but plan also to make showers available for most guests.
- Capitalize on the romance of the tub. Put two tubs in the honeymoon room as in San Diego's Britt House, or a big tub for two in front of a fireplace, as in San Francisco's Spreckels Mansion.
- A shared tub or shower room complements limited in-room bathing facilities; sinks in the rooms complement down-the-hall shared showers and toilets.

- Brass fixtures in the bathroom are old-fashioned and initially attractive, but they're costly and hard work to maintain.
- Install sinks in antique dressers to match your decor.

Comments from travelers: Bobbi Zane, publisher of the inn traveler newsletter, Yellow Brick Road, considers comfort a priority: "Furnishing a room for guests to use is more than just an exercise in interior decoration.

"We discovered this personally, and somewhat inconveniently, when a business trip took us to an inn for a four-day stay. This is a city inn, one that caters as much to business travelers as it does to weekend visitors. The innkeeper knew about the different needs of business travelers; indeed she offered to provide me with early morning coffee before I left for a breakfast meeting. And when a dress needed repair she was right there with a sewing kit. And the iron and ironing board (to straighten out wrinkles in a silk dress) were within reach.

"We had seen the room in advance and picked it. It was bright and cheery with big windows across one wall, spacious without being huge. A good place to relax between meetings, we thought. A table flanked by straight-back chairs could serve as a desk.

"Alas, the room wasn't as comfortable as we'd anticipated. The table held a tray of decorator items, some sherry and glasses; there was no place except the floor to place these when I needed to use the table. The straight-back chairs were great for desk work. But when I wanted to sit back and read I had to use the bed.

"There was a nice big armoire with plenty of hangers along one wall. That was great. However, there was no chest of drawers in which to place folding clothes. And for the four days I found myself rummaging through my bag every time I wanted something. (I have to admit that I encountered this same problem in a new elegant city hotel recently.)

"All this points up the advice that's frequently given to innkeepers: Move into your rooms. Take your luggage and stay there for a day or two. Go about your business just as you would if you were staying in your own quarters.

"This process can be very revealing. Some possible discoveries include: a need for better sound insulation, lamps that look great but don't provide enough light, bedding that's too heavy or too light, the need for a shelf in the bathroom (very common) or the need for a bigger shelf (even more common), a shower that's balky or isn't very workable, the need for a full-length mirror and enough room to step back and use it, mirrors that are too high or too low, window shades and curtains that are difficult to operate, the need for a soap dish in the shower.

"The list goes on. We have encountered every problem on this list."

- Waterproof-fabric shower curtains launder well and quickly; apply a spot cleaner to the hem (which shows the dirt first) and put them in the washing machine.
- For fabric shower curtains to be used with a plastic liner, use a sheet, making buttonholes for the rings.
- Smooth glass doors for showers clean more easily than pebbly ones.
- Sliding shower doors keep the water in its place, but the tracks are hard to keep clean.
- If space is tight in a former-closet bathroom, put the sink — or the tub — in the guest room.
- Plan plenty of space in bathrooms for makeup and shaving gear.

LIGHTING

- Guests want reading lights on both sides of the bed and lights for shaving and applying makeup.
- Plan carefully: Start with light sources for specific purposes like bed reading, makeup, and chair reading, and then determine if they're enough.
- A designer suggests three lights minimum are most flattering to rooms and guests because shadows are less harsh.
- Overhead lights are rarely installed today, but don't remove existing overheads. Just put in a rheostat to adjust light intensity for the mood, or install a fancy fan and fixtures.
- Lamps installed in the bedside wall do not take up table space. Neither do floor lamps, but they're knocked over more easily.
- Rewiring old lamps is not particularly difficult, so finding and restoring old bridge lamps can be economical.
- Modern lamps in brass or china can complement an old-fashioned decor.
- Old lampshades add a special flavor to rooms, but are difficult to find and expensive to custom-order.
- Try bulbs in various wattages in room lamps to decide on the right amount of light. Beware of dangerously high wattages; they burn lampshades and start fires.
- Every room should have a romance light that can be turned down low enough to see but not to read. Leave this one on after you turn down the beds.

FIRST IMPRESSIONS

- The entryway sets a tone for a stay and can entice a potential guest, so the first impression is important. Use a handsome antique desk, a cabinet, or a cheerful bouquet. The entryway is a priority decorating job.
- How your inn looks to passersby involves primarily landscaping and gardens, but don't forget to look from the street at your curtains, for neatness, and your lighting, for warmth. A porch swing or a well-placed armoire visible through an upstairs window can contribute to your image.

FURNITURE

- Wood and marble surfaces add richness to rooms. Guests appreciate them and generally are careful to protect them. The occasional water rings or iron marks are easily repaired.
- Marble surfaces are less susceptible to inadvertent guest damage, but are also easier to overlook when cleaning; watch for barely visible rings and dust.
- Don't be so concerned with being true to the period that you provide no comfortable furniture. A few good pieces with tasteful coordinates can give an impression of consistency.
- A round table with a cloth draped to the floor adds softness and an extra surface to the room. Make the table inexpensively from a round piece of plywood and a pedestal foot from the home building supply store, or buy a "decorator table" from the Penney's catalog.
- Varathane in a satin finish is good protection for fine wood surfaces.
- Dressers, shelves, closets, cupboards, and luggage racks should be selected based on the probable length of stay of your guests. Overnighters generally don't need a full dresser; guests staying longer than two days need space to store things outside their suitcases.
- If possible, guest rooms should have at least one comfortable chair.
- Stripping woodwork: Some of it is ugly and soft. Don't take on a stripping project without carefully evaluating whether the finished product is worth the work.
- Window seats are a charming way to add seating, and can also be used to store blankets, pillows, and Christmas decorations.
- Trunks are another decorating feature that double as storage.
- Quilted material for window-seat cushions softens hard edges of cut foam, and it's durable.
- Velcro makes cushion covers easy to remove for washing.
- Cover imperfect dresser tops with crocheted doilies.
- Glass or Plexiglas covers to protect dresser tops are easy to clean, but quickly show dust.
- Mirrors can solve space problems by creating illusions of distance.
- Utilitarian mirror placement: over the sink and long enough for short and tall users; a full-length or large, tilting, over-the-dresser mirror to dress with; a lighted or small, movable, tabletop mirror for makeup and hair.

WALL SURFACES

- Painting woodwork: Many old houses are dark, and can benefit from tasteful paint jobs.
- Wallpaper can hide many defects in old, repaired walls that might otherwise need resurfacing.
- Wallpaper will take incidental scuffs and scrapes without showing them.
- Wallpaper can set a tone for a room and be the starting place for the whole decorating scheme.

- Wallpaper accents are economical: Paper a ceiling, just one wall, or half-way up the walls.
- Use a strip of wallpaper border in a painted room around the ceiling or to frame a bed, fireplace, baseboard, or doorway. The illustrations in wall-paper sample books are a good resource for ideas.
- Good vinyl-coated wallpaper is easier to maintain than paint.
- Stain and prime woodwork before installing it as trim. Then just fill the nail holes.
- Consider covering a foam or masonite wall or fitted-doorway panel with fabric to reduce sound transmission between walls and through unused doorways.
- Use soft things to absorb sound: replace shutters with drapes, use tables and tablecloths instead of hard dressers, and hang quilts on the wall.
- Stencil borders on walls and ceilings.

FLOORS

- Paint and stencil a "rug" on a wood floor.
- Wood floors are beautiful, but they're noisy. Plan large rugs, and runners in hallways and on stairs.
- Before you choose an expensive refinishing job for your wood floors, con-sider the folk-art look of painting them.
- Different color carpets in each guest room add interest.
- Dark carpets show lint; light carpets show spots.
- Investigate the new, easy-care surfaces for refinishing wood floors. In a satin finish, they can produce a look very much like waxed floors.

WINDOWS

- Professional installation of good-quality window shades is worth the money. A shade installed slightly askew will wear out faster.
- An alternative to blinds is an under layer of blackout-fabric curtains on big rings to slide easily behind your regular curtains.
- Use window coverings for energy conservation, noise insulation, privacy, and light control, as well as decoration. Line them to extend their lives and accommodate late sleepers.

ACCESSORIES

- Bedspreads can be tablecloths, tablecloths can be curtains, and comfor-ters can be upholstery. Be creative.
- One good old quilt can provide fabric for several pillows, framed wall hangings, and quilted wreaths. Use the little scraps to make Christmas tree ornaments.
- Use wreaths for artwork on walls; make them of vines, herbs, fabric, and so on.
- Frame illustrations from old books. Use photos from family albums. Save handsome old calendars. Use them all for wall decoration.
- Switchplate and outlet covers can be made attractive with wallpaper or brass or wood covers.

- Make or buy linenlike easy-care cloth napkins bordered with lace.
- Solid-color napkins show stains more than print ones. Whites can be bleached.
- If you permit smoking, provide ashtrays and matches.
- Set out books and magazines liberally for warmth.
- Plants, dolls, old teddy bears, ducks, and shells and bottles from the beach can make a room look human and inviting. A Victorian dress or hat on a rack is another nice touch.
- But if a room looks full before the guest arrives, it will be difficult to enjoy. Put "objets" in spaces guests don't need: hatboxes atop the armoire, for example. Leave valuable surface space for the guests.

COLOR

- Color evokes a mood, creates an ambience, and changes space perceptions. You can also target customers — upper class, male or female, and so on — by choosing certain colors, says Carlton Wagner, noted designer and color consultant.
- Dark colors or patterns make a room smaller, but hide incidental spots on bedspreads and rugs. Light colors and white expand space and look fresh, but must be cleaned more often.

Noted designer Carlton Wagner on color response: "Everyone has long been aware that certain colors look good in certain situations and in certain combinations. There is an additional factor to consider: People respond to the colors they see.

"Response to color takes place at several levels. There is an inherited response to color, one that is shared with all humans of the same sex. There is a learned response to color because of your background and upbringing. There is a response to color based on climate and geography.

"To choose colors for an inn it is important to consider how people are going to respond to the colors you choose. The colors must be pleasing to the eye and appeal to the greatest number of the type of person you wish to attract to your inn. Different colors will attract different guests.

"Some basics. Shades of green will appeal to people who are upwardly mobile. Blue will appeal to most people when relieved with white and other colors. Purples and lilacs will appeal to most women, but not most men. The browns to tints of tan will have universal appeal if accented with other colors. Blue-based pinks will appeal to women and yellow-based pinks will appeal to men.

"Remember, you can not clone yourself to fill your inn. You will have to rely on others to occupy rooms. Therefore the colors you choose should be well within your "like" range, but must have sufficient appeal to attract and please the type of guests you wish to have stay with you."

- Guests seem to choose first the rooms with dark and light contrast or rooms that are bright and airy. A monochromatic color scheme is less inviting and less memorable, yet the right single color enhances the serenity of a room.
- Accent a simple door with paint, highlighting the panels.
- A common color thread running through your rooms will mean you can use the same color towels and tissues for them all.
- Avoid ice-blue color schemes in cold climates; avoid red in hot areas. Simple changes in your basic color scheme—different throw pillows and table coverings, for example—can warm rooms for winter and cool them for summer.

MISCELLANEOUS

- Make scale drawings of rooms, measuring and marking window locations, doors, fireplaces, and built-ins. Use scale furniture pieces for model arrangements and to help you figure appropriate sizes of pieces to be purchased.
- Before you renovate a room, evaluate it very carefully. Don't incur the expense of cutting in a skylight when a lighter color paint would do the trick.
- Use closets as part of the decor. Remove the doors, wallpaper in a coordinated print, and make them dressing rooms.
- Keep a notebook on decorating ideas gleaned from visits to other inns, magazines, and restoration museums.
- Don't overlook the possibility of involving a decorator or designer, especially if you have more than five rooms to do. You'll save time and possibly money, when you consider the decorator's discount purchasing power.

Before you decorate, and then on a regular schedule during your life as an innkeeper, stay a night in every room. Notice noise, cobwebs, ceiling paint problems, lighting, mirrors, down-the-hall bathroom accessibility, water pressure, and hot-water adequacy. These are all areas that affect guest comfort tremendously. And guest comfort is your chief objective.

AMENITIES

The amenities are the extras, and there are as many philosophies about providing these special suprises to your guests as there are innkeepers. The range of possibilities is also very broad. Here are things to consider when planning what you would like to offer.
- What do *you* especially appreciate when you travel?
- What will help your guests be comfortable in your area? Umbrellas and boots may be the perfect surprise for rainy-weather visitors.
- What will make the visit more enjoyable? This could be anything from bikes to hot tubs.

- What is characteristic of your area? Wineglasses, salt-water taffy, or apples?
- What will increase your competitive edge? When people call and ask about prices, what amenities will make your inn look like a good value? What will encourage a guest to come back? Balance the cost of an amenity with its effectiveness.
- Do you have the energy and the money to continue to provide the amenity? For example, bowls of fresh fruit in each room are a cinch when the orchard is full, but expensive in winter. Turning down beds may mean hiring extra staff when you plan to go out to dinner.
- Would guests miss it if you didn't provide it?
- What problems would providing it cause to other guests? Television in a game room is a plus to some guests, a minus to others, and the sound may carry up the stairs to the guest rooms.
- How will you feel if a guest takes the entire basket of bubble bath envelopes from the bathroom?

Also keep in mind that the amenities you provide can and should reinforce your inn image. Things guests take home should continue to remind them of your inn and their lovely experience there. If you can provide things guests will take to work or share with others, your amenities can extend your marketing program even further.

Here are the pluses, and in some cases the minuses, of various choices.

FLOWERS The rose garden you established to create curb appeal can also be a good source of cut flowers, as well as petals to dry for potpourri. Fresh flowers make rooms smell good as well as look lovely. When cut flowers are out of season and expensive, consider flowering plants such as poinsettia, impatiens, and flowering bulbs.

PORT OR SHERRY Many inns put small decanters in guest rooms or the common area. They look nice and are relatively inexpensive. The Bath Street Inn serves Italian Swiss Colony port; Ten Inverness Way serves Gallo's Livingston cream sherry — and guests are forever asking the names of those fine beverages!

CANDY Some inns put mints on pillows when they turn down the beds. At other inns, a candy jar in the parlor is a sweet stop on the way back from dinner.

TURN-DOWN SERVICE Five-star hotels *must* provide this, so it's a posh service. On the other hand, it can be a difficult service to staff, as you must hire someone to do it if you want to go out for the evening, and they'll have to wait around watching for guests to leave for dinner. It can cause problems for guests: interrupted naps, lovemaking, and so on. On the

---

Comments from travelers: "At one very elegant inn, it wasn't clear to us until we were leaving the next day that the sumptuous parlor was open to us to enjoy. In other inns we've visited, a decanter of something on the coffee table and an invitation to enjoy it is a nice way to get this message across."

other hand, it can give the innkeeper an opportunity for a conversation with quieter guests, as well as a chance to remove wet towels from antique furniture pieces and fragile quilts to a stand for the night.

MENU BOOK Guests really appreciate a menu book or basket of current best-restaurant menus. It also saves hours of innkeeper time making recommendations!

EVENING BEVERAGE SERVICE If your parlor is comfortable for gathering, a "wine time" encourages it. Inns should also provide something non-alcoholic, such as soft drinks, mineral water and lime, lemonade, or iced tea. At some inns, guests are specifically invited to this evening gathering; at others, they're just informed that there will be drinks in the parlor at such-and-such time. Some inns serve hors d'oeuvres. This is prime time for innkeepers and guests to spend together.

TV AREA At the Bath Street Inn, the Olympics were the catalyst for bringing a television into the inn. It's in a third-floor alcove, separate from the guest rooms. Guests watch evening news, favorite programs, or whatever; it's especially appreciated by business travelers there on their own.

VIDEO CASSETTE DECK AND VIDEOTAPES If there's little to do in your area in the evenings, you might provide a library of classic films.

STEREO AND RECORDS, TAPES Choose music that you enjoy to enhance the inn's ambience.

LIBRARY This can be a separate room or a corner of the parlor, with well-stocked bookcases and a selection of magazines. Your choice of reading material can reveal your personal tastes, and also establish an image.

SPA, TENNIS COURT, SWIMMING POOL Any or all of them, if provided in such a way as not to detract from the peacefulness guests desire, are pluses that will attract people.

TELEPHONE A small desk, message pad and pencil, directories, and good light make a comfortable spot for phone calls in the common area or in guest rooms. See Telephone Logistics for more on the pros and cons.

BATHROOM ITEMS Oversize towels or clean towels twice a day are luxurious. You might provide a basket for carrying toiletries to a shared bathroom, or stock your bathrooms with soaps, shampoos, and shaving cream.

PERSONAL NEEDS ITEMS Bathrobes, an iron and ironing board, and a hair dryer or blower all fit this category.

OVERSIZE BEDS Americans who have king-size beds at home will find it difficult to sleep in a standard double bed. You can order converter rails to make your antique double beds accommodate queen-size mattresses. You can also use two twin beds together for a king.

EXTRA PILLOWS Shams for sitting up and reading in bed are especially nice in rooms too small for easy chairs. Fancy neck rolls and heart-shaped pillows are other nice extras.

WELCOME SERVICES Some inns offer a beverage to refresh arriving guests. Others carry luggage and provide airport pickup.

ROOM KEYS Customers like the option of locking their rooms when they're out. You can ask a locksmith to make keys that will open the inn entry door and separate room doors. For example, at Ten Inverness Way, every guest-room key opens the front entry door, but no one guest-room key opens any other guest room.

ALL-DAY COFFEE AND TEA SERVICE It's easy and inexpensive to provide in vacuum serving bottles and much appreciated.

DINNER RESERVATION SERVICE This is simple to do and makes guests feel special. Because restaurants get frequent reservations from innkeepers, they often give your guests better service and more attention than they'd otherwise receive. And restaurateurs may return the favor, sending a late dinner guest your way.

BICYCLES This depends on your area, but if it's a nice place to bike, the bikes will be used and appreciated.

PICNIC LUNCHES Provide them yourself, make arrangements with another supplier, or send guests to a nearby deli for do-it-yourself.

SOCIAL DIRECTOR You'll be asked, and should be able to say, where to bike, ride horses, play tennis and golf, jog, hike, find antiques, see best scenery, and get Burt Reynold's autograph.

POSTCARDS AND STATIONERY A nice giveaway that does your promoting for you! Some inns provide stamps and do the mailing.

AIRPORT/TRAIN/BUS PICKUP This can be expensive in terms of time and gasoline, but if it's practical for you to do, it makes guests feel very special.

REFRIGERATOR Guests like to have a place to store the oysters they bring back from the beach, to chill the wine they picked up on a tour, and to hold their doggy bags from dinner until time to go home.

MISCELLANEOUS Games; coloring books and crayons; jigsaw puzzles; popcorn maker, stocked and ready; Polaroid camera to take pictures of guests for their albums; coffee mugs to take home; cuttings from your herb garden; and seasonal items, like heart cookies for Valentine's Day, Christmas ornaments, Easter eggs.

Amenities are a good topic to brainstorm with your partners. Silly things may be perfect for your inn, or you may feel that only the most elegant items reflect the image you've chosen. Whatever your direction, be innovative and have fun with this!

SOURCES AND SUPPLIERS

Before you buy basic inn items, check the Yellow Pages for industry suppliers. Motel equipment in your Craftsman bungalow? Of course you won't use motel bedspreads and frames, but under the covers, inn beds are strikingly similar to beds in other top-quality lodgings. You can say the same for soap, towels, and tablecloths, as well as other necessities, and the discounts are excellent.

If you find the perfect brass fixtures at a retailer's, contact the manufacturer directly and ask about industry prices, particularly when you can buy in quantity—even small quantities.

Industry suppliers can also provide solutions to problems that you will not have encountered as a householder. For example, buying hand and body soaps by the gallon to refill attractive dispensers in guest bathrooms is not only cheaper, it's also more convenient than stocking dozens of sixteen-ounce refill bottles.

During renovation, ask your contractors to introduce you to local suppliers of paint, plumbing, and electrical supplies, and then establish with them your own account with a trade discount.

Wholesale food warehouses are rarely the bargain you would expect. Price food carefully, with an eye to quality. For inns of twelve rooms or less, you're probably better off shopping at a local grocery.

Don't buy retail linens until you check wholesale prices. How to find a linen supplier for your area? Look in the Yellow Pages for "wholesale items," and be sure you find a lodging industry supplier, not just a wholesaler who sells to retail stores.

Other ways to identify good suppliers? Attend regional or state innkeeper conferences where there are exhibitors serving the small industry. Ask your colleagues. Check innkeeper publications, particularly the classified ads in *innkeeping* newsletter.

When you contact wholesale suppliers, use your inn stationery. You're a member of the lodging industry, so ask confidently for industry prices, especially for quantity purchases.

Marketing: You Gotta Have a Gimmick

If you're not careful, the opening day you've so long anticipated can be the longest, loneliest day of your life. Where are all the friends who asked you every two weeks when you'd be ready? Where are the neighbors who stopped by to check your progress? Where are the guests that are going to pay for the months of renovation you've just completed?

Marketing is how you let people know what you have to offer, and it's how you make them want it. Marketing is critical to success. You'll lose business if you don't do a good job of getting the message out there.

Marketing includes many things, from the obvious ones like advertising and publicity, to creating an inn image that can be presented to potential guests in an exciting, compelling way. To make sure your opening day isn't an anticlimax, put your marketing program together as you proceed with the other business of getting ready to open.

ESTABLISHING AN IMAGE

You'll have set the tone for your image before you began renovating, when you made decisions about inn ambience. You will build on your image with obvious decisions about brochure design, colors, and copy. The Joshua Grindle Inn brochure, for example, is a simple postcard, reflecting the no-nonsense New England feel of the inn's northern California coastal community of Mendocino.

But there are also other, less-obvious ways to build your inn image. You can capitalize on your community in amenities you offer. In California's Napa and Sonoma wine regions, for example, inn rooms often provide wineglasses. But don't offer something just because everyone else does, or, if it's an important service in your area, offer it differently. The Old Yacht Club in Santa Barbara is a block and a half from the beach. They provide beach chairs and towels and picnic baskets for breakfast. They capitalize on their relationship to the ocean in every way they can, including the name of the inn. Naturally, an inn in Nebraska is unlikely to offer beach chairs or wineglasses.

You can dress to convey an image. At the Rose Victorian Inn in San Luis Obispo, California, the innkeeper and staff wear long dresses and lovely aprons, in keeping with the Victorian theme. At the Glenborough Inn, some guests feel a bit uncomfortable receiving a breakfast tray in their pajamas, so Pat sometimes delivers it wearing her long-sleeved flannel nightgown.

---

*S*hirley Denison of The Raymond House Inn in Port Sanilac, Michigan, sends a mailing to former guests in the fall suggesting they give the inn as a Christmas gift. Her mailing says, in part, "Instead of a present that may find its way to the attic or back to the store, why not give a gift certificate so friends, family, and business acquaintances can enjoy the inn themselves? It will . . . make the winter seem shorter in anticipation of balmy days in Port Sanilac."

Don't overlook the contribution of your staff to your inn's image. If you have an old English country house image, hire someone with an English accent. If you emphasize hiking and the outdoors, recruit staff from the local gym or Sierra Club chapter.

You'll want to maintain and extend the image of your inn throughout its lifetime, responding to the interests of your guests. If you have decided to emphasize history and a guest suggests that a library of books about the history of your area would be interesting, consider adding one. Be willing to research the history of your inn building if guests are interested in it.

Your guests will often tell you what they like. Look for moments when you can ask.

Don't let your inn image just happen. Once it's established, it's very difficult to change. Consider carefully what your inn image should be and how you will project it. Your inn guests will return in large part for your particular style.

SELECTING A NAME

Inn image and inn name are vitally related, of course, so the work you have done on developing an image concept is a good start on choosing the name. But there are a number of additional opportunities and limitations. Let's review them one by one.

LOCATION

Use reference or allusion to your location to evoke a mental image for potential guests. The Inn by the Sea is a name opportunity for a coastal location, but since inns along hundreds of miles of American coastline could claim it, you might include the name of your town and make it The Carmel Inn by the Sea. Maybe your inn's proximity to a landmark can lead you to a name.

HISTORY

Is there a historical event or personage that hints at a name for your inn? Many inn names are taken from the former owners of the residences. The

---

Dane and Joan Wells attribute part of their success at The Queen Victoria in Cape May, New Jersey, to having spelled out to themselves "exactly whom we wanted as guests. Everything we have done in some way relates to the market image we set for ourselves," Dane says. Joan and Dane encourage new innkeepers to start defining their image by writing the most perfect thank-you letter they could hope to receive from a guest, and then build their inn around that letter. "Later on," Dane adds, "you can compare actual letters you receive with the one you wrote yourself to see how close you've come to delivering the image you set out to achieve."

Glenborough Inn considered this approach. According to Pat, "A Mr. Brooks was the original owner. But in Santa Barbara, there's a Brooks Institute, so 'Brooks Inn' would have been confusing. The most famous person who lived at our inn was named Fowler. Fowler is an okay name, except 'fowl' can also be 'foul,' with obvious negative connotations. So we decided the historical names didn't work for us."

But consider The Captain Lord Mansion in Kennebunkport, Maine. All three parts of that name connote authority and even wealth: captain, lord, and mansion. "Captain" also brings to mind the sea, which the inn overlooks from its top floors, where no doubt a waiting wife once paced.

SOUND

"The Captain Lord Mansion" is pleasant to say and to hear, both important tests for the inn name you select. How will it sound when you answer the phone? Will callers say," What?" The Bath Street Inn often gets mail addressed to Bass Street Inn. Susan makes a joke of it, telling callers it's "bath—as in taking one."

Does the name feel good coming out of your mouth? Does it sound crisp, clear, inviting? Does it come trippingly off the tongue? Chambered Nautilus is an inn name that does, and it also brings to mind the sea, "chambers," and even aquariums, all appropriate to the inn and its Seattle location.

CONNOTATIONS

Be sure the name you choose doesn't mean something different to others from what it means to you. The Bath Street Inn chose not to be called the Bath House because bathhouses have specific, inappropriate connotations in some areas of California. Nevertheless, people still occasionally call the inn the Bath House. So when you name your inn, consider whether the name will have for others some implication you don't like, or whether it invites unpleasant wordplay.

To test this, try the name out on friends and strangers. Tape record it.

The Jabberwock, an inn in Monterey, California, evokes immediately an image of playfulness, from the moment the name rolls off your tongue. If you know the Lewis Carroll poem "The Jabberwock," you're propelled instantly into the innkeepers' image of gentle fun.

Each room name comes from the poem, and so do names for the bathroom, the telephone room, and the common refrigerator. Even breakfast food has Lewis Carroll names. The property is landscaped in trills and trolls. The logo is ornate and intriguing; if you look closely, you'll see The Jabberwock. The playful theme is carried through with milk and cookies at bedtime.

Because the reference to the poem is rather erudite, while the poem itself is sheer fun, The Jabberwock appeals to both the sophisticate and the child — of any age.

Experience the name in the context of your building and the atmosphere you want to have. For many people, the word *parsonage* evokes warm feelings about their parson and their relationship to the church. For others, negative past experiences predominate. On the other hand, a name like The Parsonage has more historical connotation and softness than Minister's House. Since the name should strengthen the image for prospective guests, you wouldn't want to name an authentic British pub-style inn The Parsonage.

INNOVATION

Moving the words around in a name can sometimes create something fresh. For example, say a couple named King is opening an inn that they want to call King's Bed and Breakfast. By changing it just a little, to Bed and Breakfast with the Kings, they've made it more of an invitation. The Kings, determined to use their name, can make a rather conventional choice something different by changing the order of the words.

DESIGNING A LOGO

Your logo should be a strong visual statement of the spirit of the inn name, image, and ambience. It can be as simple as a typeface or as extravagant as an artist's design, commissioned and copyrighted for your inn alone. Whatever way you go, the trick for maximum effectiveness is repetition, using your logo in the same way on all your visual material, from brochures to T-shirts. This strengthens the image in your prospective guest's mind.

Whether you want the challenge of designing a logo yourself with a typesetter, or prefer to work with a designer-artist, there's some basic conceptual work you need to do first.

First, can you tie the logo image into the name of your inn? to a drawing of it? to the street it's on? to the skyline of your city? to the tree in front of the inn? to your locale? to a special service you offer? Capitalize on the concept that will give you the strongest image. And in general, the simpler, the better. For instance, if you're the Cuckoo's Nest Inn on Pine Street, you might be able to come up with a stylized cuckoo in a pine tree.

Second, do you want or need something more than just a typeface? Why? Do you have the budget to have a logo created for you? Is your budget so limited that it would be wise to do a less-ambitious logo very well, rather than try to do an ambitious one poorly?

Third, make a list of specific uses for your logo, along with the minimum and maximum sizes required for those purposes. Remember that as you reduce an image, the lines become thinner. As you enlarge it, the lines become thicker. To maintain the original quality of the design for each use, it's wise to have the art work done in two sizes, for large and small reproduction.

Consider the appropriateness of the overall shape of the logo. For example, a long name on an essentially horizontal logo may take the entire area of a one-inch display classified ad, leaving you no room to describe the inn. An emphatically vertical logo may be a problem on a sign for your front yard.

You will want to put your logo to a variety of uses, some immediately, others several years into the business: letterhead, ads, brochure, sign, postcard, T-shirt, matchbook, soap, and display at a conference.

DOING IT YOURSELF

If you're not a professional, but plan to design your logo yourself, you might start by finding a typesetter you can work with. Artists or public relations firms may give you recommendations of who's creative, willing to share ideas, and ready to give honest feedback. Talk to a few prospects about prices and procedure, and ask to see the selection of typefaces. Most reasonably large typesetting companies will have similarly wide selections of faces, but it's possible that one will have something unusual.

There are headline typefaces and text faces. Headline faces tend to have stronger personalities. Many firms have flyers or booklets that show their faces in available sizes. If not, ask them to photocopy samples of your favorites for you to take home. Look them over carefully. Maybe you can combine them in an interesting way. For example, an ornate first letter can set off an otherwise straightforward, readable typeface. Be sure to look at individual letters in your inn name; some of them may be hard to read in some faces.

Once you've narrowed the choices to three or four, have your inn name set in your favorite faces, in a larger size than you'll use on a business card. If you want more than just a typeset name in your logo, review

---

L ogo Logic: Karin and Manfred Wolf opened the White Goose Inn in Orford, New Hampshire, in 1984. They had originally intended to name the inn the Wild Goose — "because we didn't know what we were doing when we came here," says Karin — but discovered the name was already taken.

They've used the White Goose very successfully. It appears on all their promotional materials, including a handsome sign that attracts a lot of attention. Karin is an artist and says, "The goose is easy to paint, so I often use it. I paint geese on small canvases and they sell so well I can't keep up. Now guests and friends often give me presents of goose things they find, which also adds to the image."

the typesetter's clip-art books for border shapes or illustrations, like an apple or a tree. A typesetter can put art and type together as you request, as well as making useful suggestions for snazzing it up or simplifying, and advising on the different sizes you'll need for the various uses you plan.

FINAL PRODUCT

Whether you or someone else is the designer, now is the time to think about economy of reproduction. Your basic logo design should work well in black-and-white without halftones for shading. There may be times and purposes for color or halftones, but using a logo that requires special printing techniques and inks is costly in the long run.

Show your prospective logo designs to your partners and friends for their opinion. Ask them to choose a favorite. Do some reality testing, too. Ask what each logo says to them, what ideas and feelings are evoked. Does it say hominess, elegance, softness? Don't prompt the answer you want to hear.

Once you've made your choice, get stats in a variety of sizes at the typesetter's or from a lithographer. Stats are camera-ready art and a file of them is handy for quick response to a good ad-price offer or to use on a fast-needed flyer.

PRODUCING A BROCHURE

Producing a good brochure is astonishingly time-consuming, and it's easy to let it slip when you're up to your armpits in sawdust. But your brochure must be ready at least as soon as you open the doors of your inn. The brochure is the basic tool in your promotion kit. It represents you to prospective guests who may never have seen your area or your inn. The words, pictures, and format you choose can make or break you.

You'll almost certainly be surprised and frustrated at how long it takes to get everything done: a week to ten days for typesetting, a couple of weeks for drawings, time for you and your partners to review and react to everything, a week for the printer and another for the bindery. The operational decisions that precede these mechanical steps can be even more time-consuming: setting rates, establishing deposit policies, and deciding about credit cards. Give the entire process plenty of time.

Whether you decide to design and write your brochure yourself or pay specialists to do it, you need to have a good grasp of what you want to convey and how you want to convey it. It helps to be very analytical here, about what can become otherwise too personal. You're choosing your appropriate approach within a spectrum of what other inns do, so at least six months ahead of opening day, begin collecting brochures you like from other inns. Keep a collection to review for ideas on layout, color, typefaces, and the ability to project a feeling.

At the same time, begin collecting promotional materials of the big spenders in your area—the chamber of commerce, the department of tourism, and big hotels or motel chains. Analyze the way they sell the area and their business. This can give you a good idea of why people come to your community.

About four months before opening day, start considering how much energy and expense you want to put into developing your brochure. There are a number of approaches you can take to getting the job done. You can do it yourself, drawing the illustrations, hand-lettering the copy, and doing the layout and paste-up. If you're very good at it, this can be successful. But the truth is, a complete do-it-yourself job fails more often than it succeeds.

You can take the opposite approach and hire an agency to do the whole job. You tell them what you want, and they write the copy, commission the artwork, choose and order the type, and furnish you with printed brochures. You can build in stopping points along the way where they ask for your approval. Naturally you will want to know the price of the project before you make any agreements.

Then there's a middle ground, which you design to suit your own needs and skills. Perhaps you want to write the copy, and then hire an artist and production person to do the rest. Or you may want to do the drawings. Another option is for you to handle the legwork, getting someone to write the copy, someone else to take photographs, arranging for the typesetting, and choosing a printer. In a sense, it's like being your own contractor.

For a complete job or any one of the pieces, be careful about working with friends. Your brochure is so important that you don't want courtesy to require you to accept something less than terrific. It must be easy to say a firm no.

CONTENT

Put yourself in the position of a future guest. What would you want to know if you were shopping for a getaway inn? When you travel, what questions do you want answered? Do you look for descriptions of all the rooms or information on cancellation policies? Do you want to know what the inn looks like, as well as the surrounding city? Make a list of the questions you have as a traveler. Ask your friends, partners, and guests at inns you visit what questions they have. Using the list as a guide, start three and a half months before opening to draw up the categories of information you want to include in your own brochure. Here are some suggestions.

• How much of your policies and procedures do you want to describe? The longer an inn is in business, the more of this information innkeepers include. They learn from experience that clear information saves time, confusion, and unhappiness on all sides. It's important to describe your deposit and cancellation policies, check-in and check-out times, and smoking standards. Some innkeepers fear that this information will seem negative in what is supposed to be, after all, a sales piece. But it's only fair for guests to know what they're getting into; in practice, clarity seems to give guests a feeling of security. And besides, you should feel good about policies you have carefully designed for everyone's benefit.

- Should you include prices? Some inns put them on an insert card that can be altered less expensively than the entire brochure. Other inns list a range of room prices. Still others price each room individually.
- How will your guests find the inn? Most will probably be from out of town. Plan to include a map and/or directions. It will reduce the time you have to spend on the phone, repeating the same instructions. A map *and* instructions may be necessary if the situation is complicated. In Santa Barbara near the Glenborough Inn, there are Cabrillo, Carillo, and Castillo streets. Even when you're following directions exactly, it's easy to believe you must have misread something, or to wonder if there's a typo in the instructions. A map helps clarify directions. When you've drafted your instructions and drawn your map, have a friend who easily gets lost test them.
- How much space should you devote to describing your area and activities? If one of your major marketing challenges will be convincing people to come to your area, you may wish to devote quite a bit of space to it. On the other hand, if the inn is at Niagara Falls, the bigger challenge may be differentiating your inn from a multitude of other accommodations options.
- Should you describe each guest room? This is an area of some controversy. If you have sixteen rooms, it will be difficult to describe each without losing your audience. But if your inn is small and the rooms are decorated and priced substantially differently, detailed descriptions will save you telephone time and help the guest fantasize about the place. It's to your advantage to promote those fantasies. In some inns, the guest rooms aren't the main draw, the common area is. In that case, that is what you'd want to focus on.
- What about mentioning the innkeepers' names? It adds a nice, warm touch, but there's a risk: Some guests tend to treat staff as second-class citizens since they're not the "real" innkeepers. No matter how much you plan to be involved in your inn, you will need days off.
- Should you use the brochure to promote special services? Meetings and weddings, on-site therapeutic massage, bikes to rent, tours, gift certificates, and package deals are services you might offer. If some are integral parts of your inn image, mention them in the brochure. If you're not sure how certain services will be accepted, plan instead to promote them with brochure inserts. This gives you a chance to try ideas and discard them if they fail, without dumping your whole brochure.

These are the basic areas you'll want to consider for your brochure copy. You will probably think of others. This is the "function" part of brochure planning; "form" is next.

FORMAT

You'll mail thousands of brochures during your innkeeping career. Think about the effect of various formats on cost. Printing on both sides of a page, for instance, costs twice as much as one-sided printing. Some card-style designs take advantage of one-sided printing for an unusual, effective look, but standard brochures look more professional printed on both sides. In addition, since the costs of paper, design, and postage are fixed, the marginal cost of an additional side of information is very little. If there's a brochure format you like, before you do anything else, take it to a couple of printers for informal bids on what it would cost to do something similar.

Black ink is the cheapest. Adding other ink colors or using any color instead of black is usually somewhat more expensive, but it can be worth it in effectiveness. Ask your designer about using screens, which use shading to make one or two colors look like more, and other design techniques to make an inexpensive printing job look special.

Choose your paper carefully, and make sure you understand how the color of the paper will affect the color of the inks; your printer can show you samples. Contrast is important. In general, red ink or paper is hard to read. Remember, you're already competing for your reader's attention; don't put any unnecessary obstacles in the way.

Choose a paper that allows you consistency among promotional materials. Not all papers are available in the weights you may need for letterhead, business cards, and postcards. Consider whether your paper will fold nicely; heavy stock sometimes won't, unless you pay a little more to have it scored before folding. Consider recycled paper.

If you're on a tight budget and evaluating design, ink, and paper choices that vary widely in price, think about whether a potential guest is more likely to choose your inn if you go with a more expensive look. If your image is elegance, the answer may be "yes." If your image is more down-home, the extra cost may not be worth it.

Before you take your design to the printer, take it to the post office. A size differential of ¼ inch that makes no difference in the effectiveness of the design can nearly double your mailing costs. Putting the return address in the wrong corner of a 5½-by-8-inch mailer can do the same thing. Test how well your design and paper make it through the mails by mailing samples to friends. Do postmarks cover copy or detract too much from the look of your self-mailer? Or if you want a delicate look, is your paper too flimsy to survive the mail? A three-panel, two-fold piece will hold up better with lightweight paper than a single-fold piece.

Typefaces should be easy to read. The accepted wisdom among graphic artists is that italic isn't, all capital letters isn't, and reverse type (white letters on a dark background) isn't. On the whole, the more you're aware of the typeface, the less you're aware of the words. Type must be clear in small sizes as well as in large. Look at all the characters you will use, including numbers for your address (with zip code) and telephone number (with area code).

COPY

Few people feel obligated to read carefully any printed piece that comes before their eyes. The best format then is one that provides the basics in big letters to attract attention and detail in small letters for those who want it. Use short sentences and short paragraphs, with headings that tell the bare bones of your story to readers who routinely give material a thirty-second scan.

DOING IT YOURSELF

If you decide to write your own copy or do your own artwork, take plenty of time. Three months isn't too long. You need time to think, to work, to get others to react, and time to put your copy, drawings, or photographs away so you can come back and review them with fresh eyes.

HIRING WRITERS AND ARTISTS

Even if you're working with a pro, do your homework first. It will save you money, because your job will take less time, and you'll probably be happier with the product because it will reflect your inn as you see it. Start by writing out your identity concept. Give it to your artist or writer with a copy of your logo. Also supply any other written descriptions you may have, like the one in your business plan. Your writer will also need a list of what information must be included in the brochure.

Before any work begins, put on paper your expectations and the artist's or writer's fees, delivery dates, and restrictions. Specify whether you are buying the product outright or only limited rights to its use. For example, if you're working with a photographer, will you own a specific number of prints only or the negatives, too? Be clear about what happens if you don't like the preliminary work proposed to you. Your contract

---

When innkeeping *newsletter held a competition for best inn brochure in 1985, the norm was an 8½-by-11-inch, three-panel sheet of colored stock, with line art, one or two ink colors, and a fold that made it possible to mail the brochure in a standard business envelope. Only one brochure that fit that description was a winner, however. Another winner varied the convention with an invitation format. The top prize went to Elk, California's Harbor House for a brochure of few words and several outstanding black-and-white photographs printed on glossy stock.*

In the intervening years, as inns have proliferated and competition has increased, brochures have become increasingly professional in appearance. Perhaps 10 percent of the inns now use four-color production. Another approach is a package brochure that the innkeeper assembles from several loose sheets, depending on the season and the interests of the caller. Windham Hill Inn, for example, in West Townshend, Vermont, has a four-color folder plus sheets describing their cross-country ski program for winter, summer concert series, Thanksgiving dinner specials, seasonal rate sheets, and so on. The idea is to speak directly and compellingly to specific consumer markets.

should provide for a "kill fee" to be paid by you to end the agreement at a specified stage if you don't like the work in progress.

TYPESETTING

Getting type set for the brochure will probably take about ten days. Material to be typeset must be typed double spaced with wide margins. Keep a copy so you can check your original against the type you get back from the typesetter. The errors the typesetter makes will be corrected for free. The errors you make or alterations you request after the material has been set will be charged to you. They can be expensive.

Your typesetter may also provide layout and paste-up skills.

SELECTING A PRINTER

This is a good time to establish a working relationship with a printer, since you'll be doing plenty of printing through the years. Find someone you're comfortable with. Ask to see samples. Check to see that they're crisp and clean, not smudged, not tilted, and with folds sharp and straight.

Printing prices can vary tremendously, so get bids for your first job from more than one printer. Include this information in your bid requests:

- Name of paper, weight, and color.
- How many ink colors, identified by PMS numbers found on printer's ink color wheels.
- Size of finished piece.
- Number of halftones, screens.
- Number of folds.
- Number of finished pieces.

Always ask for price breakdowns based on volume; the price per thousand of ten thousand brochures will be substantially less than the cost of a single thousand brochures. Estimate how long your brochures

---

*A*n artist on artists: "If you decide to hire artists or other creative people, use them," says art director Nori Nisbet, a designer who spent sixteen years at the San Francisco Examiner's California Living magazine and now has his own design firm, Nisbet Studios. According to Nori, a good approach to working with artists, whether they be writers, photographers, illustrators, designers, or art directors, is to communicate the feelings or qualities you want to project and leave to them the decisions about how to do it. If you present too complete an outline or sketch, you won't get creativity.

Nori suggests this approach: Contact the artists and writers who interest you. Review their portfolios and choose among them. Spell out your parameters, leaving as much room for creative flexibility as possible. Agree to a specific number of preliminary sketches, or a draft of written material, for a certain fee. Agree that once the initial work is done, you may purchase some or all of the rights to it for a specific fee, and that final work will be delivered to you by a certain date.

will last based on how you'll distribute them. If you include room rates in your copy, you will need to reprint when prices go up, and you don't want to have to wait five years to raise rates. If you have only a few rooms, you might leave spaces to fill in prices by hand.

When you've got the bids and you've chosen your printer, provide painstakingly clear written instructions with your artwork and a mockup of the finished piece, illustrating where folds go and which end is up. Keep photocopies of the artwork in case it is lost and to make telephone discussions with the printer easier while he or she has the job. Set a date to check how the material will look when printed, before the whole job is run. Go to the printer and make sure everything's coming out right at that stage, when changes, although very expensive, can still allow you to salvage a potential catastrophe. Be sure to agree in advance on the final completion date and pickup or delivery.

Then prepare for the thrill of holding your first brochure in your hands — put the champagne on ice!

ONGOING MARKETING

Marketing is one of your most important jobs, and the one that most often gets pushed aside in favor of things like toilet repair. It's a classic example of the urgent pushing aside the important. Don't let it happen to you, or all your urgent work will be complete, and you'll have no guests to enjoy the perfect flush.

For the first three years at least, plan a regular weekly time to market, two to five hours minimum. Use the time to send promotional material to writers, track patterns of occupancy and demographics, and plan new promotional strategies.

Develop a promotion file of names and addresses of travel writers who have done articles about other inns. Keep copies of the articles so you'll know the subjects and angles that most interest particular writers; this will help you target letters, releases, and personal contacts with them. Keep copies of information you send anywhere; you can often reuse it as it is, or modify it slightly to send to someone else. Keep a careful record of what you've done, so you won't waste time contacting the same travel writers or guidebook authors more than once.

File art — drawings, logos in various sizes, and photographs — and originals of type used for ads and brochures. Much of this can be recycled, and it's all expensive to use just once. Keep additional separate files for advertising contracts, letters to guidebook publishers, and promotion ideas.

As results of your marketing begin to appear in newspaper and magazine articles and guidebooks, keep a scrapbook for your guests in the common room. It will provide them interesting information about the inn and also reconfirm their idea that yours is the best place to stay.

Whether you are suggesting a story idea to the travel editor of the *New York Times*, or asking a guidebook writer to consider including your inn in the next edition, there are basic materials you will be expected to provide.

What do you need? At least one crisp, clear line drawing. If one is all you'll have, make it a view people will see and recognize as they drive by. You need eight-by-ten or five-by-seven black-and-white glossy photographs of the exterior, a guest room, the common room, and a breakfast, plus a few color transparencies, either slides or four by fours.

Many writers say they prefer to see people in the photographs, receiving a breakfast tray or walking up the front pathway; after all, these aren't real-estate ads. And be sure your photographer is familiar with work for publication, so the contrast in the photographs will be good. Your objective is to have such appealing artwork available that editors who must choose which inn among several to highlight will pick yours so they can use your great photo. In some instances, a fine color transparency provided by an inn has appeared as the cover of a magazine! The byword is, make it easy for the media to make you famous. Have several copies of everything, so you can mail artwork at a moment's notice. Label it with your inn name and address, and request its return—but don't count on it.

You will need to provide the media with background material. Your brochure is an obvious source, but a detailed, easy-to-read description of the inn just for writers is a good idea. Describe the history of the inn, the locale, the innkeeper's biography, and what there is to do. Consider including a unique item that makes your inn stand out from the rest, just to attract the writer's attention: an acorn from your oak tree, rare seeds

---

*M*ary Nichols of Hannah Marie's Country Inn, Spencer, Iowa, uses theme teas to promote her inn. "The teas have lots of benefits," says Mary. "They give locals a chance to dress up and see the inn, they produce extra cash flow, and have resulted in great PR, from newspaper articles to a feature in a book on teas."

Mary researches her authentic teas and has presented them on such themes as Queen Victoria's chocolate tea, tea at the Ritz, Danish tea luncheon, Hannnah's country tea, and a Mad Hatter's tea party for mothers and daughters at which Mary and her staff are dressed as Queens of Hearts.

---

*P*hotographs: "Every inn should have black-and-white and color interior and exterior photos and probably a drawing. Innkeepers have actually told me they can't take a black-and-white photo and can't find a friend to do it. This is silly and self-defeating. Your photos give you a chance to present your inn in absolutely the best light. Media will omit inns that don't provide quality material that's easy to use."

—*Anthony Hitchcock and Jean Lindgren*, THE COMPLEAT TRAVELER

from your historic garden, or a bit of patchwork in the pattern of your handmade quilts.

Also include a collection of chamber of commerce material about your town and area; no need to duplicate material you probably help pay for with your membership. Reprints of articles on your inn give media people a feeling of security, that they're not alone in being interested in you. Reprints should show dates, the writer's name, and the newspaper or book title. Select the most recent and the best coverage as the quantity grows.

Many inns assemble these materials in looseleaf binders or cardboard folders. Some inns preprint covers with their logo; others find attractive ways to mount a business card or brochure on the cover. Your presentation should look professional, but don't be afraid to be innovative and creative; media people get kits by the hundreds.

Now you're ready to promote. In some cases, you'll want to introduce your inn to an important writer with your complete kit; in others, you'll select appropriate materials from it. Depending on the photos, artwork, and attention-getters your kit includes, it can be expensive. Use it judiciously, but don't be stingy. A major article is worth the price of a lot of kits!

INN GUIDEBOOKS

Innkeepers say inn guidebooks are the largest single source of business, excluding word of mouth and return guests. Because the time lag between selecting inns for a volume and getting the guide to the bookstore can be a year or two, contacting guidebook writers can begin even before you open.

The best approach is to send a letter to the author at the publishing house. Indicate that you're familiar with the author's book and understand his or her particular emphasis, which might be history, cuisine, or quality. Explain why your inn is an appropriate inclusion, particularly if it helps fill an obvious gap, such as location.

Briefly describe a few additional things that make your inn different from others. Being "romantic" and "charming" is not enough. Use specific, vivid language that will help your reader "see" your inn. Mention attractions and events in your area, and invite the writer to visit. Enclose a

---

Would I stay here? "My personal bottom line on evaluating an inn is, 'would I stay here?' I once called an innkeeper to check a few details after I'd worked for four hours on the writeup, and got a very rude response. I thought, if he's going to treat me like this, how will he treat somebody who wants a reservation? I tore up my review. I try to visit every new inn I hear about, but only include in my guidebook those that I have personally inspected and found to be extra special in every way. It's shocking to me that many guidebook writers don't visit the places they recommend."

—Jacqueline Killeen, COUNTRY INNS OF CALIFORNIA

press kit or material from it: a brochure and other information that will make a visit irresistible, particularly anything that relates specifically to the author's guidebook angle. You may also want to include some reference to yourself — hobby, life-before-innkeeping, close relationship to the House of Windsor — to convey that time spent with you will be interesting. Your tone should reflect your style as an innkeeper, just as it does with guests or prospective guests.

Keep the letter brief, a page if possible, and, before you finalize it, ask someone not connected with the inn to read it and tell you what overall impression it conveys. This is a safeguard against the errors occasioned by being too close to your subject.

Naturally, this letter is going to take some time. Once you've written it, though, you'll find that with slight modifications it's a good letter to use for many other contacts, with other media or new businesses in your area that might need accommodations for clients. And you'll modify it to send to writers of several other guidebooks, too.

Keep guidebook writers informed of price or other significant changes, and, when they do list your inn, send a thank-you note.

Should you offer a free night's stay? Many writers make it a policy not to accept free nights, to insure their objectivity. On the other hand, it's expensive to visit hundreds of inns a year, and some writers almost have to accept free nights. It doesn't hurt to suggest it.

Some guidebooks require fees to list inns. Before you pay, ask other innkeepers whether the listings are worth it. Many bed-and-breakfast homestay reservation services will list inns; if fees are charged only for bookings and you like the terms, there's no reason not to list with these services. When you receive a solicitation of information from a guidebook writer, check the deadlines and respond clearly with what they want and when.

TRAVEL WRITERS

Coverage in newspaper and magazine travel articles is one of the best free promotions for inns. Sometimes getting a story is just luck, but there are also things inns can do to attract attention. To plan the most effective approach to a travel writer, consider your story from a writer's viewpoint.

Writers need to produce good articles in a reasonable amount of time. Remember that these folks are being invited to all kinds of places, all the time; a "getaway" is not the thrill to them that it would be to you. The information you provide should reassure them that they'll get a great story without a tremendous amount of work if they take the time to visit. You must provide complete information on rates, directions, special programs and deals, and so on.

Your area is as important as your inn. Innkeepers often mistakenly believe an inn makes a story, but travel writers regard inns as places to stay, not reasons to travel. A large part of your "sell" is selling the things to do in your area.

Some innkeepers routinely send out press releases to writers; others insist personal letters are the best approach. In either case, keep in mind that travel writers get stacks of mail, and many of them have perfected the art of reducing the size of the stacks at a rate of about an inch a minute. You need to attract attention and make a compelling case in your first paragraph.

On the whole, sending a mass mailing to travel writers announcing your inn opening is probably a waste of time. It would be wiser to send out specific invitations to writers in nearby large cities. Do something catchy to attract attention, like sending a box of cookies along with the invitation to an opening of Grandmother's Inn, or delivering a hot pizza along with the invitation to the opening of Albergo Lucia. Use all the pizzazz you can muster!

When a writer arrives, have a press kit available, but present it at the end of the tour. The writer should be attentive to the inn, not the kit.

---

*L*os Angeles Times *travel editor Jerry Hulse: "You don't know about an inn until you actually look at it. I recently went to a big city and didn't want to stay in a hotel. I drove around until I saw an inn that looked promising, and went in. I like the feeling and the innkeepers; it had the proper mood.*

"I prefer to receive some brief information and pictures, rather than a press kit—too many kits are twenty-eight pages saying the same thing. I want to know what's special about the place, what the personality of the innkeepers is. I like a homey atmosphere."

---

*C*hristian Science Monitor *Travel Editor Ellen Steese: "We have a short items column, 'News for the Traveler,' which might pick up material on inns; writers should provide an address where readers can send for additional information, like a brochure.*

"When we're looking for places to stay on trips, we consult books on inns, and we keep material which has been sent to us. We do accept free stays, but often we don't have the travel budget to send a writer to the area in the first place. The larger the appeal of the area as a whole, the greater the chance one of us will get there."

---

*C*onde Nast Traveler *editor-at-large Paul Grimes: "I look at everything I am sent. There are writers I trust and guidebooks I trust, as well as word-of-mouth. We travel anonymously under my wife's name, and I write only about inns where we have actually stayed."*

SPECIAL EVENTS

Special events are gatherings done around a theme, designed to expose people to your inn, create interest, and generate publicity. The big-city paper in your area is unlikely to do more than one travel article about your inn, but if you sponsor an autumn biking tour that goes from inn to inn, Halloween ghost stories by the fire, or an annual Trivial Pursuit marathon, that's news.

The more angles you can come up with, the better. Some inns plan events calendars for a full year, so every article on one event automatically leads readers to send for the full calendar. Sometimes you can get local merchants to cosponsor, saving you money and providing more hands for the work to be done. For example, the bike tour might include stops at new wineries in the area, or it might be sponsored by a worthy nonprofit group that will do much of the promotion for you. Nonprofit sponsorship of events means you can get free public service announcements on radio and television, too.

Sometimes special events are a way to bring in paying overnight guests at slow times of the year; they can also introduce local residents to your inn, who will then think of you first for accommodating out-of-town guests. For some inns, the events themselves have provided important income during early years before occupancy could support the operation.

Special events are great opportunities for creative promoters to generate consistent publicity and to develop an image as the place to be. But they're also a lot of work. Creating a newsworthy happening is just the first step; the follow-up of letters, press releases, and phone calls to the media takes a lot of time, energy, and nerve. If you've got all those, you can make events pay off.

ADVERTISING

"Never buy ads or vacuum cleaners on the first contact." Ad salespeople always sound urgent, but there will always be another chance. Here are some guidelines to help you make wise advertising decisions.

• Remember that advertising is only one part of your overall promotion campaign, and that it needs to be integrated into the plan. A number of excellent, one-time articles on your inn won't help for long if readers can't find out how to contact you a few months later when they finally plan a trip.

---

*C*hristmas Crafts: Carl Glassman and Nadine Silnutzer of the Wedgwood Inn in New Hope, Pennsylvania, hold an annual Christmas crafts showing and sale. It grows more successful every year. Originally a four-day event, it now lasts twelve days. Four artists, from weavers to glassmakers, display their work. The event opens with an afternoon of wine and cheese.

According to Carl, "The show has become a sort of tradition. Before we get the publicity out, people are already calling to find out what the schedule will be."

- The reader, or audience, is basically passive. The more difficult you make your ad to read, the less attention it will get. Some marketing studies claim you have all of three seconds to grab a reader's attention.
- Arrange the information in the ad as clearly as possible. Use the 60–40 rule: 60 percent art and 40 percent copy, or 60 percent copy and 40 percent art. If art and copy are given equal weight, the reader will be confused about what to focus on.
- The primary goal of an ad is to give your reader the basic facts: what you do, where you are, how to reach you. The size ad you buy should determine how many more details you will be able to share.
- Are your primarily competing with inns in your area, and therefore working to differentiate your place on the basis of price, services, quality, and so on? Or is yours the only inn in the area, and you are trying to attract a new market, missionary style? Determine your position — and it may very well combine a bit of both objectives — to help construct more effective ads.
- How well will your ad compete on a page? If you are buying a small ad on a directory page, you have a lot of competition for attention. So how can you draw the reader's eye? Use bold borders, bold type, or black background with white type. Is your logo a real eye-catcher, or does it need to be strengthened when it's reduced? Can you use a combination of bold and lightweight typefaces or a combination of type sizes to balance the look of the ad?
- Leave room around the words or the design within the borders of the ad so the eye can focus. This concept is called white space by graphic designers.

Direct mail from inns: is it junk? Direct mail pros say any business's best prospects are those who have bought in the past. For inns, this means that getting former guests back should be easier than bringing in first-timers. A number of inns use direct mail techniques.

Some produce quarterly newsletters to tell former guests about the new gazebo, staff changes, and special offerings. Newsletters often include favorite recipes and, almost always, a calendar of area and inn events.

Other inns take a simpler approach. The Governor's Inn in Ludlow, Vermont, sends its charming postcard — a color reproduction of a "primitive" painting of the inn, situated in its New England village — to announce new and exciting happenings at the inn. The news is typeset and printed; the postcards are addressed by hand. Innkeepers Charlie and Deedy Marble used the cards one midsummer to announce that their famous picnic hampers were featured in a major magazine story, that the artist who painted their postcard would be exhibiting at the inn all summer, and that traditional English tea would be served at the inn on Thursdays and Sundays.

Does direct mail work for inns? Some innkeepers think so; others say the "image" value is worthwhile even if there's little impact on bookings.

Consider walking into a room with flowered wallpaper, plaid curtains, striped upholstery, and mirrors along one wall. The eye doesn't know where to look first; it has no resting place, no focus. The only obvious move is to leave the room. For the same reasons you wouldn't decorate this way, you shouldn't design ads this way.

• Repetition — alias money, money, money. A one-time placement of an ad is likely to get little or no response. When you've carefully considered all the periodicals you might buy space in, and you've made your choice(s), give the ad some time. For a reader, it's a disappointment to try unsuccessfully to find in a current issue an ad that was there last month.

• When should you advertise? Do you expect a slow time you want to bolster? Advertise *before* you hit it. In the middle of a lull is no time to make a one-month advertising appearance. Besides, you won't have any money then.

If there's a time of year when your area is flooded with tourists, you may want to advertise then, so people take your ad home to plan for the next season. You might also want to run an ad that encourages them to come back at a slower time.

Figure out exactly what the ad's purpose is, and then buy space accordingly. The only way you can gauge the effectiveness of an ad is to be very clear from the beginning about what you want it to do.

• Never, never, never let a persuasive sales representative talk you into buying an ad in the first phone call or meeting. Ask for the rate sheets and the demographics information on the subscribing population. A professional publication will have this information for you. Then tell them you'll get back to them after you review it. If the publication looks like a good possibility, request the same kind of information from its competitors. Compare them carefully to choose your best buy.

• In general, beware the little, "inexpensive" ads, those costing thirty to seventy-five dollars. The only truly inexpensive ad is one that brings in more business and income than it costs.

• Advertising lodging in the local paper is usually a waste of money. Instead, get involved in fund raisers for community causes, and advertise the events. This demonstrates your public spirit, and inclines the local media to print your media releases.

• If you're considering a particular ad buy, contact other inns that use the publication and ask about their results. Sometimes you'll get a more helpful answer from inns not in your immediate competitive area.

Advertising shouldn't be an impulse or instinct buy, and it doesn't have to be. Just make sure you know what you want your ads to do, and then run ones that accomplish your purpose and target your audience at a good price. To target your ads, you have to do your homework. Start by reviewing your guest research. From where will most of your guests come? What professions will they represent: doctors, attorneys, teachers, carpenters, artists? Finally, what will your guests come to the inn to do: ski, hike, or eat?

Using this information, develop a list of advertising target priorities.

Be as specific as you can about your target goals. For example, maybe your very best market is birdwatching dentists from the Twin Cities, and your next best, also from Minneapolis — St. Paul, is carpenters who enjoy the hot springs and mud baths. How do you reach these targets?

If your audience is chiefly professionals from the Twin Cities, there may be a business journal most of them receive. If they are in small business, a chamber of commerce publication might be good. If your guest population is very broad in terms of profession and activities, you might consider advertising in the Minneapolis *Tribune's* travel section, a publication that targets a geographic area more than a demographic one.

The next step is designing an ad that will catch the eyes of the people you want to attract. If you're after craftspeople, how about an ad with calligraphy? Professionals may be drawn to a very sophisticated, clean look. (Caution: This may be the toughest one to achieve without the assistance of a pro.)

If you plan to work with an artist on the ad, look at several portfolios to find an artist who already does the kind of thing you like. It's much easier than trying to explain to an artist, no matter how talented, an unfamiliar style that your heart's set on.

Buying Ad Space

In the same way that you compare the prices of eggs on the basis of the cost per dozen, you compare the prices of ads on the basis of cost per thousand (CPM), i.e., the cost of reaching a thousand readers. To determine this cost, telephone or write publications that interest you and request a media kit. If the publication is very small, there may not be a kit, but the publisher should be able to give you information on the number of subscribers and the objective of the publication, which will help you confirm whether its readers are your target market.

The simplest calculation of CPM would involve dividing the total number of readers by the cost of the size ad you want. A better measure would involve analyzing the demographics of the readership, figuring how many of the readers are in your target market, and dividing that number by the cost of your ad. For example, say you're considering buying ad space in a travel magazine. The demographics material you receive

---

Fireside Specialists: Rick Litchfield and his wife, Bev Davis, of The Captain Lord Mansion, in Kennebunkport, Maine, offer a "Fireside Special" at the inn. It's a special rate for a "long winter weekend at the Maine coast inn of your dreams," three nights in a fireplace suite, including taxes, firewood, and breakfast.

"We didn't believe in this kind of packaging originally," Rick says, "but we've become believers since we introduced it. During a four-month period, December to March, the special resulted in a net increase of more than two hundred room nights and just over $12,000, excluding normal growth. The cost of printing brochures and all advertising in magazines and newspapers was less than $2,000, so we believe our net income was over $10,000."

includes the information that 50 percent of the readership owns recreational vehicles. If you're selling overnight accommodations and these folks don't need them, you should reduce the readership figures by half. The more detailed the demographics information you can get, the more carefully you can calculate CPM.

Naturally, you'll want to purchase the ad space that gives you the lowest CPM. Once you've established this, start looking for ways to reduce that cost even further. Media kits usually indicate that the more frequently you run an ad, the greater the discount you'll get. So if you know the ad works for you, go ahead and commit to buying the space for a year ahead. On the other hand, when you advertise for the first time in a publication, don't let the discount attract you into buying more than you should. Determine the number of times you want to run your ad based on a reasonable trial of effectiveness there. For a weekly publication, you should probably advertise for at least a full month. For a monthly, you should give it at least three months.

Consider whether cooperative buying can save you money. There are several ways to approach this. You might advertise with a group of innkeepers. This is an especially attractive idea if you have a group reservation service.

Or, if you're in an area where there are few inns to co-op with, you might work with a restaurant or a tourist attraction. The chamber of commerce in your area may already be involved in organizing such ads, or you could suggest that they do so. Since it's to your advantage in any case to tell prospective guests that there is good food and interesting adventure in your area, why not let the other businesses that will benefit from that advertising help pay for it?

No matter how you manage to spread the cost around, advertising is still expensive. The following ad comparison chart is a guide to its value, based on innkeepers' experience, and, generally speaking, arranged according to effectiveness.

ADVERTISING MEDIA COMPARISON

Travel or Inn Directories
ADVANTAGES
Often free inclusion
Produces many bookings
Used as "bible" by inn goers
Complete information possible
Very long life-span

DISADVANTAGES
Limited audience
Review subject to author opinion
Long publication, revision lead time

Magazines
ADVANTAGES
Long life-span
Multiple readers per copy

High-quality reproduction
Preselected audience

DISADVANTAGES
Expensive space
Long lead time for submission
Limited audience
Affordable ad may be dwarfed
  by large ads
Need high-quality art to compete

Nearby Big-City Newspaper
ADVANTAGES
Short lead time, flexible
Travelers may clip ads
Good for special-package promo
Short tests for results possible
Large circulation
Likely to reach guest prospects

DISADVANTAGES
Expensive for the return
Ad placement a problem
Affordable ads get lost

Telephone Directories
ADVANTAGES
Popular consumer medium
Users are seeking lodging
Comparison shopping easy
Small ads get read

DISADVANTAGES
Annual release, revision
Inflexible format
Comparison shopping easy
Problem of which editions to buy
Unusual inn info resource

Local Newspaper
ADVANTAGES
Local visibility
Short lead time, flexible
Longevity: residents clip ads
Good community relations

DISADVANTAGES
Doesn't reach travelers
Circulation may be small, less read
Return rate low for expense
Ad placement problematic

Advertisers Sheets
ADVANTAGES
Inexpensive
Local visibility

DISADVANTAGES
Giveaway, not to target audience
Reaches nonguest locals
Limited circulation

Special Newspapers or Newsletters (Professional Organizations, Schools, Clubs, Etc.)
ADVANTAGES
Preselected audience
Longevity: often saved

DISADVANTAGES
Small audience
High cost per reader

Radio
ADVANTAGES
Some audience selectivity possible
Frequent repetition possible
Short lead time
Intrusive: listeners hear ad
Wide reach and general presence
Personal and persuasive voice
  approach

DISADVANTAGES
Repetition a must for payback
Can be annoyingly repetitive
Complete information expensive
No printed material to retain
High cost for return
High cost for professional production

Television
ADVANTAGES
Dramatic impact
Wide audience coverage

DISADVANTAGES
No printed material to retain
High cost of time and production
Nonselected audience

Outdoor (Signs, Posters, Transit, Etc.)

ADVANTAGES
Frequency of exposure
Long period of exposure
May attract travelers

DISADVANTAGES
Limited, nonselected audience
High cost for large size
Limited space for information
Clutter of signs distracting

---

*S*hirley *Denison and husband Ray opened The Raymond House Inn in Port Sanilac, Michigan, in 1983. As a child, Shirley visited grandparents in Port Sanilac and emphasizes her historic connections to the historic town as part of her inn image. She's also an artist, and developed an inn gift shop to sell her ceramic creations, including special water carafes, soap dishes, muffin plates, lamps, wine jugs, large platters, and flower pots, fired in a special blue glaze and inscribed with the name of the inn.*

GIFT CERTIFICATES AND GIVEAWAYS

Gift certificates for nights at the inn can generate income during slow times like Christmas. There's also a publicity angle on gift certificates: Inns are frequently asked to donate them as prizes for fund raisers. Every time your inn is mentioned at a raffle or a silent auction, potential guests hear it. Every guest who comes at no charge as the result of a fund raiser will be another satisfied customer to spread the word.

To help a good cause without loss of needed income, limit the certificate's validity period to times when the inn won't be full. Track the way your donation is publicized, so you can decide whether you'll want to do it again next year. Feel free to be specific about the conditions of your offer. You can donate for the silent auction only, or perhaps reserve the right to be the only inn featured.

DIRECT MAIL

Direct mail gives you the opportunity to capture a prospective guest's undivided attention—for a few seconds, at least. Compare this with magazine advertising, where readers may never see your ad at all among the competition.

Successful mail promotion makes a valuable short-term offer that is urgent, personal, and easy to understand. Even offering a percentage discount is too complex. Think about what would make you drop everything and run: "Stay two nights and get the third one free," or "Stay three

INNKEEPER'S SAMPLE DIRECT MAIL BUDGET

COST FOR PRODUCING A 1,000-PIECE MAILING

No. 10 carrier envelope
Brochure
Cover letter $.65 each
Bonus certificate   or $650 total
Postage
Mailing is done by innkeeper

BREAK-EVEN CHART

ROOM NIGHTS BOOKED	10	15	20	30
FIXED COSTS				
Mailing	$650	$650	$650	$650
VARIABLE COSTS (depending on number of guests)				
Housekeeping, breakfast, wine, and bonus offered	$200	$300	$400	$600
TOTAL COST	$850	$950	$1050	$1200
TOTAL INCOME				
Average room rate $75	$750	$1125	$1500	$2250
GROSS PROFIT	<$100>	$175	$450	$1050

Break-even point: 12 bookings (income, $900; cost, $890)

nights and we'll give you a hundred bucks!" Be sure to describe exactly how a guest can take advantage of the offer, and tell them to do it. Many innkeepers are shy about saying "Call now," but it works.

Elements of successful direct mail are a carrier envelope, a cover letter, a brochure, and an offer. Two kinds of headlines are used: the attention getter on the envelope, which makes it irresistible to open, and the master headline on the letter, which is an invitation to respond. Good headlines can make or break your direct mail effort. Naturally, they should be consistent with and extend your overall theme at the inn. Innkeepers came up with these three distinctive headlines at an *innkeeping* Intensives workshop: "Escape to an island"; "Bring your family home to Vermont"; and "A bottle of wine, a fireplace, and you, at ———."

How do you know which idea will work best? Print two different offers, randomly splitting your list. Code them so you know when you get a booking whether the guest responded to the special rate, say, or the free champagne. Stick with the most successful offer on subsequent mailings.

Who receives the mail? That depends on whom you want to come. Former guests comprise a good mailing list for many inns, particularly when you want repeat weekend or week-at-the-shore business. On the other hand, if your weekends are full and you want to book midweek rooms, you may find that your typical midweek guest is an out-of-stater. It's unlikely that many of them will come back frequently enough to justify the mailing, since vacationers tend to explore many options.

If you've got a clearly targeted audience and an irresistible idea, mail it! Once you've developed a piece that works, you can use it again and again.

TRAVEL AGENTS

For most sectors of the accommodations business, travel agents are a significant resource for booking rooms. For inns, they're the wave of the future. Innkeepers, however, have been hesitant to work with agents for several reasons. Innkeepers don't want to pay commissions; they — and their eventual guests — experience confusion over third-party reservations because inns are so different from each other; and they don't like to miss the opportunity to set the stage for the visit with a hospitable initial phone contact.

Travel Agents Pay Off: Up until a few years ago, members of the Santa Barbara Innkeepers Guild rarely used travel agents and limited paying commissions to weekdays and slow seasons. Their infrequent experiences with agent-booked guests were problematic: Guests arrived unaware of smoking rules, shared baths, and cancellation policies.

Then, in 1987, the innkeepers were challenged by a new member innkeeper, who was also a travel agent, to begin working with agents in a serious way. So they designed this cooperative display ad for the Hotel Travel Index, *the "big book" found in every agency.*

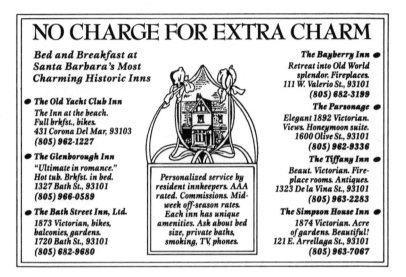
The cost of running the ad was about $225 per inn per quarter. Guild members report monthly midweek bookings at $500 to $1,000 per inn. Every inn has experienced results; this is one ad no member has ever questioned continuing!

As for the logistical problems, the innkeepers now report positive working relationships with travel agents. The innkeepers pay commissions promptly for rooms booked at any time of the week or year, and work at communicating policies to both the agent and the guest. They send confirmations directly to the client when possible, or send two confirmations to the agent with one marked "for client." "Since we've begun to work at communicating clearly with the travel agents, we've experienced no more confusion with these bookings than with a wife who books for a reluctant husband," says one innkeeper.

Make it your goal to get organized enough to avoid the confusion, and establish hospitality with a warm letter of confirmation. Commissions, usually just 10 percent of the cost of the room, are an investment, not an expense. Travel agents can fill rooms that would otherwise remain empty; the commission is a bargain.

TELEPHONE MARKETING

What is the sound of opportunity knocking? In the inn business, it's the ringing of the telephone. Great beds and great breakfasts are not enough. You need a telephone presence that conveys all you have to offer.

Skill matters, too. An inviting presence on the phone is simply an empty promise if your guests arrive to find you forgot to calendar their reservation, quoted the wrong room rate, or were too embarrassed to mention the no-smoking policy. Whoever handles the phones should understand the history, development, and relevance of your policies. There's a tendency for new staff members to apologize for policies that seem unnecessarily hardnosed. Sometimes too, staff people who don't have to follow the reservation process all the way through can be too casual about recording complete, accurate information. Getting names right, for example, avoids embarrassment and is a way of demonstrating to people that they're important to you. You can and must be professional and skilled, as well as friendly and inviting.

Get the details right and you'll find that your telephone can be a great promotional resource — on the customer's dime. You have paid for your callers through your advertising, your brochures, special promotions, word of mouth, and so on. And now, this caller is spending time and money to find out whether your inn really is as wonderful as it's billed to be.

The first rule for tapping this resource is to make sure the phone is well tended, by you or someone you have trained. Whoever answers your phone should see it as an opportunity to transform marginally interested callers, obviously shopping around by phone, into guests with confirmed reservations, so eager to stay in your inn that you know their deposits will go into the mail without hesitation.

When you or trained staff people can't answer the phone, make sure your answering machine or service tells callers what time you will be available, and encourages them to call back. Offer to return calls, and ask callers to state the best time they can be reached. Needless to say, a lot of calling back on your part is both time-consuming and costly, so keep this in mind when scheduling your work time at the phone.

A disadvantage to relying on the phone machine is the number of dial tones you'll have to listen to. Some callers can't talk to a phone machine or want immediate results. If a busy executive is trying to make reservations for a spouse's birthday, chances are he or she will want the matter to be resolved at once. Your machine may cause your place to be skipped in favor of one that can confirm the reservation immediately.

If you must use the phone machine, be sure your message is clear, friendly, and inviting. Give the caller a reason to make the extra effort to get in touch with you.

When speaking with a prospective guest, it's essential to articulate a sense of your place in a simple, appealing way. Have ready a few adjective-laden sentences that capture just what it is that makes your inn rare and wonderful. Develop a "script" and keep it by the phone for you or your reservation people to use.

Base it on a guest's-eye view of the experience of your inn, empha-sizing the things you've picked out to highlight in your brochure: archi-tecture, setting, sounds, scents, and activities. Use vivid adjectives to construct the most poetic description possible for your surroundings. You're not the last building on the right at the end of the road. You're at the back of a wooded canyon with no through-traffic, where the main sounds are singing birds and the running river. You're not on the left side of the highway; you're on a magnificent promontory jutting out over the Atlantic Ocean. You're not five miles from town; you're high in the hills with a sweeping view of the bay.

Extract the essence into two or three sentences that can be spoken comfortably, without sounding "canned." Rather than responding to the question, "What's your inn like?" with a strictly factual account of how many rooms you have and whether there are private baths, have those few lines ready to spark the interest of the caller.

But don't get so involved in what you want to say that you forget to lis-ten. Find out as much as you can about your callers' needs. For example, are they looking for a secluded place, or for one within walking distance to shops and restaurants? Point out the ways your place matches what they're seeking.

If you do have a room, your script can make your callers feel lucky to get it. If your inn sounds irresistible, callers will "shop" no further and are unlikely to cancel a reservation later.

If you don't have a room this Saturday night, get in your two-liner anyway, and volunteer information about when you do have an opening. Mention that weekends book up eight weeks (or whatever) in advance, but during the week they'll have the place pretty much to themselves. Mention how wonderful it is to walk along the beach on a Tuesday morn-ing without running into another soul, or to go bicycling along a country road with no weekend traffic.

Hildrun-Uta Triebess of the Elk Cove Inn in Elk, California, opened two new guest rooms on Labor Day one year with a contest. She invited guests to submit names for the new rooms. The prize for coming up with a winning name was a free stay at the inn.

"It was a nice incentive for guests to get involved," Hildrun-Uta says, "and besides, it's appropriate for them to name the rooms, since they occupy them." How could any guest resist talking up an inn with a room he or she had named?

If they can't come midweek but sound interested in your inn, encourage them to book the next available weekend, reminding them that most of the inns in your area fill up at least that far in advance. You might also mention something that's going to be of special interest even two or three months ahead, like whale watching or spring blossoms, and suggest they make plans now for the next outing.

If they decide to come to your area on a weekend when you are already booked, invite them to tour your inn. Seeing your place will give them a solid image to store for future vacation plans and a sample of the charm they can expect when they come back to stay.

If you can't get a booking, ask if you can send a brochure if they don't already have one. Add callers to your mailing list, too. Remember, you paid for this inquiry, so use it. At the very least, find out how they heard about your inn so you can keep track of the ads or sources that are working.

The telephone is a tool to help you make the most of all your other promotional techniques. Use it creatively, with a warm and light touch. Joke around a little; it's fun for you, and people respond to it.

Up and Running

PROFESSIONALISM

A variety of things will bring guests to your inn; professionalism will bring them back. Innkeepers must combine skill with flexibility, the warmth and intimacy of grandma's with the perfection of Buckingham Palace.

Guests are usually understanding and helpful in the face of emergencies at the inn, but they expect peace and comfort. If you accompany mopping up the water from a broken commode with a litany of how tough your day has been, you are breaking the spell.

Professionalism is obvious in numerous small things. At check-in time, for example, the mood of an entire stay is established. It's an insecure time for guests, who bring high hopes along with uncertainty about what to expect; if you're scrambling around to get organized, you add to that insecurity.

Even if you spent the last four hours cleaning rooms, comforting your sick child, and installing a new sink, and even though the groceries you raced out to purchase are still spread all over the kitchen table, what really matters is how your guest feels when you open the door and say, "Hi! Welcome to — — —!"

Among prospective and operating innkeepers, there are a few who want to escape the rat race, and "lay back." Nothing, however, will more quickly destroy your efforts to relax in your new career than a double booking, and that's just what you'll get if you refuse to run your inn in a professional way.

Do you want to be casual about innkeeping? Before you begin, take a moment to imagine what it's like to tell a young honeymoon couple that the room they booked and paid for has been given away because you forgot to note their reservation in the calendar book. This is nightmare stuff!

---

*N*o deposit, no arrival: It's Friday night, almost eleven o'clock, and you're dozing off, warm and secure in the knowledge that, no matter how empty midweek may be, at least you're always full on weekends. "Full" is an understatement, in fact; the phone rang steadily until about four hours ago with requests for this very night.

But wait a minute. Where are the Smiths, that nice man who said your place sounded just right for the anniversary getaway he was planning? That was more than three weeks ago; he certainly had plenty of time to receive your brochure and confirmation. He seemed so nice. Surely he would have let you know if he changed his mind? "Maybe we should be requiring a deposit or at least a credit card number," you think, as your stomach starts to clench up.

Is that the doorbell? No, it's the clock. Midnight.

Or how about failing to notice that the Smiths never sent their deposit for Saturday night, leaving you with an empty room on one of the few nights you can count on full occupancy? Emotionally and economically, you can't afford a lot of errors like these.

Whether evidenced by cold coffee, grungy sheets, or rude telephone manners, a too-casual approach to innkeeping can ruin you. A professional always tries harder. The conventional wisdom is that an unhappy guest tends to mention the bad experience to eleven people.

POLICIES AND PROCEDURES

Policies and procedures are major areas of controversy among innkeepers. Questions like whether or not to accept credit cards have stirred violent disagreement between those who have been burned on collecting and those who think it's only sensible to accept plastic in the modern world.

Inns are as individual as innkeepers, and one inn's set of policies is unlikely to be perfect for any other. Nevertheless, other innkeepers may have solutions you haven't thought of in problem areas like cancellation and deposit refund policies. There's also a feeling of safety in numbers: the "industry standard" is easier to assert.

Developing clear policies and putting them in writing is good for your guests as well as for you. Guests to whom you have sent a brochure or letter of confirmation describing your no-pets policy, for example, won't be able to muster up much righteous indignation when you stop them at the front door with Fido. Here are some specifics.

SMOKING

Stale cigarette odors in a guest room can take days to disperse. Not only that, fires caused by cigarettes kill more people than any other kind of fire. This is due chiefly to smoking in bed, but another common cause is cigarettes that fall into sofas and smolder until finally the upholstery ignites in the wee hours of the night. The combination of cigarettes and alcohol is especially deadly, because people become more careless when they drink. That's the down side.

On the other hand, some potential guests will undoubtedly decide against your inn if they're not permitted to smoke there. A middle ground is permitting smoking in some limited area of the inn, where it will be least hazardous and least offensive. You may also want to limit *what* can be smoked: Cigars get a pretty strong no at most inns; pipes can smell cozy or lousy. Quite a few inns simply permit no smoking inside. One inn allows smoking on the veranda, which communicates their policy while also creating a mental image of a summer day in a porch swing.

Some inns have both smoking and no-smoking guest rooms. This works especially well if you have a separate cottage or a separate floor for the purpose. With wood-burning fireplaces or wood stoves in some rooms, it may be difficult and also less important to enforce a policy against cigarettes there.

So what do you do when there's a problem and your clear policy is being ignored? Often a nice note by the pillow is enough to stop the smoke in a no-smoking guest room. Because it involves no face-to-face interaction, embarrassment on both sides is less. If it's a one-night stay, you may prefer simply to console yourself that they'll be gone in the morning. If you encounter a smoking guest in a no-smoking area, a nice line to use is, "Are you going to have trouble with our no-smoking policy?" Take it from there.

CHILDREN AND PETS

Note: In some states refusing children may be determined to be illegal; proceed carefully. Experience is the best guide to whether having children and pets works at your inn. Also, consider whether you truly like them and whether they fit your image of the inn. Children may be a problem to guests who are purposefully taking breaks from their own. They may create noise problems. In some inns, the contents are too valuable to risk to children and dogs. Some of your guests may be allergic to pets.

Setting an age limit for children is one way to tailor your policy to the kinds of problems children might create in your inn. Just decide at what age the average child will behave the way you prefer your guests to behave.

State this policy positively. Here's an example from an inn in Kennebunkport, Maine: "The 1802 House is adult-oriented. Therefore, children 12 and over are most welcome." The Lyme Inn, Lyme, New Hampshire, uses another positive approach: "The comfort of our guests is assured by our policy of no children under 8 years of age, and no pets."

"Children welcome" is a clear enough statement of the other side of the policy, and also gives a sense of the character of the inn and the innkeeper.

The Jakobstettel Guest House in St. Jacobs, Ontario, encourages children age six and older. Innkeeper Ellen Brubaker welcomes them with a tour that features the location of the cookie jar! "Kids are great! We just involve them!" says Ellen. "We post their drawings on the refrigerator, and let them 'help' make muffins." Families generally do a good job of supervising their own children, she says.

The inn uses pullout sofas in guest rooms for one or two children; they put a mattress on the floor for more, and parents bring sleeping bags.

CASH OR CHARGE?

"Do you accept cash?" Incredible as it sounds, guests ask it. Here's an outline of the advantages and disadvantages of various forms of payment.

Cash

ADVANTAGES
No bank charges
Almost always "good"

DISADVANTAGES
Risk of theft
Need to make change
Need to receipt payment

Checks

ADVANTAGES
No bank charges
No change to make
Good for mail-in deposits
Automatic receipt of payment

DISADVANTAGES
Some risk of "bouncing"

Travelers Checks

ADVANTAGES
As good as cash
Minimal fear of counterfeit

DISADVANTAGES
Some risk of theft
Need to make change
Need to receipt payments

Credit Cards

ADVANTAGES
Can confirm last-minute reservation
Convenient for guest
More "impulse" sales,
    more expensive rooms sold
Automatic receipt of payment

DISADVANTAGES
Bank charges, 2 to 4 percent
Authorizations take time
Disputed charges difficult to collect
    (protection varies)

Regardless of the pros and cons, you may find credit cards are a must if your chief market is business travelers.

DEPOSITS

A deposit is the seal on a two-way commitment: the innkeeper commits that the room will be ready and waiting for the guests to arrive, the guests commit to coming. Most inns require a deposit within a week or ten days of the date the reservation is made. For reservations made months in advance, you may wish to allow more time, but it's to your advantage in every way to get the money in hand.

Deposits can be the price of one night's stay, half the price of the total stay, the price of the first and last nights' stay, or the total amount. Base your choice on how much commitment you want. Don't ignore the interest-income potential of deposits; many seasonal inns exist off-season on early deposits and interest.

A related procedural issue involves last-minute reservations, made too late to be guaranteed with deposits (except by credit card). Should you take a phone reservation for a Saturday night when you have no way to guarantee the caller will actually take the room until you've already turned everyone else away? If you usually fill up on Saturdays with drop-ins, forget the reservation and fill the room on a first-come, first-served basis. It's probably the safest course, but it's also the hardest to explain satisfactorily to a pleading caller.

So you may want to encourage goodwill and reward the caller who thought far enough ahead to call even on a Friday. One inn accepts such reservations, requiring a confirming telephone call by ten on the morning

162

of the reserved stay; they haven't been burned on this yet. If there's no reconfirmation, there's plenty of time left in the day to fill the room.

Other inns warn callers that they will have to bill them even if they don't show for a last-minute reservation. You can ask them to take the Girl Scout Oath, or intimate that your people will be watching them. Whatever "friendly persuasion" you use, remember that establishing a personal connection with these callers makes it harder for them to disappoint you.

CANCELLATIONS

Do nice innkeepers finish last? Without any cancellation policy they will. How much notice of cancellation should you require to return a deposit? Base it on how much time you need to refill the room and the time, effort, and worry you'll experience in the meantime.

The range goes from twenty-four hours to seven and even thirty days, the latter for an inn on a tiny island near San Francisco. This inn, the East Brother Light Station, makes refunds only if the booking is subsequently filled, and even then they keep 10 percent of the deposit as a handling fee. If one party has reserved a number of your rooms, or reserved one room for an extended stay, a longer cancellation period may be necessary, since it will take you longer to refill.

Refunding deposits if you fill the room is standard practice. Cancellation fees vary from 10 percent to five and ten dollars. The fees help to reimburse you for the time on the phone you'll use calling your waiting list, postage to send out new confirmations to new guests, and so on.

Whatever notice you require, don't apologize for it if it works for you and if it's clearly communicated in advance to guests. You can always make an exception if you want to, and be a good guy.

Sorry, we can't make it after all: It's Thursday afternoon. The telephone rings. The caller sounds frantic and unhappy. "There's no way we can keep our reservation for this weekend. We're in the middle of moving and there's just too much to do." You pleasantly but firmly remind your caller of the cancellation policy described in the brochure you send as a confirmation of all reservations. You say, "Of course we'll send you a refund right away if we can rebook the rooms. In fact, I'll call and let you know as soon as that happens."

On Friday morning, the room is still empty. Your guest-that-should-have-been calls again. When she learns that her $130 deposit is still very much at risk, she decides to come anyway.

It's Sunday morning. The off again-on again guest pair is preparing to check out. Large smiles are on their faces. "Do you know how much we needed this?" they say.

Moral: You won't always come out this well, but maintaining your policies is important. Done with grace, everybody wins.

Most innkeepers are understanding and generous in cases of real emergency. On the other hand, as one innkeeper says, "A lot of grandmothers die," if you believe all the people who call to cancel.

It's always a good idea to ask whether you should just hold the deposit for another stay to be rescheduled in the future. Then if you do refill the room, you won't have to send back the money. Also, consider offering to hold late cancellations another night when you know you won't be full. If they can come midweek when your rooms would otherwise be empty, maybe you will feel all right about leaving their room empty on the weekend, and you'll have created goodwill at the same time.

CHECK-IN/CHECK-OUT

How do you decide what's the best check-in time or period for your inn? In a city inn with round-the-clock staff, you might base it solely on the time it takes you to get your rooms ready for the next guests. But if yours is a smaller, country operation, and the only desk staff is you, limiting check-in time to give yourself comfortable hours away from the inn, to shop, do promotion, or take a hike, may be important. More and more, innkeepers are indicating that check-in hours need to meet their own needs, as well as their guests'.

You can turn a potential negative into a positive here. Explaining to guests that you need time to read or go to the beach expresses something about the very personal nature of inns. In most cases, reasonable check-in hours can be established, limited to as few as two hours a day. If most of your guests arrive from nearby cities after a day's work, a five-to-seven check-in time may work. If they are chiefly vacationers, midafternoon hours may work better. You may decide to establish different check-in hours for weekends and midweek days. Given the labor-intensive nature of innkeeping and the limited number of rooms and therefore room rents, limiting check-in times can save you money you would otherwise have had to pay yourself or a staff member simply to be there.

But people will arrive without reservations and turn away when they see a sign indicating check-in time is hours away. To avoid this, some innkeepers arrange special telephone lines on the inn's front door that connect to a neighbor, who comes when called to take care of early arrivals. Other inns work out arrangements with nearby shops to take payments for rooms and assure guests of a space. This takes some coordination, but simple systems have been worked out to communicate to the people who will handle them the number of rooms available; normally they receive a flat fee for each payment they take.

Innkeepers who have established limited check-in hours find they work very well. Some inns arrange to leave keys and special notes for guests with reservations who must arrive early or late; others encourage guests to call when they arrive in town, and will check them in early if the room is ready. But don't give up too easily on a policy when you've established it to meet some very real needs of your own. As more and more inns take the initiative to do this, others feel more comfortable about it too, making life easier for everyone.

Check-out time at most inns is eleven or noon. Few guests fail to leave on time, but it's often possible to accommodate a requested late check-out time by leaving the room until last for cleaning.

Occasionally you'll have to knock on a door and ask people to leave. You might use a line like this: "I'm sorry to bother you, but it's a half hour past check-out time, and I just want to warn you that we'll be cleaning your room in about ten minutes. You can leave your bags in the office if you like, and feel free to enjoy the garden."

BREAKFAST HOURS

If it's 10:30 A.M. and nobody has shown up for breakfast, you'd better think back on whether you told them when breakfast is served, and where. You want your guests to be comfortable, and part of that is knowing the "house rules." If you serve breakfast in bed, ask your guests the night before what time they'd like it. If you serve everybody promptly at nine in the dining room, talk it up during check-in time when you show them the inn and their room. Some inns serve over a range of time, from eight to ten, for example. When establishing a breakfast schedule, consider the bathrooms situation. If they are "down the hall," you're putting considerable stress on them and your guests if you require everyone to be at the table at once. Establishing and communicating a cutoff time is also important.

Many inns offer early breakfasts to business travelers. Some also provide early coffee service in guest rooms, or in the common area where guests can help themselves.

Policies and procedures should be based on meeting your guests' needs and your own, focusing on the most efficient, effective ways to handle recurring situations. Flexibility is key; every bottom line probably has its own bottom line. As one pro puts it, "Your inn reflects you, and you have to be able to live with whatever you offer, so make it fit. Mull it over; try it out."

HANDLING RESERVATIONS

Just because you don't have fifty rooms to book doesn't mean you can afford to be casual about maintaining a proper reservations system. A well-organized reservation form is the primary source of information that performs a variety of important functions, including these:

- Ensures that all essential information is taken at one time, when the guest calls to make the reservation, so it's on the guest's dime.
- Ensures that all policies and procedures are described to the guest, even when you take the call at the busiest moment of the day.
- Provides a convenient and time-saving space to make calculations.

- Provides marketing data for future advertising and promotional planning.
- Provides the basis for a mailing list.
- Allows easy filing and retrieval of reservations.
- Becomes an all-in-one inn sitter's resource, allowing inn sitters to read or quote information accurately without hours of training.
- Helps eliminate double bookings, cancellations, misunderstandings, and unhappy guests.
- Provides easy retrieval of information on repeat guests. Happy is the guest greeted with warm words of personal recognition based on the previous stay.

Professional inns keep useful, accurate, retrievable information. Here are the basics of how it's done.

THE RESERVATION FORM

Though specific information needs vary from inn to inn, reservation forms can follow some basic rules. Most inns devise their own forms; some use standard 8½-inch by 11-inch paper, others use 4-inch by 6-inch cards. Some innkeepers fill blank pages with information in each of several categories they keep in their heads; others use preprinted cards. Some include a lot of information; others include very little. The basic information necessary to ensure a pleasant stay for your guest and a smooth transaction for you is:

NAME It's important to know who called to make the reservation, as well as the names and number of person(s) in the party.

ADDRESS This should be the preferred mailing address, whether home, work, or elsewhere.

PHONE Try to get business and home phones. Calling home numbers on evenings and weekends when rates are low will save you money.

DATE(S) AND DAY(S) OF RESERVATION Potential mistakes usually show up here, when callers request a day and date that do not occur simultaneously. Ask for both to improve your chance of catching the error. This information can also assist you in tracking business patterns, especially midweek and weekend variations.

ROOM Inn goers often book a specific room and expect to have it.

ROOM PRICE, DEPOSIT, WHEN DUE You'll probably request a deposit equivalent to a night's lodging price, half the total, full prepayment, or some other formula. Record clearly the total price quoted for the stay, the amount requested in deposit, and the date by which the deposit must arrive.

METHOD OF PAYMENT Leave room for credit card number, cardholder name, and expiration date.

POLICIES You will no doubt have a separate rate and policy sheet to refer to when there are questions, but it's also a big help to have policies written out on the reservation form in a conversational style you can actually read over the phone. There should also be a space to check off when the policy is read or described to the caller, so if Guest Jones arrives with cigar in hand and complains about the no-smoking policy, you can recheck the reservation form and, if necessary, actually show him the record.

CHECK-IN TIME Although the only way to make sure guests arrive during a specific check-in time is to ferry them in to an island inn, the odds of their showing up on time improve if you are clear about your check-in time. You may want to work out special arrangements with guests for whom your regular check-in hours are inconvenient.

HOW THEY FOUND OUT ABOUT YOUR INN This information, which guests are happy to share, is essential for evaluating your advertising and promotional program.

WHO TOOK THE RESERVATION If more than one person takes reservations at your inn, note who took the booking in case questions arise later.

DATE RESERVATION MADE If you require prepayment within a certain period, the date of the booking is very important. It may also prove useful or interesting to see how far in advance most reservations are made.

SPECIAL OCCASION AND OTHER NOTES Important information could be that they're coming on an anniversary or honeymoon, driving up in a day from New York, once lived in your area, hate carrots, or want dinner reservations.

BOOKKEEPING Save space on the reservation form to record when payment arrives, the date you send confirmation, and the balance due.

THE FINE PRINT

RATES include breakfast, hot tub use, evening beverage in the parlor; rates subject to change without notice; rates do not include applicable taxes; all rooms are designed for two persons (additional persons may use the sofa beds in the suites at $10/per person extra); singles subtract $5 from listed price.

RESERVATIONS held one week only, pending receipt of full prepayment; two-night minimum stay on weekends; MasterCard and VISA accepted.

CANCELLATIONS require 7 days notice prior to date of arrival for refund less $15 cancellation processing fee. If reserving more than 2 rooms, 14-day notice required.

FOR THE COMFORT OF OTHERS there is no smoking in the Main House; courteous smokers accepted in the Cottage; no children or pets.

CHECK-IN time: 3–6 P.M. Special arrangements must be made if you plan to arrive later than 6 P.M. If you wish an earlier check-in, please call on the morning of your arrival about the possibilities. Hot tub sign-ups made at check-in.

CHECK-OUT time: 11 A.M.

A lmost verbatim from major hotel-chain desk: "Now was that a corner mini suite with wet bar and a partial ocean view, or an inside room with refrigerator only and a complete ocean view, or did you say you wanted a view of the trees and mountains with a full suite and kitchen area? And was that for the Friday/Saturday special, the Sunday 'solo,' or the regular midweek rate?"

TEN INVERNESS WAY RESERVATIONS

Names: _____ Date(s) of stay _____

Address: _____ Circle: Su, M, T, W, Th, F, Sa

_____ Number of Days _____

Phone (day): _____ (night): _____

Circle one: Double / Twins / Queen   Room number requested _____

Caller's name: _____ Phone: _____

Address: _____

Policies:

1. _____ To hold your room, we must receive the full amount as a deposit, within a week from today. With tax, that would be $ _____. Do you have our brochure? If no: OK, we'll send you one with a note of confirmation when we get your check. If yes: We'll send you a note of confirmation . . .

2. _____ Our normal check-in time is 5 to 7 P.M. Will that fit in with your plans?
   Early: 12–1 only _____ Regular: 5–7 P.M. _____ Late: after 7 P.M. _____
If for any reason we're not here when you arrive, we'll put a note and key in an envelope for you on the front door.

3. _____ How did you hear about us? _____

4. Thanks a lot. We'll expect your check then within the week, and we'll see you on _____ _____.
        (date)

Notes:

Check one: send confirmation brochure? _____ Or postcard? _____
Payment received, confirmed ___ Reservation taken by: _____
Today's date: _____ Calendar? _____

RATE INFORMATION

The lodging industry is notorious for complicated rate structures. Books may come in one basic hardback format at one regular price, but rooms vary in price from Monday to Saturday, from February to June, and for one person, two people, and three people. And you may get a different price if you're a corporate traveler or a tourist.

The reason inns get into the same complexities of rates, amenities, and package deals as the big hotels is because our objective is the same; a full house. Whatever rate variations you work with at your inn, be sure the people who take reservations can find the appropriate rates quickly and communicate them accurately to callers. Whether the rate card is taped to the reservations book, the refrigerator, or the telephone desk, it must be handy, readable, and complete.

GIVING INFORMATION

After you've collected all the information *you* need from your callers, consciously take a moment to inquire about their needs. Perhaps they would like further information about their room, the inn, or the town. Offer to send additional tourist information on what to do and see in the area, or about special events during their stay. Ask if they'd like directions to the inn, especially if you've become aware through experience that the map or directions on your brochure are inadequate.

Describe the parking situation or any other important procedural matter. Some innkeepers have devised ingenious ways of dealing with late arrivals: staying up to greet them even at 3:00 A.M.; specially coding lock boxes for keys; leaving notes with maps and keys; installing intercoms to rouse the innkeepers; or maintaining a firm policy that no one is admitted after midnight. Whatever the late-arrival policy, it shouldn't be a surprise to an expectant guest.

THE CALENDAR

You've just gotten a four-day midweek reservation! Don't get so excited that you forget the crucial step: recording the information on your calendar. Whether you use a special form that lists rooms, dates, and so on, or simply a standard daily/weekly/monthly appointment book, post the name and the specific room on the appropriate dates immediately.

At day's end, most inns apply some form of a checks-and-balances system. Check all reservations taken that day against your calendar. If there are discrepancies, correct them as soon as possible.

FILING RESERVATION FORMS

Most inns file individual reservation forms chronologically for easy retrieval if there's a question or problem, to record payment received, or to prepare a weekly schedule of arriving guests.

ONCE PAYMENT HAS BEEN RECEIVED

When the money is in your hand, first pull the form and verify that the date, the room, and the amount received are correct. Note on the form the amount paid, the date the confirmation is being sent, and the balance due, if any.

Next, note on the master calendar that payment has been received, and send a confirmation or receipt. Finally, refile the form and go to the bank!

Wendy Hatfield, innkeeper at The Gingerbread Mansion in Ferndale, California, designed the reservation calendar on the next page. It records names, arrival dates, and date reservation made. An X shows the deposit has been paid. There's also a wait-list column. Wendy runs off these forms at the printer's, then writes in the dates for the weeks. She keeps the pages in a half-inch-thick three-ring binder, large enough to hold the pages and small enough to carry around the inn. Blank reservation forms and a rate information sheet are tucked inside for convenience.

	Bookings				Wait List
Room	Fountain	Rose	Garden	Heron	Name Dates Room(s)
M	Winger 7/7 X	Heyer 8/8 X	Rogers 3/15 X	Hagstrom 9/10	1. Johnson 10/15 Heron 2. Meyers 10/15-16 Fountain
T		Williams 9/1		X ↓	1. 2. 3. 4. 5.
W		↓	X		1. 2. 3. 4. 5.
Th	Jones 8/26 X ← together →	Armstrong 8/26 X	X		1. 2. 3. 4. 5.
F	Laudy 9/13	Beecham w/mother → 9/14	X	← w son Beecham (1) 9/14	1. Hillsdale 10/19 Heron 2. 3. 4. 5.
Sa	Michner (3 persons) 9/11	Markham 7/30 X	↓		1. 2. 3. 4. 5.
Su	↓	Foxworth 7/21 X	Markham X		1. 2. 3. 4. 5.

MODIFICATIONS AND CANCELLATIONS

While some inns use a separate form for recording this information, most inns put it on the reservation form. The essential points to note are:

- Previous arrival and departure dates.
- New arrival and departure dates.
- Name.
- Who is making the change, their address, phone number, position or relationship to the guest.
- What monetary differences are created by the change. Who owes what to whom.
- Today's date.
- The reason for the change.

When a change is made by phone, ask the previous arrival date and name, then retrieve the reservation form from the file, so you have the guest's history in front of you before you proceed. Be sure to erase the booking on your calendar immediately so the room will show as vacant and can be rerented. If you use a separate form for modifications and cancellations, clip it to the top of the reservation form, along with any other correspondence; the cancellation form is now the most critical information in that particular batch.

ORGANIZING FOR GUEST ARRIVALS

There should be a regular point when you prepare for the next day, week, or some definite period of time. Inns do this in a variety of ways. One pulls reservation cards weekly and pins them to the kitchen wall, ready for guest arrivals. Another keeps arriving guests' cards in a desk drawer. Still another makes a weekly chart listing dates, rooms with guest names, and, in a different color ink, notes estimated arrival times, money owed, repeat guest, special occasion, and so on. This sheet is taped to the back of the kitchen door, next to the room keys.

Each of these very different systems appears to work well for the inn using it. Each is a way of streamlining the usefulness of the information collected at reservation time, so it can be used at check-in time. At check-in, do ask your guests to register in some way; a big book or registration cards are two choices. Do not leave them waiting more than half a minute while you get their room key. Guests should feel welcome and expected.

ORGANIZING FOR THE FUTURE

The guest has come and gone. Retrieve the reservation forms from the kitchen wall, the desk drawer, or wherever you keep them to streamline your welcoming routine. These cards are filled with information about people you hope to see again. What do you do with them now? Here are several options for storage and retrievability.

- A simple filing system includes one expandable date file with numbers one through thirty-one on the tabs, plus twelve file folders, one for each month. The expandable file is used for the current month's reservation forms. All other months are filed chronologically in the monthly file folders, kept in a file drawer. Reservations can be filed by arrival date, then within that date section by name.
- File cards alphabetically on a Rolodex. They can be flipped through quickly and pulled out. Keep a separate Rolodex for each year.
- Computerize. Standard inexpensive software, available for most home systems, allows you to enter a number of different fields for each file record. You can enter not only names and addresses for future mailings, but also other demographics, such as reservation date, room selected, special occasion, and advertising source. This will allow you to print lists by categories, such as referral source, effectiveness of specific ad, length of stay, where guests come from (geographically), special-occasion business, and business travelers.

STAFFING

"What! You want to come in here and mess up my clean inn?" When you answer the doorbell feeling like that, it's time to think about getting help.

Many innkeepers start out doing everything themselves, often thinking they'll continue this way forever. They usually are concerned about the expense, paperwork, and loss of autonomy that hiring staff means. And there's no question that the intimate, homey feeling of an inn changes when hired help takes over the jobs owners previously did. Innkeepers often fear the public reaction to this, and, in addition, feel that "no one else does things the way I want them done."

When innkeepers do hire staff, it's often to make time for the things only they can do, or things they can do better than anyone else, like some kinds of promotion, planning, and financial projections. Staff can also free owners to do the things they enjoy most, such as gardening, perhaps, or spending extra time with guests. In some cases, staffers provide expertise owners don't have. But most important, owners hire staff to give themselves time off and to avoid jobs they dislike.

A good way to decide what staff to hire is to make a list of all the tasks done in the inn. Here's a start:

Cook and serve breakfast	Confirm reservations
Clean rooms	Bookkeeping
Clean common areas and kitchen	Promotion
Take phone reservations	Flower arranging

Now put four columns next to your list, for things you like to do, things you don't like to do, things someone else can do, and things only you can do. Review your list and put check marks in the appropriate columns; ask the other partners to do so as well. This process will make clear to you which tasks you might hire for. And it's also a beginning on writing a job description.

The job description should include each task to be done, the number of hours and days of the week required, the pay scale, and the experience and education required. In figuring hours and wages, be careful to consider seasonal variations, so you don't give applicants unrealistic expectations. Type the job description and keep it on file. It should be the first thing you give an applicant to review.

Where do you find applicants? Most innkeepers prefer word of mouth as a method for recruiting new staff members, including asking their present staffers for recommendations. One innkeeper uses a "network" technique, calling ten people and describing his staff needs; the word spreads from there.

Ads usually work well for locating dishwashing and cleaning staff. Local schools sometimes have internship programs that are ideal sources for larger establishments that need extra help during summer seasons. Nearby military bases and senior-citizen organizations may also be good sources.

Different kinds of people seem to do well in different inn jobs. Some inns prefer to hire people who are a bit older and give them more responsibility; other inns hire young people to do jobs like housekeeping and dishwashing. Innkeepers say high school and young college students can be expected to present scheduling problems, and their priorities may not be yours.

If there are few suitable applicants, consider offering benefits that are especially appealing or valuable in your area. These might include the opportunity to bring children to the job, avoiding the expense and uncertainty of good child care. Some inns can develop a small apartment for a staffer, or provide meals for students. Inns also offer other pluses for staff, including varied tasks and flexible scheduling, a chance to interact with guests, and often an opportunity to become an integral part of the business. Don't hesitate to mention these.

THE HIRING PROCESS

Screen applicants on the phone. Ask your good prospects to fill out application forms (available at office supply stores if you don't have your own) or supply a resumé. Then schedule and perform a regular interview.

For the interview, dress and act like an employer, not a harried innkeeper, to establish a tone of professionalism. If you have several people to see, schedule them consecutively, about thirty minutes apart. Be sure someone else will handle phones while you interview, and find a quiet, private part of the inn away from guests and other staffers.

Indicate clearly to the prospective employees what the position is; don't glamorize it. Ask questions that help you assess the applicants' commitment to the area, future plans, attitude toward work, background, and present situation. Do *not* ask questions about marital status, age, race, or pregnancy; it's illegal to consider these issues in hiring. If you're concerned about age or pregnancy because it might affect a candidate's strength for certain tasks, ask about strength.

Follow a consistent format during the interviews. It will help you compare candidates more effectively. Here are sample interview questions to ask after you've introduced yourself, toured some or all of the inn, and described the job.

• Why do you think you could do this job?
• What are your strengths and weaknesses?
• Who are you? How would you describe yourself?
• Why do you want this job? What circumstances bring you to apply for it?

---

*A*nn and Gene Swett of the Old Monterey Inn in Monterey, California, often hire college students from the area. "The people working for me are like my kids," Ann says. "I feel they're here to learn things, probably many things I'm not even aware of. I don't want anyone to feel obligated to stay here. We had a wonderful manager here for two years, for example, and she started to get frustrated when she'd learned all there was to learn. It started to become a battle over whether this was my inn or hers. Finally I just hugged her one day and said, 'You're a really neat person and I think it's time for you to move on.' There comes a time when they need to leave the nest.

"There's no doubt about who's in charge here. At the same time, making a wrong decision is not the end of the world. The innkeeper has to let go a little. But it is my inn, and they have to deal with my idiosyncracies. They have to cut up the fruit the way I want it, but that doesn't mean there's anything wrong with their technique — for them."

- What was your favorite previous job, and why? What other jobs have you had and why did you leave them?
- What other jobs are you applying for?
- What things do you think would be problems with this job?
- How long a time commitment can you make to this job?
- What are your plans for the future? What do you hope or expect to be doing in five years?

You may want to send your best candidates directly to a second interview, ideally with someone else who'll supervise the new employee. After you've interviewed all candidates, check references on your best prospect(s). Get a name and phone number of a previous and a present employer, if possible. Here's a format for a reference check.

- Describe your job opening, and ask about X's suitability for it.
- Ask what kind of work X did for the reference, for how long, and why X left.
- Ask whether the reference would hire X again.
- Ask about X as an employee. Listen hard for key words here and write them down.
- Ask what was the major problem with X. If the problem sounds like it could also be troublesome to you, ask how it was worked out in the previous position.
- Ask about X's strengths and weaknesses, and for any other information that the reference believes would be helpful.

Once you've made your choice, take a night to think about the decision, then call and offer the job. Be very specific: Reconfirm the job title, salary or hourly rate, and hours. Suggest a specific time on a specific day to begin work, suggest appropriate attire, and describe what will happen on the first day and how much time it will take.

TRAINING

Be prepared for your new employee on the first day. Have a training plan and a time card ready. It's obvious to most innkeepers that detail is necessary to task training, but don't overlook the importance of values training. Equipping your staff to understand what the inn is about will contribute immensely to their ability to convey the spirit of the inn and to meet your expectations. Consider spending an hour to cover the areas outlined here.

History
- Why and how you got into innkeeping. This will tell them a lot about your expectations for innkeepers and the inn. And besides, guests will ask staff for the story.
- Why you chose the area and the structure you did. Much of your own image of the inn will be revealed in this.
- What personal values were involved in your decision to open an inn. This can be especially revealing if you left another career or saw innkeeping as a way to earn a living and still spend time with your young children.

Objectives
- Complete this sentence: I will feel successful when _____. You may define success in terms of money, smooth operation, free time, or fame. Your definition makes a big difference in how you run your inn and what your staff people understand to be important.
- Set specific goals if you can, such as a regular 10 percent increase in occupancy year to year or getting paperwork and cleaning out of the way by 1:00 P.M. Make charts that convey your objectives visually and help you and your staff evaluate your achievements.

Organization

- Are you the head honcho in every area and your staff people are assistants? Or do you see your organization as a team with different people responsible for specific areas like maintenance, food preparation, and paperwork? Assistants behave differently from "division managers." Staff people like and need to know not only their own roles, but the roles of their co-workers and how they fit together into a total structure.
- What about the future staff structure you envision? Is there room for advancement? Will a good housekeeper ever get a chance to be a weekend innkeeper or manage the office?

Management Practices

- If you encourage staff ideas and suggestions, make it known. And act on them when they come!
- Is there a regular period, perhaps six months or a year, after which you review performances and consider giving raises? Is there a standard increase staff people can expect?
- Describe the criteria you use for determining whether and how large a raise to give. It will probably be helpful to you and to your staff to have a formal list of standards; it gives them something to work for, as well as a very tangible demonstration of your work values, and helps you maintain consistency and fairness in decisions about pay levels.

Then describe your method for task training. List the skills to be learned and the criteria for success. For example, the goal for a cleaning person might be to change a bed, arrange the flowers, and dust and vacuum a room in thirty minutes. You might use a checklist that shows every task involved in getting a room ready for the next guests. Be sure to plan enough time in your own schedule to explain things, demonstrate, check progress, give feedback, and correct errors. Let your new staff people know what standards must be met before they are on their own in the job.

As you go through this hiring process, developing a training notebook will make subsequent hiring much easier. It also provides a reminder and refresher to staff, and reduces the need for repeating details. A loose-leaf notebook indexed for various subjects is perfect; include breakfast, room cleaning, reservations policy, cancellation procedures, and so on.

KEEPING GOOD STAFF

Making your staff people feel part of the inn team is important in keeping them. Inns usually can't offer large salaries, so you need to make other job benefits clear. Be a caring, fair employer, respecting the ideas and feelings of your staff. Reward good performance. Everybody likes to be appreciated, and encouraging and rewarding good work pays off in the spirit as well as the economics of your inn. Here are some ideas:

CONTESTS Start a competition among staff members who handle the telephones and reservations. Give the one who gets the most midweek bookings during a specific period a night's stay at another inn. You can probably arrange a trade, so the room won't cost you anything. A bonus for you — in addition to increased midweek bookings — may be that your staff will see the inn in a new light as they look for the words to bring in the business.

AWARDS Corporations reward employees who come up with cost-saving and money-making ideas. Why not do this at your inn? At Ten Inverness Way, a staff member came up with an idea for saving $300 a year in the cost of dairy products by dealing directly with the local delivery company. Shopping time was reduced as well. Mary and her partner were so impressed with the idea that they instituted a standing incentive award. The rule is that any idea that produces continuing, quantifiable savings or earnings is rewarded with a check in the amount of 50 percent of the first year's cash benefits.

GRATITUDE It is surprising how important it is to thank staff. And it's equally surprising how often we forget to do it. Look for and mention things your staff members do especially well. It could be the smooth handling of a difficult phone call. It could be a creative touch with making bouquets out of next to nothing from your frostbitten garden. It could be handling a complex agenda item particularly well. You will almost certainly be amazed at how many people you will please by noticing their good work.

PROMOTION AND RAISES

Base employee rewards on the value of staff people to your business. Take care that the more responsible jobs command the higher pay, and that pay scales also reward length of employment at the inn. Don't raise pay prematurely or capriciously. Pay increases should be based on regular, individual evaluations of established criteria. If you're not entirely satisfied with a job, say, "I'd like to raise your pay to X dollars, but I need to feel confident you'll ———. When I see that this is happening regularly for a month, I'll give you the raise."

When you promote someone, they're often taking on a whole new job. Just because they've been on staff in another capacity doesn't mean they don't need thorough training in the new slot.

Don't promote and give raises just before your slow season unless you're sure you can afford it.

THE BOOKWORK

When you hire employees, you become responsible for maintaining records for unemployment insurance, disability insurance, state and federal income taxes, and social security. Your state employment service office should be able to give you current information about your legal responsibilities as an employer.

For your own purposes, you'll probably want to keep a personnel file for employees, including their applications, up-to-date addresses, reference information, and work history. A payroll file with time cards, W-4 and W-2 tax forms, payroll cards, quarterly tax records, time sheets, and other records should be kept current and retained for several years. Stationery stores can provide time cards and payroll systems that help you create records for yourself and your staff people.

FIRING EMPLOYEES

It doesn't have to be that awful, if you've clearly communicated your expectations and standards all along. For example, staffers need to understand the job description and duties, and your expectations about hours, dress, and pace. If "attitude" is a problem, describe it in concrete terms. For example, courtesy to guests and staff is concretely exhibited in saying "please" and "thank you."

Put in writing any warning or ultimatum that could result in dismissal. When you fire someone, explain again your reasons for it. In many states, dismissal for incompetence does not preclude former employees from collecting unemployment compensation; as an employer, you're responsible for screening out the incompetents before you hire them.

Laying off employees for lack of work is a different matter completely. Be sure to discuss the situation and the possibility of rehiring when conditions change. Sometimes you can negotiate a reduced-hours arrangement with an employee you want to keep but can't presently afford.

INDEPENDENT CONTRACTORS

Independent contractors can sometimes perform necessary services, but they will not be employees. They have their own businesses, provide their own tools, and establish their own work parameters. For example, it's not up to you to set a contractor's hours; they are arrived at by mutual agreement. Independent contractors pay their own social security, taxes, and unemployment and disability insurance. If your contractors have not covered their employees for worker's compensation, you're responsible if they're hurt.

At year end, you need to fill out an IRS Form 1099 for each contractor to whom you have paid $600 or more. Copies must be sent to the IRS, the state income tax agency, and the contractor. The rules defining independent contractors are specific; when in doubt, check with your accountant on whether your planned arrangement applies. Always sign a contract, such as the one shown here or in Appendix 5.

In some work areas, innkeepers can choose whether to hire an employee or work with a contractor. Gardening services are a perfect example. If you're not already an employer, it would probably be wisest

INDEPENDENT CONTRACTOR AGREEMENT

Nonemployee Compensation Contract

This Agreement is entered into on this _____ day of _____ 19_____ by and between _____ ("Contractor") and _____ ("Client"). Contractor and Client hereby agree to the following:

1. Contractor agrees to perform the following services on behalf of Client: (Insert description of services to be performed or completed.)

2. Contractor will commence work on or before _____ and will perform same on a _(insert daily or weekly)_ basis. This work will continue until _(date)_.

3. Client will pay to Contractor the following sums (rate) on the schedule set forth below.

4. Contractor and Client intend this Agreement to be one of independent contractor and employer. Accordingly, Contractor retains the sole right to control or direct the manner in which the services described herein are to be performed, subject to the foregoing, Client retains the right to inspect, to stop work, to prescribe alterations, and generally to supervise the work to insure its conformity with that specified in this Agreement. Contractor and Client understand that it is Contractor's sole responsibility to provide for all employment taxes, including withholding and social security, and insurance, including worker's compensation coverage and public liability insurance, arising out of or relating to this Agreement.

5. Other provisions (Specify):

_____   _____
Contractor   Client

to work with an independent gardening service rather than to set up the necessary structure and paperwork systems to hire a gardener as an inn employee.

INSURANCE

An elderly guest has a heart attack and tumbles down three flights of polished stairs in your vintage Victorian. Are you liable?

It's noon on the dot and your cleaning staff gets no response from repeated knocks at the door of a guest room. They open it and find the bed occupied. Invasion of privacy?

A staffer, straightening the kitchen, slashes his hand on your bread knife. Worker's compensation?

Mrs. Nice Person in the Camellia Room chokes on your magnificent eggs Benedict, permanently injuring her voice. Products hazard?

According to an attorney who works with innkeepers, "The question isn't *whether* you'll be sued, it's *when*." People with small businesses are among the most vulnerable. No longer a Jane or John Q. Citizen, innkeepers will be viewed by juries as business owners with marketable assets. On the other hand, inns aren't big enough to have the protection of a corporate legal department. If you need to retain an attorney to defend you in a lawsuit, you can plan on spending at least $10,000 for a case that goes to superior court. This is one of the catastrophes for which insurance is designed.

Fire, theft, and serious personal injury are others. In addition, your sign may blow down or valuable property may be broken. An accident at the Glenborough Inn once resulted in a loss of $700 worth of antique Haviland china.

Dreary, isn't it? Fortunately, hospitality insurance has been designed to package appropriate protection for the contingencies hotels and motels face routinely. Equally specialized policies have been developed for inns and innkeepers, combining business and personal property and liability coverages.

So shop carefully. The inn packages are likely to get you the right coverage at a lower price than you could buy it in pieces. Whether packaged or not, policy prices vary from company to company, agent to agent. Ask for detailed comparisons of proposals, and ask about special payment plans. Agents wear many hats, representing themselves, various insurance companies, and clients, including you. Be sure you feel your interests are not coming in a poor third.

Whoever insures you, you will need to prepare a complete inventory of your possessions, not only to determine how much insurance you need, but also to substantiate subsequent claims. It's wise to supplement a written inventory with color photographs or even videotape records, separately held in a safe-deposit box.

If you lease your inn property, the building should be insured by its owner. Be sure it is. And whether the building belongs to you or someone else, be sure your insurance protection begins right away. You'll need to be covered during remodeling, but you probably won't need all the coverages of an operating inn.

If you have any doubt about the best way to spend your insurance dollar, look at liability coverage first. Most inns can survive even a major property loss, but could lose everything over a bodily injury or death claim. Ask your agent about umbrella policies, which extend the limits of coverage for underlying property and liability policies. Umbrellas are good bargains in light of the extra protection they give for comparatively little additional expense.

QUESTIONS INNKEEPERS ASK ABOUT INSURANCE

"I know what is says, but what does it mean?"

Let's start with a few terms and their definitions, which may clarify the insurance language used in policies.

- *Actual cash value or replacement cost value.* Property value is determined on the basis of one of these two concepts. Actual cash value (ACV) takes depreciation into consideration; replacement cost value coverage (RCV) replaces items without depreciating their value. Since clothing, for example, depreciates 90 percent in the first year, the choice of ACV or RCV coverage can make quite a difference in the limit you insure for and the limit the insurance company will pay in case of a claim.

- *Named peril or all risk.* A named-peril policy will specifically name all the perils it will cover: fire, windstorm, smoke, and so on. An all-risk policy will cover all perils *except* the ones named. This means that if the insurance company didn't think to exclude the peril, it will be covered. For example, if an elephant in a peanut frenzy runs through your house and soils the rug, an all-risk policy would cover it; a named-peril policy wouldn't. All-risk policies normally exclude earthquake, flood, vermin, war, and wear and tear.

- *Coinsurance clause or agreed amount/stipulated amount.* An insurance policy is a legal contract between two parties. Each has a role and, legally, they are considered coinsurers. The insurance company agrees to pay for covered losses, less a deductible. The insured agrees in turn to pay the premium, disclose necessary information to the insurance company, and insure to the full value of the property within the coinsurance clause.

Let's say your building has a value of $100,000 and an 80 percent coinsurance clause. If you insure the building for less than $80,000, the amount you will receive in case of a loss will be the ratio of the amount of insurance carried to the amount required. For example:

amount carried ($50,000)
amount required ($80,000)

So if the insurance company finds that the building is insured for $50,000, for example, they will only pay you five-eighths of the value of the claim, regardless of its total size. In no case will you receive more than the value of the insurance you bought, in this case, $50,000.

An agreed amount or stipulated amount endorsement, on the other hand, states that the insurance company agrees that the value of the insurance on the building and the value of the building are the same. Even if the building turns out at the time of a loss to have been underinsured, there will be no proportional reduction of the award because of it.

It's important to come up with realistic replacement costs and get an agreed amount endorsement, particularly when the structures involved are historic and intricate, such as many inns. Normally there are no additional charges for such endorsements.

How do you figure out what the replacement amount should be? You are probably one of the best judges of the value of the gingerbread on your front veranda, the redwood beams in the living room, and the marble floors in the bath—especially if you were involved in restoring them in the first place.

- *Products coverage.* Products liability is designed to protect you from claims occurring as a result of injuries to your guests other than those caused by property. For example, products coverage would protect you from a suit by a guest who became ill upon finding half a worm in a half-eaten apple.

• *Personal injury.* This term is a perfect example of the insurance industry's unique interpretation of the language. Personal injury does *not* cover injuries like broken feet, but *does* cover hurt feelings. The perils covered include libel, slander, invasion of privacy, unlawful entry, and so on. This is extremely important coverage for anyone dealing with the general public, especially in a business where it's possible to walk in accidentally on someone taking a bath.

"As an innkeeper, should I have commerical coverage or homeowner's?"

In some areas of the country, special policies have been developed for bed-and-breakfast inns, to meet the special needs of businesses that are also homes. If this special type of policy is not available in your area, probably the smartest way to go is with commercial coverage for your building, contents of the public areas, and liability. Combine this with a tenant's policy to protect your own personal property in your private area of the inn, as well as family bicycles and so on.

It is critical to have commercial liability coverage. Some agents have reportedly told innkeepers that they don't need commercial liability protection, believing this is risky. At the very least, get it in writing.

"Do I need high liability limits?"

Innkeepers should probably carry a $5,000,000 minimum excess liability policy. Property losses can usually be absorbed as business expenses, but a large liability claim can put you out of business and take away your home and car. Put your premium dollars where they are most cost effective. Consider taking a higher deductible on property and using the premium savings to increase your liability limit.

The courts are granting high awards and, with the public on your premises, your exposure to lawsuits is high. The public is increasingly suit-conscious, too: It used to be that if Johnny fell down on the neighbor's sidewalk, you took him to the doctor. Today, more and more people are taking him to the lawyer instead.

It's sometimes hard for innkeepers to believe that among their guests, almost all of whom are very nice people, might be any of the growing number of individuals who go around looking for a reason to sue someone. But all you need is one such guest, and you could be in big trouble.

"What about punitive damages? Am I covered?"

Many states do not permit insurers to cover the costs of punitive damages, the award given the plaintiff to punish the defendant for gross negligence. In well-known cases, auto manufacturers have had to pay large damage awards for designing and selling unsafe or defective vehicles. Obviously the punishment — and the deterrent — is not effective if the insurer, rather than the offender, pays it.

Punitive damages can be awarded if the court decides there has been gross negligence in something like knowing your wiring is substandard or defective, and nevertheless inviting the public onto your premises without regard for their safety. You can't insure for this peril, but you need to be aware of it.

"What do you mean, my garage isn't covered?"

Under a commercial policy, your fences, signs, windows, and appurtenant structures (also known as garages and such) are usually not covered unless there is an endorsement stating that they *are* covered. Commercial property coverages differ from a homeowner's policy, where appurtenant structures and windows are normally covered. Such coverage may be added to commercial policies, at an additional charge.

"How do I figure out how much contents coverage I need?"

Most people underestimate the value of their furniture and other household contents. The best way to determine the value is to list your property room by room. Such a complete record of your belongings is a pain to prepare, but it's invaluable.

Here's an experiment that may help you judge whether your contents coverage is adequate. Sit at the kitchen table and make a list of the contents in some other room of the house. Then put a value on each item; replacement value is best for this. Now go into the room you inventoried mentally, and check your list. Most people find their original estimate low — as low as 50 percent.

If the contents of your inn are insured for only half their value, you've got a major problem on your hands in case of a loss. Have you priced sheets, mattresses, dishes, glasses, and so on lately?

An itemized list of all your contents will not only establish the proper level of coverage, it will also make the claim process a lot easier for you and your insurer. Trying to remember everything in a room and establish values for it is difficult enough on a tranquil afternoon. Imagine what it's like after a major fire.

"So if my contents limit matches my inventory, I'm okay, right?"

Wrong. Furs, jewelry, coin collections, silver, china, crystal, paintings, and things like camera equipment, musical instruments, or other tools that you use professionally are subject to specified limits in normal policies. Ask your agent to list such limitations. If you find that under the limit your mink will be covered, but not your chinchilla or your sable, ask about "inland marine" coverage for them. (Try not to wonder about why coverage for furs and such would be named "inland marine"; it's really not worth puzzling out.)

In addition, things made of glass, including beveled mirrors and chandeliers, are not covered for breakage unless specified in an endorsement.

Endorsements to protect them are usually inexpensive; they're another item you should probably ask about.

"Is there insurance that would protect our guests from neighborhood vandalism?"

No, there is not. Even if you have innkeeper's legal liability coverage, damage or loss to your guests' property will be covered only when you are legally responsible for the damage or loss. The key phrase here is "legally responsible," which means that the law would find you responsible.

This does not include situations where the neighbor kids do damage, where contents are stolen from a guest car parked in your lot or in front of the inn, or where a guest is mugged two doors down the street. Although you will feel terrible about any of these incidents, the law would not hold you responsible, and therefore the insurance company won't pay for such losses. Tea and sympathy are probably about the best you can do.

(There are nevertheless plenty of situations where innkeeper's legal liability coverage is very beneficial. For example, if your children broke an auto antenna, the damage would be covered. If faulty wiring caused a fire in one of your rooms, any loss of guest property would be covered.)

The bright side of this question, from the guest perspective, is that most guests would find that such situations are covered under their own homeowner or automobile policies.

"If we serve complimentary sherry at our inn, do we need special liability coverage?"

The rule of thumb here is, it's better to give than to receive. Anyone who *sells* liquor, including wine, needs liquor law liability coverage. The law will hold you responsible for any bodily injury or property damage caused by an intoxicated person you served or helped to become intoxicated. It is your legal duty to stop serving liquor when a customer has had enough. But how much is too much? Your grandmother may consider one glass of blueberry wine before 8:00 P.M. too much; someone else may find three drinks too few to begin unwinding after a hard day of sightseeing. The only way to protect yourself truly is with liquor law liability coverage and careful control over how much you allow your guests to consume.

If you don't have a bar and don't sell liquor, you don't face these problems. You may not be fully in the clear, however, even if you only serve at a Christmas party, for example, or during the 6:00 P.M. sherry gathering in the library. The question of the liability of private individuals for the drunken behavior of guests to whom they have served liquor is still open.

Host liquor law liability coverage can be purchased separately for minimal cost, or purchased under the extended or broadening liability endorsement. Standard liquor law liability rates are based on annual liquor sales figures, and are auditable.

"Is there any way to reduce the cost of my worker's compensation coverage?"

Worker's compensation premium rates are set by each state, and they vary by job classification. There is usually no variation in the rate among insurance companies. There are some ways to reduce your costs, however.

- *Minimum premium:* Different insurance companies and state programs have minimum premium charges per classification. The minimum premium is stated in each policy. If your earned premium — the estimated payroll times the rate per $100 of insurance — is less than the stated minimum charge, you are paying too much. You should either have your agent change insurance companies or investigate the state program, which usually has lower minimum premiums.
- *Correct classification:* The correct classification for innkeepers, even for bed and breakfast, is "hotel." However, if you have employees who do nothing except clerical work, they can be classified clerical. This will substantially reduce your premium, since the clerical classification costs about one-fifth as much as the hotel classification. Do not cheat; your clerical person may not carry bags or help with breakfast even occasionally. The state does audit worker's compensation.
- *Participation/dividend plan:* It's often possible to become part of a larger group that will be paid dividends based on its claims history. A dividend means that some percentage — 15 percent is common — will be returned to you. There are also sliding-scale dividend programs for individuals, offered by different insurance companies.
- *Experience modification:* An experience modification is assigned by the state to individuals who pay larger premiums, for example, $5,000 or more a year for three consecutive years. This experience modification is assigned to each insured based on its individual past loss experience compared with the state average. This modification can increase or decrease the premium. The modification is assigned by the state, not by insurance companies. However, states often fail to start this procedure, so if you think you could qualify for a premium reduction, request a modification.
- *Annual, semiannual, quarterly, or monthly audits or payments:* If your payroll varies with the time of year, or if you are not sure what this year's payroll will be because you are adding rooms, for example, you can state that you would like to have semiannual or quarterly audits. Audits give you a chance to see what your payroll figures actually are and make any revisions in your original estimate. Not only can audits be done quarterly, but payments can be made quarterly also, with or without audits. Different payment plans and/or audits can help you budget better and pay your way as you go, rather than making large advance payments. This will not change the actual premium you'll have to pay, but it can help you stay in charge of your money longer.

"What about 'loss of rents' or business interruption insurance?"

As a business owner, you need it. If you experience a loss that is covered by your insurance policy, business interruption insurance will reimburse you for lost revenues during repair or rebuilding. For example, if an oak tree falls through the roof of the inn, you'll need to close for repairs. Many of your expenses will continue. Business interruption insurance will enable you to meet your obligations.

"What if the tree falls through our quarters? Can we get insurance to pay for our expenses to live elsewhere during repair?"

Yes, you can, and it's automatic coverage under a homeowner's or tenant's policy, but it's not usually needed and is not normally included in commercial packages. Ask about special protection.

"How high a deductible should I take?"

Insurance should be considered protection against a catastrophe, not just an everyday problem. A $1,000 deductible seems to be the best buy, dollar for dollar, on property coverages. Set aside a self-insurance fund to cover those under-$1,000 items, and invest the premium you save!

GENERAL INSURANCE TIPS

ASK QUESTIONS If you feel uncertain about any of the issues raised here, make an appointment with your agent and ask questions. Insurance is supposed to give you security; think how secure you'll feel when you're sure you're covered.

REPORT ALL LOSSES Insurance is confusing and there are unquestionably occasions when what *is* covered and what *isn't* is unclear. Wind-driven rain damage, for example, is not normally covered. Rain damage because shingles blew off a roof during a storm and then rain caused further damage is covered under an all-risk policy.

Since these issues aren't clear-cut, it's a good plan always to call your agent and report any loss. Agents are there to serve you; any question you ask helps you make better decisions about limits, perils, and coverages.

KEEP RECORDS Pieces of paper with numbers on them are very impressive to insurance claims people. Remember that they run into a lot of crooks, so they're probably as suspicious of you as you are of them. (Think about it: how would you feel if the first time your insureds mention they own the Hope Diamond is when they submit a claim for umpty-zillion dollars after their house burns to the ground?) So keeping good records of contents, appraisals, and receipts makes things easier for everyone concerned.

RISK MANAGEMENT Insurance is just one aspect of a complete program to protect you, your guests, and your inn property. Another element is risk management. Many insurance companies provide risk management information and consulting, even for small businesses. Something as simple as putting nonslip pads under the oriental runners can avoid a multimillion dollar lawsuit, and providing staff with instructions on the proper way to lift can avoid worker's compensation claims. Ask your insurance agent about information and assistance in this area.

WHERE HAS ALL THE MONEY GONE? CASH FLOW MANAGEMENT

Almost every inn has high seasons, months when income is high, and slower periods when income is low. Many expenses, however, remain more or less constant. Cash flow management is the art of staying solvent year-round. Planning is key. Here are some solvency strategies that work for existing inns.

- Establish a reserve account for large annual payments, such as property tax and liability insurance.
- Establish a credit line with your bank.
- Take out credit cards and use as necessary.
- Prioritize the order of bill paying. Take into consideration the cost of interest charged for late payment versus the cost of borrowing to pay now.
- Take advantage of cash discounts for immediate payment in fat times to establish credibility for negotiating late or partial payment in lean times.
- Plan major purchases for the high season.
- Put money away regularly for such big-ticket items as washing machines that will eventually have to be replaced.
- Plan special events or a gift certificate push to bring money in for slow periods.
- Plan staffing with seasonal variations in mind; be realistic in the expectations you give your staff about hours.
- Consider taking a part-time job.
- Sell products at the inn—your homemade jam, note cards, or potpourri—or have a holiday bazaar.
- Barter for services such as printing, carpet cleaning, or legal advice.
- Collect deposits early for the fall foliage season or summer at the shore.
- Close off-season or midweek to cut expenses.

---

*L*ake to Lake Bed and Breakfast, Michigan: Eight years ago, a small group *of innkeepers from the southern Lower Peninsula banded together for promotional purposes. Since then Lake to Lake has grown to become a professionally staffed innkeeper association. Their scope today covers not only promotion, but also education, legislation, and insurance and other member services, including design input and participation in industry studies in cooperation with Michigan State University.*

They worked on the enactment of state legislation to define "bed-and-breakfast." Their Lake to Lake members' directory has been published annually since 1985 and is now distributed by the State Travel Bureau at highway Welcome Centers and via a toll-free number. The association has assembled a travel writers' database; the press release announcing their 1989 directory resulted in 1,000 requests within the first month, from every corner of the United States.

THE INN GROUP: INNKEEPER ASSOCIATIONS

The existing inns in your area can be a great resource. In many places, innkeepers have banded together on a variety of fronts for their mutual benefit:

- Group marketing, including advertising, brochure, media campaign, and special events.
- A single referral or reservation number for area inns.
- Volume buying at a discount.
- Group membership in high-cost visitor/convention centers.
- Political clout.
- Group health insurance.
- Sounding board, professional support system, communications network.
- Fun.

If you join an association that is already doing many of these things, expect to pay a special fee, in addition to monthly dues, to buy in. The group will already have done a lot of work and spent a lot of money to get the program to its present stage; you'll benefit from that, and should be willing to pay for it.

Inns are competitors, and problems do occur in innkeeper associations. Like marriage, these associations are no cinch. On the other hand, like marriage they have benefits you can't easily get elsewhere: common concerns, someone to share expenses, and complementary interests and talents.

When problems surface, apply some marriage strategies. Consider these:

- One of the biggest hurdles in marriages is making peace with the realization that, despite your expectations, your partner isn't responsible for your happiness or success. By the same token, no inn association can "fix" your occupancy rate or cash flow problems. But this doesn't mean that either the marriage or the association is a worthless relationship.

Nine Inns on Whidbey Island, Washington, formed a group in December 1982 that counts among its accomplishments:

- *Joining the Seattle-King County Convention and Visitors' Bureau, which then included them in an umbrella tour package as well as stocking and distributing their brochures.*
- *Convincing the Yellow Pages office to list bed-and-breakfast. Innkeeper Sharon Drew of Home by the Sea says, "It took us fifteen minutes to explain to the business office what it is."*
- *Being included for the first time on the Cascade Loop, a travel route through the Cascade Mountains and down the coast.*

    "Our main objective," says Sharon, "is making Whidbey Island known as a new destination, especially from Seattle, which is an hour away."

- When people in your group seem unreasonable, try really seeing them as the whole individuals they are, and not just as sources of support or frustration for your purposes. They too have goals and disappointments and babies that keep them up all night.
- If you feel you're doing more than your share, in terms of time or money, either accept it or change it, but don't be a martyr. Being unhappy is dull, and, in addition, it will cause you to create sideshow problems that will hamper the effectiveness of the group.
- Make it a policy never to talk about anyone. If people are behaving in ways you don't like, handle it with *them*. What's more destructive than the unbridled tongue?
- As to who's getting the glory, it's a waste of time to be jealous of anyone else's success. You do the best you can.
- Spend fun time together. Smiles do good things for the face. And as Sophia Loren reputedly said, "By the time you're forty, you'll have the face you deserve."

TAKING CARE OF YOURSELF

Burnout is the number-one reason innkeepers quit. It is the result of months and years of long hours and devotion that fail to produce the bookings, income, and satisfaction you expect. Every innkeeper experiences burnout, sooner or later, and to a greater or lesser degree. Innkeepers seem to be continuously reevaluating the way they live, trying to find a way to balance fatigue against their own and others' expectations.

But there are ways to recognize the danger signals and minimize the burnout. The first step is believing it can happen to you. Discuss with your partner the way you react to fatigue, and talk about how you would like to be "handled" in those situations. Maybe you want permission and encouragement to take time off. Maybe you prefer a kick out the door. Make specific plans about how you can care for each other.

Unfortunately, instead of helping detect and defuse each other's burnout, partners often feed it. One demands an impossible performance of the other, or feels guilty when a partner outperforms him or her. Married couples frequently run into problems when one partner works outside the inn. The innkeeping partner often wants more help in the inn while the outside partner feels that he or she is doing plenty by working to cover the income deficit. Or the outside partner won't know the inn procedures well enough to help out very satisfactorily, but may feel guilty about relaxing when the innkeeping partner is still taking reservations at 10:00 P.M. Don't buy into these guilt trips. It's important for each partner to encourage and celebrate the other partner's taking care of him- or herself.

SPACE

No matter how well you plan your living quarters, space will probably still be a factor in burnout, so hold out for the best living situation you can manage. Consider the matters below in your plans.

- Do you want a bedroom in private quarters, or can it be part of the guest traffic area? Some innkeepers live out of suitcases and closets, moving from guest room to guest room depending on what is rented. Usually this doesn't last long, and innkeepers who start out with a bedroom accessible to guest areas often move to a more private area as soon as they can.
- Do you want a separate sitting area/living room, or don't you mind being asked what's for breakfast when you're nine pages from the end of a Robert Ludlum novel?
- How do you feel about sharing your kitchen, including your peanut butter and onion sandwiches at midnight?
- How will you accommodate other family members who live at the inn or come home for vacations?
- Where will friends stay? Will they always need to rent a room? Is there some space in your quarters that can be planned to accommodate a futon or sofabed?
- Do you prefer to do paperwork uninterrupted, or will you be comfortable having your office/desk, and possibly your inn records, in a guest area?

Discuss these questions together before making space decisions. Respect both partners' needs for space; frequently one will need more distance or privacy, or need it in a different way. Acknowledge and appreciate these differences.

The less you accommodate your space needs initially, the bigger issue space will become. Even if you can't provide yourselves with the quarters you want and need at the outset, at least develop a plan for them and a timetable, so you will see a light at the end of the tunnel.

WORK SCHEDULES

Work patterns and responsibilities should be divided so partners can truly spell each other. If one partner does breakfast and rooms and greets guests, he or she will get little time off, unless partners alternate being fully in charge from day to day. Another approach is to share the tasks, so one handles breakfast, breaks for the afternoon while the other does rooms, then comes back "on duty" at five to greet guests.

No matter how you divide up the jobs, there is always more to do, so get a work schedule down on paper, *including breaks*. The work will get done; the breaks are what tend to be forgotten.

INN STYLE AND BURNOUT

Burnout prevention strategies are often reflected in inn policies and procedures. Many innkeepers have planned check-in and check-out times to meet their needs to take a breather, to leave the afternoon free for a concert or the evening for a dinner date instead of waiting around for a single late arrival.

The services you provide also affect your personal time during the day. Offering coffee and tea all day restricts your freedom, but there are ways to minimize the attention required of you. One inn puts a large crockery pot in their shaded, beachside courtyard for guests. At another inn, coffee is available all day in the kitchen. Still another sets out coffee, tea, and instant hot beverages on rainy days only.

Extra services, such as drinks, food, and making dinner reservations, take extra time. But they are wonderful touches and guests appreciate them. Try to evaluate whether the lack of any particular service will be a disappointment to guests, or whether providing it will really help to bring them back again. Balance the benefits against the personal cost to you.

Be creative about the way you provide services. Develop materials for guests that will augment your presence. Instead of describing to every individual guest the process of renovating the inn, provide a scrapbook of before and after photographs. Make a folder of information about what there is to do in your area. Fill a basket with collected restaurant menus, and let guests fill a blank book with their own "reviews." Maintain a scrapbook of articles about the inn and the innkeepers. All these are ways to meet guest needs for information without the personal involvement of the innkeeper.

Plan a reasonable way for guests to reach you. You shouldn't have to leap up every time someone appears in the parlor, and guests shouldn't have to wander around calling your name. A bell on the door to your quarters, or office space in an accessible but tranquil corner, communicates that you're available, while preserving your privacy and that of your guests.

PLAN FOR PRODUCTIVITY

Since burnout occurs when you're busy but don't feel productive, make long- and short-range plans that will help you minimize worry and see results. For example, if you want to increase occupancy this year by 5 percent overall, figure out what that means in terms of a daily or weekly increase in business. How many more rooms must you rent this week to accomplish your goal? Or say you want to replace all the drapes in the guest rooms this year. Plan a monthly schedule for doing it room by room, or ordering fabric one month, purchasing hardware the next, and so on. Seeing the day's work in relation to a grander scheme makes the little jobs seem more meaningful and less routine.

STRESS PREVENTION

Plan ahead to design your innkeeping lifestyle for stress prevention. Consider these:

• When will you get regular exercise? At least three days a week of fifteen to thirty minutes of heart-pumping, heavy-breathing exercise will give you stamina, and you'll need it.
• How will you arrange time off for each working partner? Begin that pattern early, so it will feel like a right—which it is!
• How can you arrange unhurried, balanced meals? Plan for good nutrition and meals that are an event: a late breakfast in the kitchen, a sandwich

in the park, a family supper around the fire when the inn is empty. This sounds easy now, but just wait!

- Don't finish off the breakfast coffee, the cocktail sherry, and the cheese and crackers without thinking. Moderation is healthy.
- Find an escape location outside the inn, perhaps a membership club, a gym, or the beach. You need a place where you can rejuvenate.
- Analyze your ways of getting focused and centered; develop and make room for them. If attending church, writing, or getting a massage are important for you, don't let innkeeping push them out of your life.
- If you're an innkeeping couple, you will need to work at maintaining and enjoying closeness. Plan ways to nurture your relationship. Some innkeepers regularly "kidnap" one another for a special day or night every month. Others play guest in various rooms of the inn on low-occupancy nights.

---

*B*eating burnout: *Bob and Marily Kavanaugh opened the Bed and Breakfast Inn in San Francisco in 1967. They've been so successful that dealing with success has been a challenge. "It was four years before we felt we could sneak off for even a day or two," Marily recalls. "After six years of steady, growing pressure, feeling responsible for every detail, our bodies, our families, and our relationship with each other were becoming undernourished.*

"So much of the time there are touching things — weddings, reunions, wonderful meetings of all kinds — and you begin to want to make that happen always. I've finally accepted that I can do my best to provide for a good experience, but essentially I can't make it happen. A good time is, in the end, the guest's responsibility."

"Part of the problem," Bob adds, "is that we're part of a generation that needs approval. We tried too hard to make innkeeping look easy to the guests. If we experienced a double-booking situation, we'd move out of our own apartment, even when we knew it wasn't our mistake."

How to solve the problem? The Kavanaughs figured out that to get truly away and to spend "quality time" with guests they had to share innkeeping duties with topnotch assistants.

Appendices

WORKSHEET: FINDING THE RIGHT LOCATION FOR YOUR INN

Property Address: _____

_____

A. General Area
_____ Proximity to large metropolitan area (within three hours)
_____ Convenient public transportation to area, airport, train, bus
_____ Close to major highways or interstates
_____ Tourist attractions, good restaurants, entertainment, shopping
_____ Good climate and environment, mountains, beach, desert
_____ Businesses, manufacturers, government offices, retailers (commercial businesses)
_____ Meets your family's environmental needs (weather, ocean, desert, mountains)
_____ Meets your family's educational and employment needs
_____ Cost of utilities, possibility for solar

B. Neighborhood
_____ Close to, but not too close to, restaurants, retailers, tourist attractions
_____ Low crime rate and safe environment
_____ Convenient to freeways
_____ Within service area for fire, police, medical, utilities
_____ Resale value

C. Specific Structure: House, Barn, Inn
_____ Zoning, master plan _____
_____ Structurally sound foundation _____
_____ Curb appeal, charm, character, historical significance _____
_____ Room for expansion _____
_____ Adjoining property, dogs barking, types of neighbors _____
_____ Outdoor area, patio, garden, spa, croquet, barbecue _____
_____ Innkeepers' quarters, privacy, storage _____
_____ Garage, parking for guests' and innkeepers' cars _____
_____ Adequate heating, air conditioning (if needed) _____
_____ Plumbing, septic tank or sewer, water heater, potable water _____
_____ Electricity, age, type, 220 available _____
_____ Landscaping, big trees, sound insulation for traffic _____
_____ Laundry facilities or in area _____
_____ Storage facilities for linens, rollaway, cleaning equipment _____

D. Rooms (Consider size, ventilation, sun and wind exposure, noise from traffic and neighbors, entry and exit, fireplace)
Living room or parlor _____
Dining room _____
Kitchen, including equipment _____
Other common areas _____
Guest rooms and bathrooms or space/closets to create bathrooms (list each)

PERSONAL FINANCIAL STATEMENT: AN INVENTORY

ASSETS

Liquid Assets (Cash is readily obtainable from these.)

Cash on hand $_____

Checking account(s) (banks and amounts) _____

Savings account(s) (passbook, money market, etc., banks and amounts)

Stocks (companies and cash values) _____

Bonds (companies and cash values) _____

Insurance (whole life—companies and cash values) _____

Other (autos, jewelry, silver, gold, coins) _____

TOTAL LIQUID ASSETS $_____

Nonliquid Assets (These take time to tap, due to rollover dates, the need to sell, etc. Can be used as collateral.)

Property/real estate (market value)

Location $_____

Location _____

Time certificates of deposit

Location _____

Pension fund

Name _____

Other _____

TOTAL NONLIQUID ASSETS $_____

Other Assets (Assets that are not necessarily liquid or collaterable, but show wealth.)

Personal property (china, silver, furs, art, clothing) $_____

Furnishings _____

Livestock, pedigreed animals _____

Subchapter S or privately held stock _____

TOTAL OTHER ASSETS $_____

TOTAL ASSETS $_____

LIABILITIES

Property mortgages (current balances, banks and expiration dates) _____

Loans

Auto _____

Other _____

Credit accounts (banks and department store names and current balances) _____

Other _____

TOTAL LIABILITIES $_____

NET WORTH Total assets less total liabilities $_____

ANNUAL INCOME

Employment (salary) $_____

Business operations (your own business) _____

Spousal/child support _____

Interest _____

Rentals _____

Dividends _____

Other _____

TOTAL ANNUAL INCOME $_____

ANNUAL EXPENSES

Property taxes/assessments $_____

Income and other taxes _____

Mortgage payments and interest _____

Other contract payments _____

Insurance _____

Living expense _____

Spousal/child support _____

Auto payments _____

Children's educational _____

Rent _____

Other _____

TOTAL ANNUAL EXPENSES $_____

CREDIT AVAILABILITY
(Itemize and state limits for each)

Bank credit line $_____

Bank credit cards _____

Department store credit cards _____

WORKSHEET:
PROPERTY EVALUATION

Address: _____

_____ All amounts and percentages are estimates.

Area occupancy rate ___ %

Area room rate: shared bath $ ___

Area room rate: private bath $ ___

Number of guest rooms: original house ___

proposed addition ___

Number of guest bathrooms: original house ___

proposed addition ___

A. Financial Needs: Purchase/Renovation Phase

Purchase: Total price _____

Mortgage(s) _____

_____

Down payment _____

Closing costs, loan fees, etc.

Moving costs

Working capital

Renovation and furnishings

Additional guest rooms:
construction

Additional bathrooms:
construction

Additional guest rooms:
furnishings

Other _____ _____

TOTAL $ _____

GUIDE

$35,000–$75,000 per guest room

Usual is 20–25% of price

_____ Get realtor or banker estimate

_____

_____ Expenses from purchase period
(___-month renovation)

_____ Estimate $20,000 (good condition) to
$40,000 per guest room in original house

_____ Estimate new construction at $60–$125 sq. ft.
(room 200–250 sq. ft.)

_____ Estimate $5,000–$10,000 each

_____ Estimate $5,000 per room

_____

B. Income

_____ rooms × 365 days ×
average room rate $ _____ = income @ 100% occupancy $ _____

1st year projection:

50% of area rate _____ % = _____ % × 100% occupancy = $ _____

2nd year projection:

1st year _____ % + 10% = _____ % × 100% occupancy = $ _____

3rd year projection:

2nd year _____ % + 10% = _____ % × 100% occupancy = $ _____

C. Expenses

innkeeping Newsletter Survey:

Five-room inn: $15,000

Seven-room inn: $13,500

Ten-room inn: $11,000

Use detailed expense percentages shown in E and adjust accordingly _____

D. Cash Flow Projection

	1st Year	2nd Year	3rd Year
Income (B)	$ _____	$ _____	$ _____
Expenses (C)	_____	_____	_____
+ or − Cash flow	_____	_____	_____

To break even:

$$\frac{\text{Expenses}}{\text{Income @ 100\%}} = \$ \underline{\hspace{3cm}} = \underline{\hspace{1cm}} \% \text{ occupancy needed}$$

E. Detailed Expenses

Standard Percentages of Expenses	Expenses Category	Annual Expenses Using Standard Percentages	Adjustments For Reality	Comments
9	Food	_____	_____	
4	Room and house-keeping supplies	_____	_____	
7.5	Hourly/part-time employees and payroll taxes	_____	_____	
6	Utilities	_____	_____	
1.5	Towels and linens	_____	_____	
8	Marketing, advertising, promotion	_____	_____	
2.5	Travel commissions and bank charges	_____	_____	
2	Office supplies and postage	_____	_____	
2	Telephone	_____	_____	
2	Travel and entertainment	_____	_____	
1	Dues and subscriptions	_____	_____	
2	Auto expenses	_____	_____	
4	Maintenance, repairs, and fixtures	_____	_____	
4	Outside services	_____	_____	
5	Insurance	_____	_____	
1	Legal and accounting fees	_____	_____	
3.5	Business and property taxes and fees	_____	_____	
30	Interest and/or lease expense	_____	_____	
5	Salaried or permanent employees	_____	_____	
100%	Total	$ _____	$ _____	

CASH FLOW PROJECTION
MONTH BY MONTH

	Jan.	Feb.	Mar.	Apr.	May	June	July	Aug.	Sep.	Oct.	Nov.	Dec.
Projected Occupancy %												
Income												
Room rental revenues												
Product sales												
Total Income												
Expenses												
Food												
Room and housekeeping supplies												
Hourly/part-time employees and payroll taxes												
Utilities												
Towels and linens												
Marketing, advertising, promotion												
Travel commissions and bank charges												
Office supplies and postage												
Telephone												
Travel and entertainment												
Dues and subscriptions												
Auto expenses												
Maintenance, repairs, and fixtures												
Outside services												
Insurance												
Legal and accounting fees												
Business and property taxes and fees												
Interest and/or lease expenses												
Salaried or permanent employees												
Total expenses												
Cash flow												

PROPOSAL AND CONTRACT

Date _____ , 19 _____

TO _____

_____

Dear Client:

_____ propose to furnish all materials and perform all labor necessary to complete the following:

_____

_____

_____

_____

_____

_____

All of the above work to be completed in a substantial and workmanlike manner according to standard practices for the sum of _____

Dollars ($_____)

Progress payments to be made _____

_____ as the work progresses to the value of _____ percent (_____%) of all work completed. The entire amount of contract to be paid within _____ days after completion.

Any alteration or deviation from the above specifications involving extra cost of material or labor will only be executed upon written orders for same, and will become an extra charge over the sum mentioned in this contract. All agreements must be made in writing.

Name and Registration Number of any salesperson who solicited or negotiated this contract:

Respectfully submitted,

By _____

Address

Telephone

Name _____ No. _____

Contractors are required by law to be licensed and regulated by the Contractor's State License Board. Any questions concerning a contractor may be referred to the registrar of the board whose address is:

Contractor's State License No. _____

You, the buyer, may cancel this transaction at any time prior to midnight of the third business day after the date of this transaction.

Contractor's State License Board,
1020 N Street,
Sacramento, California 95814

ACCEPTANCE

You are hereby authorized to furnish all materials and labor required to complete the work mentioned in the above proposal, for which _____ agree to pay the amount mentioned in said proposal, and according to the terms thereof.

ACCEPTED _____ Date _____ , 19 _____

Appendix 6

ROOM PLANNING WORKSHEET

Room name (or location): _____

Type of room: _____

Atmosphere desired: _____

Natural light: _____

Colors: _____

ITEMS TO BE PURCHASED
OR INSTALLED   **Budgeted**   **Spent**   **Ordered**   **Installed**

Item	Budgeted	Spent	Ordered	Installed
Bed				
Headboard				
Mattress/springs				
Dining Table				
Light				
Chairs				
1				
2				
3				
Nightstands				
Table for lamps				
Bed lights				
Dresser				
Firewood container				
Armoire				
Desk/dressing table				
Mirrors				
Makeup				
Dressing				
Heating/air conditioning				
Wall treatment				
Window treatment				
Floor treatment				
Bed covering				
Fireplace tools				
Linens				
Accessories				

In the format above, make a master list of items needed in more than one room, such as beds, linens, carpeting, draperies, and accessories, which you may be able to purchase in quantity.

RESOURCES

INNS

The Guide to Guidebooks. An annotated bibliography of the books published as guides for inn travelers; where you'd like your inn listed. Available through *innkeeping* newsletter.

innkeeping, The Innkeeper's Newsletter. Published monthly since 1982; $56/year. PAII, P.O. Box 90710, Santa Barbara, CA 93190. Ask for the index to back issues. Don't open an inn without it!

Inn Review Catalog Directory. Inn Review, P.O. Box 1789, Kankakee, IL 60901. "The complete Yellow Pages for bed & breakfasts, country inns."

Oates, William A. *Innquest.* Published ten times a year since November 1984; $30/year. P.O. Box 1162, Brattleboro, VT 05301. Written for people interested in buying existing inns.

Professional Association of Innkeepers International. Trade association for country inn/bed-and-breakfast industry. Also, the best resource for aspiring innkeepers. Send for Innkeepers Library Catalog. P.O. Box 90710, Santa Barbara, CA 93190.

So You Think You Want To Be an Innkeeper? The semiannual workshops of the Santa Barbara Innkeepers Guild. For information on dates, contact Pat Hardy at 805-965-0707, or c/o PAII, P.O. Box 90710, Santa Barbara, CA 93190.

HOMESTAY HOW-TO'S

Notarius, Barbara, and Brewer, Gail. *Open Your Own Bed & Breakfast.* New York: John Wiley & Sons, 1987.

Stankus, Jan. *How to Open and Operate a Bed & Breakfast Home.* Chester, Ct: Globe Pequot Press, 1989.

BUSINESS

Banks, Jr., David H. *Business Planning Guide.* Dover, NH: Upstart Publishing, 1989. A handbook to help you write a business plan and financing proposal.

McKeever, Mike P. *Start-Up Money: How to Finance Your New Small Business.* Berkeley: Nolo Press, 1984. A great guide to writing a business plan.

Phillips, Michael, and Rasberry, Salli. *Honest Business.* New York: Random House, 1981. A good general introduction to doing any kind of business of your own.

Small Business Administration. Ask for the current catalog and send for the titles that look relevant, such as "Planning and Goal Setting for Small Business," "Learning about Your Market," "Marketing for Small Business," "Advertising — Retail Store," "Selecting the Legal Structure for your Firm," "Checklist for Going into Business," and "The ABC's of Borrowing."

RENOVATION AND DECORATION

National Trust for Historic Preservation. *A Guide to Tax-Advantaged Rehabilitation*. National Trust, 1785 Massachusetts Avenue NW, Washington, D.C. 20036.

The Old House Journal. Magazine and catalog published by Old House Journal Corporation, 69A Seventh Avenue, Brooklyn, NY 11217.

Victorian Warehouse Catalog. 190 Grace Street, Auburn, CA 95603.

Vintage Woodworks Catalog. 513 South Adams, Fredericksburg, TX 28624.

Wagner, Carlton. *Color Power* and *The Color Response Report*. Color Communication, 4242 West Fillmore Street, Chicago, IL 60624. Understanding color and putting it to work for you.

MARKETING AND PROMOTION

innkeeping Newsletter. *The Innkeepers Marketing Handbook*. PAII, P.O. Box 90710, Santa Barbara, CA 93190.

innkeeping Newsletter. *The Guide to Guidebooks*. PAII, P.O. Box 90710, Santa Barbara, CA 93190.

Beals, Melba. *Expose Yourself: Using the Power of Public Relations to Promote Your Business and Yourself*. San Francisco: Chronicle Books.

Lant, Jeffrey. *The Unabashed Self-Promoter's Guide*. J. Lant Associates, 50 Follen Street, Suite 507, Cambridge, MA 02138.

Phillips, Michael, and Rasberry, Salli. *Marketing Without Advertising*. Berkeley: Nolo Press, 1987.

FOOD AND RECIPES

Bristow, Linda Kay. *Bread & Breakfast*. San Francisco: 101 Productions/ Ortho Information Services, 1988.

Dragonwagon, Crescent. *The Dairy Hollow House Cookbook*. New York: MacMillan, 1986. In addition to recipes, this book conveys the spirit of innkeeping. Out of print, but available from the author at The Dairy Hollow House, 515 Spring Street, Eureka Springs, Arkansas 72632. 501-253-7444.

POLITICS

Anderson, Kare. *Cutting Deals with Unlikely Allies, An Unorthodox Approach to Playing the Political Game*. Anderson Negotiations/ Communications, Inc., 321 Karen, Tiburon, CA 94940. If you get into political trouble, this is the practical guide to getting out.

EXPERT COUNSEL

Inn Valuation and Appraisal

Michael Yovino-Young and Alison Teeman, Yovino-Young Associates, 2716 Telegraph Avenue, Berkeley, CA 94705; 415-548-1210.

William A. Oates, William Oates & Associates, P.O. Box 1162, Brattleboro, VT 05301; 802-254-5931.

Inn Traveler Publications.
"Country Inns/Bed & Breakfast," P.O. Box 457, Mt. Morris, IL 61054;
$15/year.
"Discerning Traveler," 504 West Mermaid Lane, Philadelphia, PA 19118;
$65/year.
"Inn Review," P.O. Box 1789, Kankakee, IL 60901; $35/year.
"Innsider," 821 Wanda, Ferndale, MI 48220; $18/year.
"Yellow Brick Road," 2445 Northcreek Lane, Fullerton, CA 92631; $29/
year.

Staff
innkeeping Newsletter. *My Staff Manual.* PAII, P.O. Box 90710, Santa
Barbara, CA 93190.

SO YOU THINK YOU WANT TO BE AN INNKEEPER? WORKSHOPS

The Santa Barbara Innkeepers Guild, a pioneer in professional organizations begun by innkeepers, offers twice yearly an in-depth three-full-day workshop on the delights and headaches of opening an inn. Students are "in residence" at one of the participating Santa Barbara inns.

Workshop sessions are given by experienced owner-innkeepers with a collective total of fifty years in the business. These leaders have also had careers that range from professional educator, nationally renowned designer, chef, personnel manager, and antique dealer, to psychiatric social worker and executive director of a nonprofit agency. Additional expertise includes an attorney/certified public accountant. The greatest advantage of this training is the twenty-four-hour availability of these experts to answer questions and to give a glimpse into the lifestyle of an innkeeper.

After eight years, the guild is proud not only of the thirty-nine wonderful inns (from Park City, Utah to Arrow Rock, Missouri) opened by former students, but also of the many participants who took away a renewed commitment to pursue their dreams and those who reoriented their time line or their fantasy.

Much of the content of this book grew out of the original framework of these workshops, although more detailed examples, personalized attention to individual questions during nonclass time, and more depth in numerous areas typify the on-site workshop situation.

For descriptive brochure and/or reservations, write Guild Workshop, c/o PAII, P.O. Box 90710, Santa Barbara, CA 93190. For questions, contact Pat Hardy or JoAnn Bell, 805-965-0707.

PROFESSIONAL ASSOCIATION OF INNKEEPERS INTERNATIONAL

The trade association of the country inn/bed-and-breakfast industry, providing services and information to innkeepers, aspiring innkeepers and innkeeper organizations. For information, contact PAII, P.O. Box 90710, Santa Barbara, CA 93190.

innkeeping NEWSLETTER

Coauthors Pat Hardy and JoAnn Bell are also editor and publisher of *innkeeping*, the national monthly newsletter for people who own and run bed-and-breakfast and country inns. Because it's written and published by former innkeepers, the information relates to the real world—you can put it right to work in your own inn. Here's a sampling of subscriber comments:

"I like the well-researched and comprehensive articles on inn problems. I save all the issues and refer to them frequently."
Sandra Allembert, Four Columns Inn, Newfane, VT
"Your suggestions have proven the most helpful in the business."
Colette Bailey, The Grey Whale Inn, Fort Bragg, CA
"Articles are germane and to the point, tips are useful. Yours is one of the best trade newsletters I've seen."
Joan and Dane Wells, the Queen Victoria, Cape May, NJ
"Of the fifty or so business and trade magazines we receive each month, *innkeeping* is one of the few publications read (and enjoyed!) by everyone in our office. The best ideas come from operators themselves rather than from those in ivory towers."
William J. Hoffman, President, Trigild Corporation, San Diego
"We have really gained a lot from your *innkeeping* newsletter over the past three years. We really need you."
Shirley Dittloff, Barrow House, St. Francisville, LA
"Your newsletter is the only one I keep, reread, highlight, etc. Thank you a thousand times for being there!"
Jean Wu, Prescott Pines, Prescott, AZ

A year's worth of monthly issues, eight pages each, costs $56. If the ideas in *innkeeping* enable you to fill just one more room a year, avoid one no-show, or reduce your brochure budget, the newsletter will have paid for itself. Most subscribers feel that it pays for itself over and over again.
TO SUBSCRIBE Simply send a check for $56 to *innkeeping*, c/o PAII, P.O. Box 90710, Santa Barbara, CA 93190, along with your name, inn name (if you're already in business), and address.
THE GUARANTEE When you receive your first issue—or at any other time in the year—if you don't think the newsletter is worth the price, ask for a refund. No hassle.

INDEX

76, 86; reasons to buy existing, 76–77; selling, 86–90; size of, 2, 67–71, 78, 96; upgrading of, 81–82; valuation of, 78–81, 88, 203

Insurance, 9, 178, 179–86; buying from agent, 180; choosing agent, 47; information from agent, 186; questions about, 180–86; during renovation, 100; worker's compensation, 100, 178, 185

K

Kitchens: and health department, 40, 105, 108; furnishing, 115; licensing standards, 40; organization of, 104–05

L

Laundry, 102, 113

Leasing inns, 90–92

Legal structure of inn business, 30–37

Licenses, 40, 76, 84; business, 40

Lighting, 118

Linens, 113, 127

Loans: for existing inns, 77; to purchaser of inn, 88; sources of, 73–74

Location, researching a, 26–30

Logo, designing a, 132–34

M

Maintenance, skills needed, 20

Marketing, 19–20, 140–57, 203; and business plan, 52; creating an image, 129–30; direct mail, 152–53; materials needed for, 140, 142–43; ongoing, 140; reasons for, 129; and sale of inn, 90; skills needed, 19–20; telephone 155–57; through travel agents, 153–55; use of brochure in, 134; use of special events in, 146, 152 (*see also* Promotions)

Meals, planning considerations, 104. *See also* Breakfast

N

Newsletter, innkeeping, vii, 9, 59, 60, 61, 70, 77, 78, 90, 127, 204, 205

O

Occupancy rates, projection of, 63

P

Parking, 29, 39, 98

Partnership, 31–33, 36–37; types of, 32

Payment: policies concerning, 161; received, 170

Permits, sales tax, 38

Personnel. *See* Staff

Pets, policies concerning, 161

Policies, 135, 160–65, 167–68; breakfast, 165; cancellation, 163–64; check-in/out, 164–65; children and pets, 161; deposit, 159, 162–63; hiring and staff, 176–78; payment, 162; smoking, 160–61

Professional Association of Innkeepers International (PAII), 204

Profit and loss statement, 73

Promotions, 20, 43, 85–86, 136, 146, 149, 156

Properties: adjoining, 30, 69; comparison of, 67–71

Property evaluation forms, 64–71, 197–98

Publications, innkeeping, 78, 202–04. *See also* Newsletter

Local, state, Fed / Taxes, permits,
  Licences, Zoning, covenants,

Anything having to do w/ Area:
  Attractions, Financial + other
  influences to viability, etc
  Trends

City (town), county Sov't

Appliances age